MEMOIRS OF COURT OF LOUIS XIV

AND OF THE REGENCY
Being the Secret Memoirs of the Mother of the Regent

BY
MADAME ELIZABETH-CHARLOTTE OF BAVARIA DUCHESSE D'ORLEANS

Complete

BOOK 1.

PREFACE.

The Duchesse d'Orleans, commonly though incorrectly styled the Princess of Bavaria, was known to have maintained a very extensive correspondence with her relations and friends in different parts of Europe. Nearly eight hundred of her letters, written to the Princess Wilhelmina Charlotte of Wales and the Duke Antoine-Ulric of Brunswick, were found amongst the papers left by the Duchess Elizabeth of Brunswick at her death, in 1767. These appeared to be so curious that the Court of Brunswick ordered De Praun, a Privy Councillor, to make extracts of such parts as were most interesting. A copy of his extracts was sent to France, where it remained a long time without being published. In 1788, however, an edition appeared, but so mutilated and disfigured, either through the prudence of the editor or the scissors of the censor, that the more piquant traits of the correspondence had entirely disappeared. The bold, original expressions of the German were modified and enfeebled by the timid translator, and all the names of individuals and families were suppressed, except when they carried with them no sort of responsibility. A great many passages of the original correspondence were omitted, while, to make up for the deficiencies, the editor inserted a quantity of pedantic and useless notes. In spite of all these faults and the existence of more faithful editions, this translation was reprinted in 1807. The existence of any other edition being unknown to its editor, it differed in nothing from the preceding, except that the dates of some of the letters were suppressed, a part of the notes cut out, and some passages added from the Memoirs of Saint-Simon, together with a life, or rather panegyric, of the Princess, which bore no slight resemblance to a village homily.

A copy of the extracts made by M. de Praun fell by some chance into the hands of Count de Veltheim, under whose direction they were published at Strasburg, in 1789, with no other alterations than the correction of the obsolete and vicious orthography of the Princess.

In 1789 a work was published at Dantzick, in Germany, entitled, Confessions of the Princess Elizabeth-Charlotte of Orleans, extracted from her letters addressed, between the years 1702 and 1722, to her former governess, Madame de Harling, and her husband. The editor asserts that this correspondence amounted to nearly four hundred letters. A great part of these are only repetitions of what she had before written to the Princess of Wales and the Duke of Brunswick. Since that period no new collections have appeared, although it is sufficiently well known that other manuscripts are in existence.

In 1820 M. Schutz published at Leipsig the Life and Character of Elizabeth-Charlotte, Duchesse d'Orleans, with an Extract of the more remarkable parts of her Correspondence. This is made up of the two German editions of 1789 and 1791; but the editor adopted a new arrangement, and suppressed such of the dates and facts as he considered useless. His suppressions, however, were not very judicious; without dates one is at a loss to know to what epoch the facts related by the Princess ought to be referred, and the French proper names are as incorrect as in the edition of Strasburg.

Feeling much surprise that in France there should have been no more authentic edition of the correspondence of the Regent-mother than the miserable translation of 1788 and 1807, we have set about rendering a service to the history of French manners by a new and more faithful edition. The present is a translation of the Strasburg edition, arranged in a more appropriate order, with the addition of such other passages as were contained in the German collections. The dates have been inserted wherever they appeared necessary, and notes have been added wherever the text required explanation, or where we wished to compare the assertions of the Princess with other testimonies. The Princess, in the salons of the Palais Royal, wrote in a style not very unlike that which might be expected in the present day from the tenants of its garrets. A more complete biography than any which has hitherto been drawn up is likewise added to the present edition. In other respects we have faithfully followed the original Strasburg edition. The style of the Duchess will be sometimes found a little singular, and her chit-chat indiscreet and often audacious; but we cannot refuse our respect to the firmness and propriety with which she conducted herself in the midst of a hypocritical and corrupt Court. The reader, however, must form his own judgment on the correspondence of this extraordinary woman; our business is, not to excite a prejudice in favour of or against her, but merely to present him with a faithful copy of her letters.

Some doubts were expressed about the authenticity of the correspondence when the mutilated edition of 1788 appeared; but these have long since subsided, and its genuineness is no longer questioned.

SECRET COURT MEMOIRS.
MADAME ELIZABETH-CHARLOTTE OF BAVARIA, DUCHESSE D' ORLEANS.

SECTION I.

If my father had loved me as well as I loved him he would never have sent me into a country so dangerous as this, to which I came through pure obedience and against my own inclination. Here duplicity passes for wit, and frankness is looked upon as folly. I am neither cunning nor mysterious. I am often told I lead too monotonous a life, and am asked why I do not take a part in certain affairs. This is frankly the reason: I am old; I stand more in need of repose than of agitation, and I will begin nothing that I cannot, easily finish. I have never learned to govern; I am not conversant with politics, nor with state affairs, and I am now too far advanced in years to learn things so difficult. My son, I thank God, has sense enough, and can direct these things without me; besides, I should excite too much the jealousy of his wife—[Marie-Francoise de Bourbon, the legitimate daughter of Louis XIV. and of Madame de Montespan, Duchesse d'Orleans.]—and his eldest daughter,—[Marie-Louise-Elizabeth d'Orleans, married on the 17th of July, 1710, to Charles of France, Duc de Berri.]—whom he loves better than me; eternal quarrels would ensue, which would not at all suit my views. I have been tormented enough, but I have always forborne, and have endeavoured to set a proper example to my son's wife and his daughter; for this kingdom has long had the misfortune to be too much governed by women, young and old. It is high time that men should now assume the sway, and this is the reason which has determined me not to intermeddle. In England, perhaps, women may reign without inconvenience; in France, men alone should do so, in order that things may go on well. Why should I torment myself by day and by night? I seek only peace and repose; all that were mine are dead. For whom should I care? My time is past. I must try to live smoothly that I may die tranquilly; and in great public affairs it is difficult, indeed, to preserve one's conscience spotless.

I was born at Heidelberg (1652), in the seventh month. I am unquestionably very ugly; I have no features; my eyes are small, my nose is short and thick, my lips long and flat. These do not constitute much of a physiognomy. I have great hanging cheeks and a large face; my stature is short and stout; my body and my thighs, too, are short, and, upon the whole, I am truly a very ugly little object. If I had not a good heart, no one could endure me. To know whether my eyes give tokens of my possessing wit, they must be examined with a microscope, or it will be difficult to judge. Hands more ugly than mine are not perhaps to be found on the whole globe. The King has often told me so, and has made me laugh at it heartily; for, not being able to flatter even myself that I possessed any one thing which could be called pretty, I resolved to be the first to laugh at my own ugliness; this has succeeded as well as I could have wished, and I must confess that I have seldom been at a loss for something to laugh at. I am naturally somewhat melancholy; when anything happens to afflict me, my left side swells up as if it were filled with water. I am not good at lying in bed; as soon as I awake I must get up. I seldom breakfast, and then only on bread and butter. I take neither chocolate, nor coffee, nor tea, not being able to endure those foreign drugs. I am German in all my habits, and like nothing in eating or drinking which is not conformable to our old customs. I eat no soup but such as I can take with milk, wine, or beer. I cannot bear broth; whenever I eat anything of which it forms a part, I fall sick instantly, my body swells, and I am tormented with colics. When I take broth alone, I am compelled to vomit, even to blood, and nothing can restore the tone to my stomach but ham and sausages.

I never had anything like French manners, and I never could assume them, because I always considered it an honour to be born a German, and always cherished the maxims of my own country, which are seldom in favor here. In my youth I loved swords and guns much better than toys. I wished to be a boy, and this desire nearly cost me my life; for, having heard that Marie Germain had become a boy by dint of jumping, I took such terrible jumps that it is a miracle I did not, on a hundred occasions, break my neck. I was very gay in my youth, for which reason I was called, in German, Rauschenplatten-gnecht. The Dauphins of Bavaria used to say, "My poor dear mamma" (so she used always to address me), "where do you pick up all the funny things you know?"

I remember the birth of the King of England

[George Louis, Duke of Brunswick Hanover, born the 28th of May, 1660; proclaimed King of England the 12th of August, 1714, by the title of George I.]

as well as if it were only yesterday (1720). I was curious and mischievous. They had put a doll in a rosemary bush for the purpose of making me believe it was the child of which my aunt

[Sophia of Bavaria, married, in 1658, to the Elector of Hanover, was the paternal aunt of Madame. She was the granddaughter of James I, and was thus declared the first in succession to the crown of England, by Act of Parliament, 23rd March, 1707.]

had just lain in; at the same moment I heard the cries of the Electress, who was then in the pains of childbirth. This did not agree with the story which I had been told of the baby in the rosemary bush; I pretended, however, to believe it, but crept to my aunt's chamber as if I was playing at hide-and-seek with little Bulau and Haxthausen, and concealed myself behind a screen which was placed before the door and near the chimney. When the newly born infant was brought to the fire I issued from my hiding-place. I deserved to be flogged, but in honour of the happy event I got quit for a scolding.

The monks of the Convent of Ibourg, to revenge themselves for my having unintentionally betrayed them by telling their Abbot that they had been fishing in a pond under my window, a thing expressly forbidden by the Abbot, once poured out white wine for me instead of water. I said, "I do not know what is the matter with this water; the more of it I put into my wine the stronger it becomes." The monks replied that it was very good wine. When I got up from the table to go into the garden, I should have fallen into the pond if I had not been held up; I threw myself upon the ground and fell fast asleep immediately. I was then carried into my chamber and put to bed. I did not awake until nine o'clock in the evening, when I remembered all that had passed. It was on a Holy Thursday; I complained to the Abbot of the trick which had been played me by the monks, and they were put into prison. I have often been laughed at about this Holy Thursday.

My aunt, our dear Electress (of Hanover), being at the Hague, did not visit the Princess Royal;

[Maria-Henrietta Stuart, daughter of Charles I. of England, and of Henriette-Marie of France, married, in 1660, to William of Nassau, Prince of Orange; she lost her husband in 1660, and was left pregnant with William-Henry of Nassau, Prince of Orange, and afterwards, by the Revolution of 1688, King of England. This Princess was then preceptress of her son, the Stadtholder of Holland.]

but the Queen of Bohemia

[Elizabeth Stuart, daughter of James I. of England, widow of Frederic V., Duke of Bavaria, Count Palatine of the Rhine, King of Bohemia until the year 1621, mother of the Duchess of Hanover.]

did, and took me with her. Before I set out, my aunt said to me, "Lizette, now take care not to behave as you do in general, and do not wander away so that you cannot be found; follow the Queen step by step, so that she may not have to wait for you."

I replied, "Oh, aunt, you shall hear how well I will behave myself."

When we arrived at the Princess Royal's, whom I did not know, I saw her son, whom I had often played with; after having gazed for a long time at his mother without knowing who she was, I went back to see if I could find any one to tell me what was this lady's name. Seeing only the Prince of Orange, I accosted him thus,—

"Pray, tell me who is that woman with so tremendous a nose?"

He laughed and answered, "That is the Princess Royal, my mother."

I was quite stupefied. That I might compose myself, Mademoiselle Heyde took me with the Prince into the Princess's bedchamber, where we played at all sorts of games. I had told them to call me when the Queen should be ready to go, and we were rolling upon a Turkey carpet when I was summoned; I arose in great haste and ran into the hall; the Queen was already in the antechamber. Without losing a moment, I seized the robe of the Princess Royal, and, making her a low curtsey, at the same moment I placed myself directly before her, and followed the Queen step by step to her carriage; everybody was laughing, but I had no notion of what it was at. When we returned home, the Queen went to find my aunt, and, seating herself upon the bed, burst into a loud laugh.

"Lizette," said she, "has made a delightful visit." And then she told all that I had done, which made the Electress laugh even more than the Queen. She called me to her and said,—

"Lizette, you have done right; you have revenged us well for the haughtiness of the Princess."

My brother would have had me marry the Margrave of Dourlach, but I had no inclination towards him because he was affected, which I never could bear. He knew very well that I was not compelled to refuse him, for he was married long before they thought of marrying me to Monsieur. Still he thought fit to send to me a Doctor of Dourlach, for the purpose of asking me whether he ought to obey his father and marry the Princess of Holstein. I replied that he could not do better than to obey his father; that he had promised me nothing, nor had I pledged myself to him; but that, nevertheless, I was obliged to him for the conduct he had thought fit to adopt. This is all that passed between us.

Once they wanted to give me to the Duke of Courlande; it was my aunt d'Hervod who wished to make that match. He was in love with Marianne, the daughter of Duke Ulric of Wurtemberg; but his father and mother would not allow him to marry her because they had fixed their eyes on me. When, however, he came back from France on his way home, I made such an impression on him that he would not hear of marriage, and requested permission to join the army.

I once received a very sharp scolding in a short journey from Mannheim to Heidelberg. I was in the carriage with my late father, who had with him an envoy, from the Emperor, the Count of Konigseck. At this time I was as thin and light as I am now fat and heavy. The jolting of the carriage threw me from my seat, and I fell upon the Count; it was not my fault, but I was nevertheless severely rebuked for it, for my father was not a man to be trifled with, and it was always necessary to be very circumspect in his presence.

When I think of conflagrations I am seized with a shivering fit, for I remember how the Palatinate was ravaged for more than three months. Whenever I went to sleep I used to think I saw Heidelberg all in flames; then I used to wake with a start, and I very narrowly escaped an illness in consequence of those outrages.

[The burning of the Palatinate in 1674—a horrible devastation   commanded by Louis, and executed by Turenne.]

Upon my arrival in France I was made to hold a conference with three bishops. They all differed in their creeds, and so, taking the quintessence of their opinions, I formed a religion of my own.

It was purely from the affection I bore to her that I refused to take precedence of our late Electress; but making always a wide distinction between her aid and the Duchess of Mecklenbourg, as well as our Electress of Hanover, I did not hesitate to do so with respect to both the latter. I also would not take precedence of my mother. In my childhood I wished to bear her train, but she would never permit me.

I have been treated ill ever since my marriage this is in some degree the fault of the Princess Palatine,—[Anne de Gonzague, Princess Palatine, who took so active a part in the troubles of the Fronde.]—who prepared my marriage contract; and it is by the contract that the inheritance is governed. All persons bearing the title of Madame have pensions from the King; but as they have been of the same amount for a great many years past they are no longer sufficient.

I would willingly have married the Prince of Orange, for by that union I might have hoped to remain near my dear Electress (of Hanover).

Upon my arrival at Saint-Germain I felt as if I had fallen from the clouds. The Princess Palatine went to Paris and there fixed me. I put as good a face upon the affair as was possible; I saw very well that I did not please my husband much, and indeed that could not be wondered at, considering my ugliness; however, I resolved to conduct myself in such a manner towards Monsieur that he should become accustomed to me by my attentions, and eventually should be enabled to endure me. Immediately upon my arrival, the King came to see me at the Chateau Neuf, where Monsieur and I lived; he brought with him the Dauphin, who was then a child of about ten years old. As soon as I had finished my toilette the King returned to the old Chateau, where he received me in the Guards' hall, and led me to the Queen, whispering at the same time,—"Do not be frightened, Madame; she will be more afraid of you than you of her." The King felt so much the embarrassment of my situation that he would not quit me; he sat by my side, and whenever it was necessary for me to rise, that is to say, whenever a Duke or a Prince entered the apartment, he gave me a gentle push in the side without being perceived.

According to the custom of Paris, when a marriage is made, all property is in common; but the husband has the entire control over it. That only which has been brought by way of dowry is taken into the account; for this reason I never knew how much my husband received with me. After his death, when I expected to gain my cause at Rome and to receive some money, the disagreeable old Maintenon asked me in the King's name to promise that if I gained the cause I would immediately cede the half of the property to my son; and in case of refusal I was menaced with the King's displeasure. I laughed at this, and replied that I did not know why they threatened me, for that my son was in the course of nature my heir, but that it was at least just that he should stay until my death before he took possession of my property, and that I knew the King was too equitable to require of me anything but what was consistent with justice. I soon afterwards received the news of the loss of my cause, and I was not sorry for it, on account of the circumstance I have just related.

When the Abby de Tesse had convinced the Pope that his people had decided without having read our papers, and that they had accepted 50,000 crowns from the Grand Duke to pronounce against me, he began weeping, and said, "Am I not an unhappy man to be obliged to trust such persons?" This will show what sort of a character the Pope was.

When I arrived in France I had only an allowance of a hundred louis d'or for my pocket-money; and this money was always consumed in advance. After my mother's death, when my husband received money from the Palatinate, he increased this allowance to two hundred louis; and once, when I was in his good graces, he gave me a thousand louis. Besides this, the King had given me annually one thousand louis up to the year before the marriage of my son. That supported me, but as I would not consent to the marriage I was deprived of this sum, and it has never been restored to me. On my first journey to Fontainebleau, the King would have given me 2,000 pistoles, but that Monsieur begged him to keep half of them for Madame, afterwards the Queen of Spain.—[Marie-Louise d'Orleans, born in 1662, married, in 1679, to Charles II., King of Spain.]

I cared very little about it, and, nevertheless, went to Fontainebleau, where I lost all my money at Hoca. Monsieur told me, for the purpose of vexing me, of the good office he had done me with the King; I only laughed at it, and told him that, if Madame had chosen to accept the thousand pistoles from my hands, I would very freely have given them to her. Monsieur was quite confused at this, and, by way of repairing the offence he had committed, he took upon himself the payment of 600 louis d'or, which I had lost over and above the thousand pistoles.

I receive now only 456,000 francs, which is exactly consumed within the year; if, they could have given me any less they would. I would not be thought to make claims to which I am not entitled, but it should be remembered that Monsieur has had the money of my family.

I was very glad when, after the birth of my daughter,

[Elizabeth-Charlotte d'Orleans, born in 1676, married, in 1697, to the Duc de Lorraine. Philippe d'Orleans, afterwards Regent of France, was born in 1674; there were no other children by this marriage.]

my husband proposed separate beds; for, to tell the truth, I was never very fond of having children. When he proposed it to me, I answered, "Yes, Monsieur, I shall be very well contented with the arrangement, provided you do not hate me, and that you will continue to behave with some kindness to me." He promised, and we were very well satisfied with each other. It was, besides, very disagreeable to sleep with Monsieur; he could not bear any one to touch him when he was asleep, so that I was obliged to lie on the very edge of the bed; whence it sometimes happened that I fell out like a sack. I was therefore enchanted when Monsieur proposed to me in friendly terms, and without any anger, to lie in separate rooms.

I obeyed the late Monsieur by not troubling him with my embraces, and always conducted myself towards him with respect and submission.

He was a good sort of man, notwithstanding his weaknesses, which, indeed, oftener excited my pity than my anger. I must confess that I did occasionally express some impatience, but when he begged pardon, it was all forgotten.

Madame de Fiennes had a considerable stock of wit, and was a great joker; her tongue spared no one but me. Perceiving that she treated the King and Monsieur with as little ceremony as any other persons, I took her by the hand one day, and, leading her apart, I said to her, "Madame, you are very agreeable; you have a great deal of wit, and the manner in which you display it is pleasant to the King and Monsieur, because they are accustomed to you; but to me, who am but just arrived, I cannot say that I like it. When any persons entertain themselves at my expense, I cannot help being very angry, and it is for this reason that I am going to give you a little advice. If you spare me we shall be mighty good friends; but if you treat me as I see you treat others, I shall say nothing to you; I shall, nevertheless, complain of you to your husband, and if he does not restrain you I shall dismiss him."

He was my Equerry-in-Ordinary.

She promised never to speak of me, and she kept her word.

Monsieur often said to me, "How does it happen that Madame de Fiennes never says anything severe of you?"

I answered, "Because she loves me."

I would not tell him what I had done, for he would immediately have excited her to attack me.

I was called sometimes 'Soeur Pacifique', because I did all in my power to maintain harmony between Monsieur and his cousins, La Grande Mademoiselle,

[Anne-Marie-Louise d'Orleans, Duchesse de Montpensier, and Marguerite-Louise d'Orleans, Duchess of Tuscany, daughters of Gaston, Duc d'Orleans, but by different wives.]

and La Grande Duchesse:

[Charlotte-Eleonore-Maddleine de la Motte Houdancourt, Duchesse de Ventadour; she was gouvernante to Louis XV.]

they quarrelled very frequently, and always like children, for the slightest trifles.

Madame de Ventadour was my Maid of Honour for at least sixteen years. She did not quit me until two years after the death of my husband, and then it was by a contrivance of old Maintenon; she wished to annoy me because she knew I was attached to this lady, who was good and amiable, but not very cunning. Old Maintenon succeeded in depriving me of her by means of promises and threats, which were conveyed by Soubise, whose son had married Madame de Ventadour's daughter, and who was an artful woman. By way of recompense she was made gouvernante. They tried, also, to deprive me of Madame de Chateau Thiers; the old woman employed all her power there, too, but Madame de Chateau Thiers remained faithful to me, without telling of these attempts, which I learnt from another source.

Madame de Monaco might, perhaps, be fond of forming very close attachments of her own sex, and Madame de Maintenon would have put me on the same footing; but she did not succeed, and was so much vexed at her disappointment that she wept. Afterwards she wanted to make me in love with the Chevalier de Vendome, and this project succeeded no better than the other. She often said she could not think of what disposition I must be, since I cared neither for men nor women, and that the German nation must be colder than any other.

I like persons of that cool temperament. The poor Dauphine of Bavaria used to send all the young coxcombs of the Court to me, knowing that I detested such persons, and would be nearly choked with laughter at seeing the discontented air with which I talked to them.

Falsehood and superstition were never to my taste.

The King was in the habit of saying, "Madame cannot endure unequal marriages; she always ridicules them."

Although there are some most delightful walks at Versailles, no one went out either on foot or in carriages but myself; the King observed this, and said, "You are the only one who enjoys the beauties of Versailles."

All my life, even from my earliest years, I thought myself so ugly that I did not like to be looked at. I therefore cared little for dress, because jewels and decoration attract attention. As Monsieur loved to be covered with diamonds, it was fortunate that I did not regard them, for, otherwise, we should have quarrelled about who was to wear them. On grand occasions Monsieur used formerly to make me dress in red; I did so, but much against my inclination, for I always hated whatever was inconvenient to me. He always ordered my dresses, and even used to paint my cheeks himself.

I made the Countess of Soissons laugh very heartily once. She said to me, "How is it, Madame, that you never look in a mirror when you pass it, as everybody else does?"

I answered, "Because I have too great a regard for myself to be fond of seeing myself look as ugly as I really am."

I was always attached to the King; and when he did anything disagreeable to me it was generally to please Monsieur, whose favourites and my enemies did all they could to embroil me with him, and through his means with the King, that I might not be able to denounce them. It was natural enough that the King should be more inclined to please his brother than me; but when Monsieur's conscience reproached him, he repented of having done me ill offices with the King, and he confessed this to the King; His Majesty would then come to us again immediately, notwithstanding the malicious contrivances of old Maintenon.

I have always had my own household, although during Monsieur's life I was not the mistress of it, because all his favourites derived a share of profit from it. Thus no one could buy any employment in my establishment without a bribe to Grancey, to the Chevalier de Lorraine, to Cocard, or to M. Spied. I troubled myself little about these persons; so long as they continued to behave with proper respect towards me, I let them alone; but when they presumed to ridicule me, or to give me any trouble, I set them to rights without hesitation and as they deserved.

Finding that Madame la Marechale de Clerambault was attached to me, they removed her, and they placed my daughter under the care of Madame la Marechale de Grancey, the creature of my bitterest enemy, the Chevalier de Lorraine, whose mistress was the elder sister of this very Grancei. It may be imagined how fit an example such a woman was for my daughter; but all my prayers, all my remonstrances, were in vain.

Madame de Montespan said to me one day that it was a shame I had no ambition, and would not take part in anything.

I replied, "If a person should have intrigued assiduously to become Madame, could not her son permit her to enjoy that rank peaceably? Well, then, fancy that I have become so by such means, and leave me to repose."

"You are obstinate," said she.

"No, Madame," I answered; "but I love quiet, and I look upon all your ambition to be pure vanity."

I thought she would have burst with spite, so angry was she. She, however, continued,—

"But make the attempt and we will assist you."

"No," I replied, "Madame, when I think that you, who have a hundred times more wit than I, have not been able to maintain your consequence in that Court which you love so much, what hope can I, a poor foreigner, have of succeeding, who know nothing of intrigue, and like it as little?"

She was quite mortified. "Go along," she said, "you are good for nothing."

Old Maintenon and her party had instilled into the Dauphine a deep hatred against me; by their direction she often said very impertinent things to me. They hoped that I should resent them to the Dauphine in such manner as to afford her reason to complain to the King of me, and thus draw his displeasure upon me. But as I knew the tricks of the old woman and her coterie, I resolved not to give them that satisfaction; I only laughed at the disobliging manner in which they treated me, and I gave them to understand that I thought the ill behaviour of the Dauphine was but a trick of her childhood, which she would correct as she grew older. When I spoke to her she made me no reply, and laughed at me with the ladies attendant upon her.

"Ladies," she once said to them, "amuse me; I am tired;" and at the same time looked at me disdainfully. I only smiled at her, as if her behaviour had no effect upon me.

I said, however, to old Maintenon, in a careless tone, "Madame la Dauphine receives me ungraciously; I do not intend to quarrel with her, but if she should become too rude I shall ask the King if he approves of her behaviour."

The old woman was alarmed, because she knew very well that the King had enjoined the Dauphine always to behave politely to me; she begged me immediately not to say a word to the King, assuring me that I should soon see the Dauphine's behaviour changed; and indeed, from that time, the Dauphine altered her conduct, and lived upon much better terms with me. If I had complained to the King of the ill treatment I received from the Dauphine he would have been very angry; but she would not have hated me the less, and she and her old aunt would have formed means to repay me double.

Ratzenhausen has the good fortune to be sprung from a very good family; the King was always glad to see her, because she made him laugh; she also diverted the Dauphine, and Madame de Berri liked her much, and made her visit her frequently. It is not surprising that we should be good friends; we have been so since our infancy, for I was not nine years old when I first became acquainted with her. Of all the old women I know, there is not one who keeps up her gaiety like Linor.

I often visited Madame de Maintenon, and did all in my power to gain her affections, but could never succeed. The Queen of Sicily asked me one day if I did not go out with the King in his carriage, as when she was with us. I replied to her by some verses (from Racine's Phedre).

Madame de Torci told this again to old Maintenon, as if it applied to her, which indeed it did, and the King was obliged to look coldly on me for some time.

During the last three years of his life I had entirely gained my husband to myself, so that he laughed at his own weaknesses, and was no longer displeased at being joked with. I had suffered dreadfully before; but from this period he confided in me entirely, and, always took my part. By his death I saw the result of the care and pains of thirty years vanish. After Monsieur's decease, the King sent to ask me whither I wished to retire, whether to a convent in Paris, or to Maubuisson, or elsewhere. I replied that as I had the honour to be of the royal house I could not live but where the King was, and that I intended to go directly to Versailles. The King was pleased at this, and came to see me. He somewhat mortified me by saying that he sent to ask me whither I wished to go because he had not imagined that I should choose to stay where he was. I replied that I did not know who could have told His Majesty anything so false and injurious, and that I had a much more sincere respect and attachment for His Majesty than those who had thus falsely accused me. The King then dismissed all the persons present, and we had a long explanation, in the course of which the King told me I hated Madame de Maintenon. I confessed that I did hate her, but only through my attachment for him, and because she did me wrong to His Majesty; nevertheless, I added that, if it were agreeable to him that I should be reconciled to her, I was ready to become so. The good lady was not prepared for this, or she would not have suffered the King to come to me; he was, however, so satisfied that he remained favourable to me up to his last hour. He made old Maintenon come, and said to her, "Madame is willing to make friends with you." He then caused us to embrace, and there the scene ended. He required her also to live upon good terms with me, which she did in appearance, but secretly played me all sorts of tricks. It was at this time a matter of indifference to me whether I went to live at Montargis or not, but I would not have the appearance of doing so in consequence of any disgrace, and as if I had committed some offence for which I was driven from the Court. I had reason to fear, besides, that at the end of two days' journey I might be left to die of hunger, and to avoid this risk I chose rather to be reconciled to the King. As to going into a convent, I never once thought of it, although it was that which old Maintenon most desired. The Castle of Montargis is my jointure; at Orleans there is no house. St. Cloud is not a part of the hereditary property, but was bought by Monsieur with his own money. Therefore my jointure produces nothing; all that I have to live on comes from the King and my son. At the commencement of my widowhood I was left unpaid, and there was an arrear of 300,000 francs due to me, which were not paid until after the death of Louis XIV. What, then, would have become of me if I had chosen to retire to Montargis? My household expenses amounted annually to 298,758 livres.

Although Monsieur received considerable wealth with me, I was obliged, after his death, to give up to my son the jewels, movables, pictures—in short, all that had come from my family; otherwise I should not have had enough to live according to my rank and to keep up my establishment, which is large. In my opinion, to do this is much better than to wear diamonds.

My income is not more than 456,000 livres; and yet, if it please God, I will not leave a farthing of debt. My son has just made me more rich by adding 150,000 livres to my pension (1719). The cause of almost all the evil which prevails here is the passion of women for play. I have often been told to my face, "You are good for nothing; you do not like play."

If by my influence I can serve any unfortunate persons with the different branches of the Government, I always do so willingly; in case of success I rejoice; in a less fortunate event I console myself by the belief that it was not the will of God.

After the King's death I repaired to St. Cyr to pay a visit to Madame de Maintenon. On my entering the room she said to me, "Madame, what do you come here for?"

I replied, "I come to mingle my tears with those of her whom the King I so much deplore loved most.—that is yourself, Madame."

"Yes, indeed," she said, "he loved me well; but he loved you, also."

I replied, "He did me the honour to say that, he would always distinguish me by his friendship, although everything was done to make him hate me."

I wished thus to let her understand that I was, quite aware of her conduct, but that, being a Christian, I could pardon my enemies. If she possessed any sensibility she must have felt some pain at thus. receiving the forgiveness of one whom she had incessantly persecuted.

The affair of Loube is only a small part of what I have suffered here.

I have now no circle, for ladies a tabouret—[Ladies having the privilege of seats upon small stools in the presence.]—seldom come to me, not liking to appear but in full dress. I begged them to be present as usual at an audience, which I was to give to the ambassador of Malta, but not one of them came. When the late Monsieur and the King were alive, they were more assiduous; they were not then so much accustomed to full dresses, and when they did not come in sufficient numbers Monsieur threatened to tell the King of it.

But this is enough, as M. Biermann said, after having preached four hours together.

SECTION II.—LOUIS XIV.

When the King pleased he could be one of the most agreeable and amiable men in the world; but it was first necessary that he should be intimately acquainted with persons. He used to joke in a very comical and amusing manner.

The King, though by no means perfect, possessed some great and many fine qualities; and by no means deserved to be defamed and despised by his subjects after his death.

While he lived he was flattered, even to idolatry.

He was so much tormented on my account that I could not have wondered if he had hated me most cordially. However, he did not; but, on the contrary, he discovered that all which was said against me sprang from malice and jealousy.

If he had not been so unfortunate as to fall into the hands of two of the worst women in the world Montespan, and that old Maintenon, who was even worse than the other, he would have been one of the best kings that ever lived; for all the evil that he ever did proceeded from those two women, and not from himself.

Although I approved of many things he did, I could not agree with him when he maintained that it was vulgar to love one's relations. Montespan had instilled this into him, in order that she might get rid of all his legitimate blood connections, and might suffer none about him but her bastards; she had even carried matters so far as to seek to confine the royal favour to her offspring or her creatures.

Our King loved the chase passionately; particularly hawking and stag hunting.

One day all the world came to Marly to offer their compliments of condolence; Louis XIV., to get rid of the ceremony, ordered that no harangues should be made, but that all the Court should enter without distinction and together at one door, and go out by the other. Among them came the Bishop of Gap, in a sort of dancing step, weeping large, hot tears, and smiling at the same moment, which gave to his face the most grotesque appearance imaginable. Madame, the Dauphine, and I, were the first who could not restrain ourselves; then the Dauphin and the Duc de Berri, and at last the King, and everybody who was in the chamber burst out into loud laughter.

The King, it must be allowed, gave occasion to great scandal on account of his mistresses; but then he very sincerely repented of these offences.

He had good natural wit, but was extremely ignorant; and was so much ashamed of it that it became the fashion for his courtiers to turn learned men into ridicule. Louis XIV. could not endure to hear politics talked; he was what they call in this country, 'franc du collier'.

At Marly he did not wish the slightest ceremony to prevail. Neither ambassadors nor other envoys were ever permitted to come here; he never gave audience; there was no etiquette, and the people went about 'pele-mele'. Out of doors the King made all the men wear their hats; and in the drawing-room, everybody, even to the captains, lieutenants, and sublieutenants of the foot-guards, were permitted to be seated. This custom so disgusted me with the drawing-room that I never went to it.

The King used to take off his hat to women of all descriptions, even, the common peasants.

When he liked people he would tell them everything he had heard; and for this reason it was always dangerous to talk to him of that old Maintenon.

Although he loved flattery, he was very often ready to ridicule it. Montespan and the old woman had spoiled him and hardened his heart against his relations, for he was naturally of a very affectionate disposition.

Louis XIV., as well as all the rest of his family, with the exception of my son, hated reading. Neither the King nor Monsieur had been taught anything; they scarcely knew how to read and write. The King was the most polite man in his kingdom, but his son and his grandchildren were the most rude.

In his youth he had played in the comedy of 'Les Visionnaires', which he knew by heart, and in which he acted better than the comedians. He did not know a note of music; but his ear was so correct that he could play in a masterly style on the guitar, and execute whatever he chose.

It is not astonishing that the King and Monsieur were brought up in ignorance. The Cardinal (Mazarin) wished to reign absolutely; if the princes had been better instructed, he would neither have been trusted nor employed, and this it was his object to prevent, hoping that he should live much longer than he did. The Queen-mother found all that the Cardinal did perfectly right; and, besides, it suited her purpose that he should be indispensable. It is almost a miracle that the King should have become what he afterwards was.

I never saw the King beat but two men, and they both well deserved it. The first was a valet, who would not let him enter the garden during one of his own fetes. The other was a pickpocket, whom the King saw emptying the pocket of M. de Villars. Louis XIV., who was on horseback, rode towards the thief and struck him with his cane; the rascal cried out, "Murder! I shall be killed!" which made us all laugh, and the King laughed, also. He had the thief taken, and made him give up the purse, but he did not have him hanged.

The Duchesse de Schomberg was a good deal laughed at because she asked the King a hundred questions, which is not the fashion here. The King was not well pleased to be talked to; but he never laughed in any one's face.

When Louvois proposed to the King for the first time that he should appoint Madame Dufresnoy, his mistress, a lady of the Queen's bedchamber, His Majesty replied, "Would you, then, have them laugh at both of us?" Louvois, however, persisted so earnestly in his request that the King at length granted it.

The Court of France was extremely agreeable until the King had the misfortune to marry that old Maintenon; she withdrew him from company, filled him with ridiculous scruples respecting plays, and told him that he ought not to see excommunicated persons. In consequence of this she had a small theatre erected in her own apartments, where plays were acted twice a week before the King. Instead of the dismissed comedians,

[These dismissed comedians had, as appears by the edition of 1788, renounced their profession, and had been admitted to the communion. After that, Madame de Maintenon no longer saw any sin in them.]

she had the Dauphine, my son, the Duc de Berri, and her own nieces, to play; in her opinion this was much better than the real comedians. The King, instead of occupying his usual place, was seated behind me in a corner, near Madame de Maintenon. This arrangement spoilt all, for the consequence was that few people saw him, and the Court was almost deserted.

Maintenon told me that the King said to her, "Now that I am old my children get tired of me and are delighted to find any opportunity of fixing me here and going elsewhere for their own amusement; Madame alone stays, and I see that she is glad to be with me still." But she did not tell me that she had done all in her power to persuade him of the contrary, and that the King spoke thus by way of reproaching her for the lies she had invented about me. I learned that afterwards from others. If the King had been my father I could not have loved him more than I did; I was always pleased to be with him.

He was fond of the German soldiers, and said that the German horsemen displayed more grace in the saddle than those of any other nation.

When the King had a design to punish certain libertines, Fagon—[Guy Crescent Fagon, appointed the King's chief physician in 1693, died in 1718.]—had an amusing conversation with him. He said,—

"Folks made love long before you came into the world, and they will always continue to do so. You cannot prevent them; and when I hear preachers talking in the pulpit and railing against such as yield to the influence of passion, I think it is very much as if I should say to my phthisical patients, 'You must not cough; it is very wrong to spit.' Young folks are full of humours, which must be dispersed by one way or another."

The King could not refrain from laughing.

He was only superstitious in religious matters; for example, with respect to the miracles of the Virgin, etc.

He had been taught to believe that to make friends with his brother was a great political stroke and a fine State device; that it made a part of what is called to reign well.

Since the time of this King it has not been the custom for ladies to talk of the affairs of the State.

If the King heard that any one had spoken ill of him, he displayed a proud resentment towards the offender; otherwise it was impossible to be more polite and affable than he was. His conversation was pleasing in a high degree. He had the skill of giving an agreeable turn to everything. His manner of talking was natural, without the least affectation, amiable and obliging. Although he had not so much courage as Monsieur, he was still no coward. His brother said that he had always behaved well in occasions of danger; but his chief fault lay in being soon tired of war, and wishing to return home.

From the time of his becoming so outrageously devout, all amusements were suspended for three weeks (at Easter); and before, they were only discontinued a fortnight.

The King had a peculiarity of disposition which led him easily to behave harshly to persons who were disagreeable to such as he loved. It was thus that La Valliere was so ill-treated at the instigation of Montespan.

He was much amused with the Comte de Grammont,—[Philibert, Comte de Grammont, St. Evremond's hero, and so well known by means of the Memoirs of Count Antoine Hamilton, his brother-in-law.]—who was very pleasant. He loaded him with proofs of his kindness, and invited him to join in all the excursions to Marly, a decided mark of great favour.

The King frequently complained that in his youth he had not been allowed to converse with people generally, but it was the fault of his natural temper; for Monsieur, who had been brought up with him, used to talk to everybody.

Louis XIV. used to say, laughingly, to Monsieur that his eternal chattering had put him out of conceit with talking. "Ah, mon Dieu!" he would say, "must I, to please everybody, say as many silly things as my brother?"

In general, they would not have been taken for brothers. The King was a large man, and my husband a small one: the latter had very effeminate inclinations; he loved dress, was very careful of his complexion, and took great interest in feminine employments and in ceremonies. The King, on the contrary, cared little about dress, loved the chase and shooting, was fond of talking of war, and had all manly tastes and habits. Monsieur behaved well in battle, but never talked of it; he loved women as companions, and was pleased to be with them. The King loved to see them somewhat nearer, and not entirely en honneur, as Monsieur did.

[Madame is not a good authority on this point. The memoirs of the time will show either that she cannot have known or must have wilfully concealed the intrigues of various kinds in which her husband was engaged.]

They nevertheless loved one another much, and it was very interesting to see them together. They joked each other sensibly and pleasantly, and without ever quarrelling.

I was never more amused than in a journey which I took with the King to Flanders. The Queen and the Dauphine were then alive. As soon as we reached a city, each of us retired to our own quarters for a short time, and afterwards we went to the theatre, which was commonly so bad that we were ready to die with laughing. Among others, I remember that at Dunkirk we saw a company playing Mithridates. In speaking to Monimia, Mithridates said something which I forget, but which was very absurd. He turned round immediately to the Dauphine and said, "I very humbly beg pardon, Madame, I assure you it was a slip of the tongue." The laugh which followed this apology may be imagined, but it became still greater when the Prince of Conti,

[Louis-Armaud de Bourbon, Prince de Conti, married in 1780 to Marie-Anne, commonly called Mademoiselle de Blois, one of the legitimated daughters of Louis XIV. by Madame de la Valliere. She was called at Court La Grande Princesse, on account of her beauty and her stature.]

the husband of La Grande Princesse, who was sitting above the orchestra, in a fit of laughing, fell into it. He tried to save himself by the cord, and, in doing so, pulled down the curtain over the lamps, set it on fire, and burnt a great hole in it. The flames were soon extinguished, and the actors, as if they were perfectly indifferent, or unconscious of the accident, continued to play on, although we could only see them through the hole. When there was no play, we took airings and had collations; in short, every day brought something new. After the King's supper we went to see magnificent artificial fireworks given by the cities of Flanders. Everybody was gay; the Court was in perfect unanimity, and no one thought of anything but to laugh and seek amusement.

If the King had known the Duchess of Hanover, he would not have been displeased at her calling him "Monsieur." As she was a Sovereign Princess, he thought it was through pride that she would not call him "Sire," and this mortified him excessively, for he was very sensitive on such subjects.

One day, before Roquelaure was made a Duke, he was out when it rained violently, and he ordered his coachman to drive to the Louvre, where the entrance was permitted to none but Ambassadors, Princes and Dukes. When his carriage arrived at the gate they asked who it was.

"A Duke," replied he.

"What Duke?" repeated the sentinel.

"The Duc d'Epernon," said he.

"Which of them?"

"The one who died last." And upon this they let him enter. Fearing afterwards that he might get into a scrape about it, he went directly to the King. "Sire," said he, "it rains so hard that I came in my coach even to the foot of your staircase."

The King was displeased. "What fool let you enter?" he asked.

"A greater fool than your Majesty can imagine," replied Roquelaure, "for he admitted me in the name of the Duc d'Epernon who died last."

This ended the King's anger and made him laugh very heartily.

So great a fear of hell had been instilled into the King that he not only thought everybody who did not profess the faith of the Jesuits would be damned, but he even thought he was in some danger himself by speaking to such persons. If any one was to be ruined with the King, it was only necessary to say, "He is a Huguenot or a Jansenist," and his business was immediately settled. My son was about to take into his service a gentleman whose mother was a professed Jansenist. The Jesuits, by way of embroiling my son with the King, represented that he was about to engage a Jansenist on his establishment.

The King immediately sent for him and said "How is this, nephew? I understand you think of employing a Jansenist in your service."

"Oh, no!" replied my son, laughing, "I can assure your Majesty that he is not a Jansenist, and I even doubt whether he believes in the existence of a God."

"Oh, well, then!" said the King, "if that be the case, and you are sure that he is no Jansenist, you may take him."

It is impossible for a man to be more ignorant of religion than the King was. I cannot understand how his mother, the Queen, could have brought him up with so little knowledge on this subject. He believed all that the priests said to him, as if it came from God Himself. That old Maintenon and Pere la Chaise had persuaded him that all the sins he had committed with Madame de Montespan would be pardoned if he persecuted and extirpated the professors of the reformed religion, and that this was the only path to heaven. The poor King believed it fervently, for he had never seen a Bible in his life; and immediately after this the persecution commenced. He knew no more of religion than what his confessors chose to tell him, and they had made him believe that it was not lawful to investigate in matters of religion, but that the reason should be prostrated in order to gain heaven. He was, however, earnest enough himself, and it was not his fault that hypocrisy reigned at Court. The old Maintenon had forced people to assume it.

It was formerly the custom to swear horridly on all occasions; the King detested this practice, and soon abolished it.

He was very capable of gratitude, but neither his children nor his grandchildren were. He could not bear to be made to wait for anything.

He said that by means of chains of gold he could obtain anything he wished from the ministers at Vienna.

He could not forgive the French ladies for affecting English fashions. He used often to joke about it, and particularly in the conversation which he addressed to me, expecting that I would take it up and tease the Princesses. To amuse him, I sometimes said whatever came into my head, without the least ceremony, and often made him laugh heartily.

Reversi was the only game at which the King played, and which he liked.

When he did not like openly to reprove any person, he would address himself to me; for he knew that I never restrained myself in conversation, and that amused him infinitely. At table, he was almost obliged to talk to me, for the others scarcely said a word. In the cabinet, after supper, there were none but the Duchess—[Anne of Bavaria, wife of Henri-Jules, Duc de Bourbon, son of the great Conde; she bore the title of Madame la Princesse after his death.]—and I who spoke to him. I do not know whether the Dauphine used to converse with the King in the cabinets, for while she was alive I was never permitted to enter them, thanks to Madame de Maintenon's interference; the Dauphine objected to it; the King would willingly have had it so; but he dare not assert his will for fear of displeasing the Dauphine and the old woman. I was not therefore suffered to enter until after the death of the Dauphine, and then only because the King wished to have some one who would talk to him in the evening, to dissipate his melancholy thoughts, in which I did my best. He was dissatisfied with his daughters on both sides, who, instead of trying to console him in his grief, thought only of amusing themselves, and the good King might often have remained alone the whole evening if I had not visited his cabinet. He was very sensible of this, and said to Maintenon, "Madame is the only one who does not abandon me."

Louis XIV. spoiled the Jesuits; he thought whatever came from them must be admirable, whether it was right or wrong.

The King did not like living in town; he was convinced that the people did not love him, and that there was no security for him among them. Maintenon had him, besides, more under her sway at Versailles than at Paris, where there was certainly no security for her. She was universally detested there; and whenever she went out in a carriage the populace shouted loud threats against her, so that at last she dared not appear in public.

At first the King was in the habit of dining with Madame de Montespan and his children, and then no person went to visit him but the Dauphin and Monsieur. When Montespan was dismissed, the King had all his illegitimate children in his cabinet: this continued until the arrival of the last Dauphine; she intruded herself among the bastards to their great affliction. When the Duchess—

[Louise-Francoise, commonly called Mademoiselle de Nantes, the legitimated daughter of Madame de Montespan and the King, was married to the Duc de Bourbon in 1685.]

became the favourite of the Dauphin, she begged that no other persons of the royal house might have access to the cabinet; and therefore my request for admission, although not refused, was never granted until after the death of the Dauphin and Dauphine. The latter accompanied the King to places where I did not, and could not go, for she even, went with him upon occasions when decency ought to have forbidden her presence. Maintenon did the same thing, for the purpose of having an opportunity of talking to the King in secret.

Louis XIV. loved the young Dauphine so well that he dared refuse her nothing; and Maintenon had so violent a hatred against me that she was ready to do me all the mischief in her power. What could the King do against the inclinations of his son and his granddaughter? They would have looked cross, and that would have grieved him. I had no inclination to cause him any vexation, and therefore preferred exercising my own patience. When I had anything to say to the King, I requested a private audience, which threw them all into despair, and furnished me with a good laugh in my sleeve.

The King was so much devoted to the old usages of the Royal Palace that he would not for the world have departed from them. Madame de Fiennes was in the habit of saying that the Royal Family adhered so strictly to their habits and customs that the Queen of England died with a toguet on her head; that is, a little cap which is put upon children when they go to bed.

When the King denied anything it was not permitted to argue with him; what he commanded must be done quickly and without reply. He was too much accustomed to "such is our good pleasure," to endure any contradiction.

He was always kind and generous when he acted from his own impulses. He never thought that his last will would be observed; and he said to several people, "They have made me sign a will and some other papers; I have done it for the sake of being quiet, but I know very well that it will not stand good."

The good King was old; he stood in need of repose, and he could not enjoy it by any other means than by doing whatever that old Maintenon wished; thus it was that this artful hussy always accomplished her ends.

The King used always to call the Duc de Verneuil his uncle.

It has been said and believed that Louis XIV. retired from the war against Holland through pure generosity; but I know, as well as I know my own name that he came back solely for the purpose of seeing Madame de Montespan, and to stay with her. I know also many examples of great events, which in history have been attributed to policy or ambition, but which have originated from the most insignificant trifles. It has been said it was our King's ambition that made him resolve to become the master of the world, and that it was for this he commenced the Dutch war; but I know from an indisputable source that it was entered upon only because M. de Lionne, then Minister of State, was jealous of Prince William of Furstenberg, who had an intrigue with his wife, of which he had been apprised. It was this that caused him to engage in those quarrels which afterwards produced the war.

It was not surprising that the King was insensible to the scarcity which prevailed, for in the first place he had seen nothing of it, and, in the second, he had been told that all the reports which had reached him were falsehoods, and that they were in no respect true. Old Maintenon invented this plan for getting money, for she had bought up all the corn, for the purpose of retailing it at a high price. [This does not sound like M. Maintenon. D.W.] Everybody had been requested to say nothing about it to the King, lest it should kill him with vexation.

The King loved my son as well as his own, but he cared little for the girls. He was very fond of Monsieur, and he had reason to be so; never did a child pay a more implicit obedience to its parents than did Monsieur to the King; it was a real veneration; and the Dauphin, too, had for him a veneration, affection and submission such as never son had for a father. The King was inconsolable for his death. He never had much regard for the Duke of Burgundy; the old sorceress (Maintenon) had slandered him to the King, and made the latter believe that he was of an ambitious temper, and was impatient at the King's living so long. She did this in order that if the Prince should one day open his eyes, and perceive the manner in which his wife had been educated, his complaints might have no effect with the King, which really took place. Louis XIV. at last thought everything that the Dauphine of Burgundy did was quite charming; old Maintenon made him believe that her only aim was to divert him. This old woman was to him both the law and the prophets; all that she approved was good, and what she condemned was bad, no matter how estimable it really was. The most innocent actions of the first Dauphine were represented as crimes, and all the impertinences of the second were admired.

A person who had been for many years in immediate attendance upon the King, who had been engaged with him every evening at Maintenon's, and who must consequently have heard everything that was said, is one of my very good friends, and he has told me that although while the old lady was living he dare not say a word, yet, she being dead, he was at liberty to tell me that the King had always professed a real friendship for me. This person has often heard with his own ears Maintenon teasing the King, and speaking ill of me for the purpose of rendering me hateful in his eyes, but the King always took my part. It was in reference to this, I have no doubt, that the King said to me on his death-bed:

"They have done all they could to make me hate you, Madame, but they have not succeeded." He added that he had always known me too well to believe their calumnies. While he spoke thus, the old woman stood by with so guilty an air that I could not doubt they had proceeded from her.

Monsieur often took a pleasure in diminishing or depriving me of the King's favour, and the King was not sorry for some little occasions to blame Monsieur. He told me once that he had embroiled me with Monsieur by policy.

I was alarmed, and said immediately, "Perhaps your Majesty may do the same thing again."

The King laughed, and said, "No, if I had intended to do so I should not have told you of it; and, to say the truth, I had some scruples about it, and have resolved never to do so again."

Upon the death of one of his children, the King asked of his old medical attendant, M. Gueneau: "Pray, how does it happen that my illegitimate children are healthy and live, while all the Queen's children are so delicate and always die?" "Sire," replied Gueneau, "it is because the Queen has only the rinsings of the glass."

He always slept in the Queen's bed, but did not always accommodate himself to the Spanish temperament of that Princess; so that the Queen knew he had been elsewhere. The King, nevertheless, had always great consideration for her, and made his mistresses treat her with all becoming respect. He loved her for her virtue, and for the sincere affection she bore to him, notwithstanding his infidelity. He was much affected at her death; but four days afterwards, by the chattering of old Maintenon, he was consoled. A few days afterwards we went to Fontainebleau, and expected to find the King in an ill-humour, and that we should be scolded; but, on the contrary, he was very gay.

When the King returned from a journey we were all obliged to be at the carriage as he got out, for the purpose of accompanying him to his apartments.

While Louis XIV. was young all the women were running after him; but he renounced this sort of life when he flattered himself that he had grown devout. His motive was, Madame de Maintenon watched him so narrowly that he could not, dare not, look at any one. She disgusted him with everybody else that she might have him to herself; and this, too, under the pretext of taking care of his soul.

Madame de Colonne had a great share of wit, and our King was so much in love with her, that, if her uncle, the Cardinal, had consented, he would certainly have married her. Cardinal Mazarin, although in every other respect a worthless person, deserved to be praised for having opposed this marriage. He sent his niece into Italy. When she was setting out, the King wept violently. Madame de Colonne said to him, "You are a King; you weep, and yet I go." This was saying a great deal in a few words. As to the Comtesse de Soissons, the King had always more of friendship than of love for him. He made her very considerable presents, the least of which was to the amount of 2,000 louis.

Madame de Ludres, the King's mistress, was an agreeable person; she had been Maid of Honour to Monsieur's first wife,—[Henrietta of England.]—and after her death she entered the Queen's service, but when these places were afterwards abolished, Monsieur took back Ludres and Dampierre, the two Ladies of Honour he had given to the Queen. The former was called Madame, because she was canoness of a chapter at Lorraine.

It is said that the King never observed her beauty while she was with the Queen, and that it was not until she was with me that he fell in love with her. Her reign lasted only two years. Montespan told the King that Ludres had certain ringworms upon her body, caused by a poison that had been given her in her youth by Madame de Cantecroix. At twelve or thirteen years of age, she had inspired the old Duc de Lorraine with so violent a passion that he resolved to marry her at all events. The poison caused eruptions, covered her with ringworms from head to foot, and prevented the marriage. She was cured so well as to preserve the beauty of her figure, but she was always subject to occasional eruptions. Although now (1718) more than seventy years old, she is still beautiful; she has as fine features as can be seen, but a very disagreeable manner of speaking; she lisps horribly. She is, however, a good sort of person. Since she has been converted she thinks of nothing but the education of her nieces, and limits her own expenses that she may give the more to her brother's children. She is in a convent at Nancy, which she is at liberty to quit when she pleases. She, as well as her nieces, enjoy pensions from the King.

I have seen Beauvais, that femme de chambre of the Queen-mother, a one-eyed creature, who is said to have first taught the King the art of intriguing. She was perfectly acquainted with all its mysteries, and had led a very profligate life; she lived several years after my arrival in France.

Louis XIV. carried his gallantries to debauchery. Provided they were women, all were alike to him peasants, gardeners' girls, femmes de chambre, or ladies of quality. All that they had to do was to seem to be in love with him.

For a long time before his death, however, he had ceased to run after women; he even exiled the Duchesse de la Ferte, because she pretended to be dying for him. When she could not see him, she had his portrait in her carriage to contemplate it. The King said that it made him ridiculous, and desired her to retire to her own estate. The Duchesse de Roquelaure, of the house of Laval, was also suspected of wishing to captivate the King; but his Majesty was not so severe with her as with La Ferte. There was great talk in the scandalous circles about this intrigue; but I did not thrust my nose into the affair.

I am convinced that the Duchesse de la Valliere always loved the King very much. Montespan loved him for ambition, La Soubise for interest, and Maintenon for both. La Fontange loved him also, but only like the heroine of a romance; she was a furiously romantic person. Ludres was also very much attached to him, but the King soon got tired of her. As for Madame de Monaco, I would not take an oath that she never intrigued with the King. While the King was fond of her, Lauzun, who had a regular though a secret arrangement with his cousin, fell into disgrace for the first time. He had forbidden his fair one to see the King; but finding her one day sitting on the ground, and talking with His Majesty, Lauzun, who, in his place as Captain of the guard, was in the chamber, was so transported with jealousy that he could not restrain himself, and, pretending to pass, he trod so violently on the hand which Madame de Monaco had placed upon the ground, that he nearly crushed it. The King, who thus guessed at their intrigue, reprimanded him. Lauzun replied insolently, and was sent for the first time to the Bastille.

Madame de Soubise was cunning, full of dissimulation, and very wicked. She deceived the good Queen cruelly; but the latter rewarded her for this in exposing her falsehood and in unmasking her to the world. As soon as the King had undeceived Her Majesty with respect to this woman, her history became notorious, and the Queen amused herself in relating her triumph, as she called it, to everybody.

The King and Monsieur had been accustomed from their childhood to great filthiness in the interior of their houses; so much so, that they did not know it ought to be otherwise, and yet, in their persons, they were particularly neat.

Madame de la Motte, who had been at Chaillot, preferred the old Marquis de Richelieu to the King. She declared to His Majesty that her heart was no longer disposable, but that it was at length fixed.

I can never think, without anger, of the evil which has been spoken of the late King, and how little His Majesty has been regretted by those to whom he had done so much good.

I hardly dare repeat what the King said to me on his death-bed. All those who were usually in his cabinet were present, with the exception of the Princess, his daughter, the Princesse de Conti, and Madame de Vendome, who, alone, did not see the King. The whole of the Royal Family was assembled. He recommended his legitimated daughters to live together in concord, and I was the innocent cause of his saying something disagreeable to them. When the King said, "I recommend you all to be united," I thought he alluded to me and my son's daughter; and I said, "Yes, Monsieur, you shall be obeyed." He turned towards me, and said in a stern voice, "Madame, you thought I spoke of you. No, no; you are a sensible person, and I know you; it is to the Princesses, who are not so, that I speak:"

Louis XIV. proved at his death that he was really a great man, for it would be impossible to die with more courage than he displayed. For eight days he had incessantly the approach of death before his eyes without betraying fear or apprehension; he arranged everything as if he had only been going to make a journey.

Eight or ten days before his death a disease had appeared in his leg; a gangrene ensued, and it was this which caused his death. But for three months preceding he had been afflicted with a slow fever, which had reduced him so much that he looked like a lath. That old rogue, Fagon, had brought him to this condition, by administering purgatives and sudorifics of the most violent kind. At the instigation of Pere Letellier, he had been tormented to death by the cursed constitution,—[The affair of the Bull Unigenitus]—and had not been allowed to rest day or night. Fagon was a wicked old scoundrel, much more attached to Maintenon than to the King. When I perceived how much it was sought to exault the Duc du Maine, and that the old woman cared so little for the King's death, I could not help entertaining unfavourable notions of this old rascal.

It cannot be denied that Louis XIV. was the finest man in his kingdom. No person had a better appearance than he. His figure was agreeable, his legs well made, his feet small, his voice pleasant; he was lusty in proportion; and, in short, no fault could be found with his person. Some folks thought he was too corpulent for his height, and that Monsieur was too stout; so that it was said, by way of a joke at Court, that there had been a mistake, and that one brother had received what had been intended for the other. The King was in the habit of keeping his mouth open in an awkward way.

An English gentleman, Mr. Hammer, found him an expert fencer.

He preserved his good looks up to his death, although some of my ladies, who saw him afterwards, told me that he could scarcely be recognized. Before his death, his stature had been diminished by a head, and he perceived this himself.

His pronunciation was very distinct, but all his children, from the Dauphin to the Comte de Toulouse, lisped. They used to say, Pahi, instead of Paris.

In general, the King would have no persons at his table but members of the Royal Family. As for the Princesses of the blood, there were so many of them that the ordinary table would not have held them; and, indeed, when we were all there, it was quite full.

The King used to sit in the middle, and had the Dauphin and the Duke of Burgundy at his right, and the Dauphine and the Duchesse de Berri on his left; on one of the sides Monsieur and I sat; and on the other, my son and his wife; the other parts of the table were reserved for the noblemen in waiting, who did not take their places behind the King, but opposite to him. When the Princesses of the blood or any other ladies were received at the King's table, we were waited on, not by noblemen, but by other officers of the King's household, who stood behind like pages. The King upon such occasions was waited on by his chief Maitre d'Hotel. The pages never waited at the King's table, but on journeys; and then upon no person but the King. The Royal Family had persons to attend them who were not noble. Formerly all the King's officers, such as the butler, the cupbearer, etc., etc., were persons of rank; but afterwards, the nobility becoming poor could not afford to buy the high offices; and they fell, of necessity, into the hands of more wealthy citizens who could pay for them.

The King, the late Monsieur, the Dauphin, and the Duc de Berri were great eaters. I have often seen the King eat four platefuls of different soups, a whole pheasant, a partridge, a plateful of salad, mutton hashed with garlic, two good-sized slices of ham, a dish of pastry, and afterwards fruit and sweetmeats. The King and Monsieur were very fond of hard eggs.

Louis XIV. understood perfectly the art of satisfying people even while he reproved their requests. His manners were most affable, and he spoke with so much politeness as to win all hearts.

SECTION III.—MADEMOISELLE DE FONTANGE.

I had a Maid of Honour whose name was Beauvais; she was a very well-disposed person: the King fell in love with her, but she remained firm against all his attempts. He then turned his attention to her companion, Fontange, who was also very pretty, but not very sensible. When he first saw her he said, "There is a wolf that will not eat me;" and yet he became very fond of her soon afterwards. Before she came to me she had dreamt all that was to befall her, and a pious Capuchin explained her dream to her. She told me of it herself long before she became the King's mistress. She dreamt that she had ascended a high mountain, and, having reached the summit, she was dazzled by an exceedingly bright cloud; then on a sudden she found herself in such profound darkness that her terror at this accident awoke her. When she told her confessor he said to her: "Take care of yourself; that mountain is the Court, where some distinction awaits you; it will, however, be but of short duration; if you abandon your God He will forsake you and you will fall into eternal darkness."

There is no doubt that Fontange died by poison; she accused Montespan of being the cause of her death. A servant who had been bribed by that favourite destroyed her and some of her people by means of poison mixed with milk. Two of them died with her, and said publicly that they had been poisoned.

Fontange was a stupid little creature, but she had a very good heart. She was very red-haired, but, beautiful as an angel from head to foot.

SECTION IV.-MADAME DE LA VALLIERE.

When one of Madame de Montespan's children died, the King was deeply affected; but he was not so at the death of the poor Comte de Vermandois (the son of La Valliere). He could not bear him, because Montespan and that old Maintenon had made him believe the youth was not his but the Duc de Lauzun's child. It had been well if all the King's reputed children had been as surely his as this was. Madame de La Valliere was no light mistress, as her unwavering penitence sufficiently proved. She was an amiable, gentle, kind and tender woman. Ambition formed no part of her love for the King; she had a real passion for him, and never loved any other person. It was at Montespan's instigation that the King behaved so ill to her. The poor creature's heart was broken, but she imagined that she could not make a sacrifice more agreeable to God than that which had been the cause of her errors; and thought that her repentance ought to proceed from the same source as her crime. She therefore remained, by way of self-mortification, with Montespan, who, having a great portion of wit, did not scruple to ridicule her publicly, behaved extremely ill to her, and obliged the King to do the same.

He used to pass through La Valliere's chamber to go to Montespan's; and one day, at the instigation of the latter, he threw a little spaniel, which he had called Malice, at the Duchesse de La Valliere, saying: "There, Madam, is your companion; that's all."

This was the more cruel, as he was then going direct to Montespan's chamber. And yet La Valliere bore everything patiently; she was as virtuous as Montespan was vicious. Her connection with the King might be pardoned, when it was remembered that everybody had not only advised her to it, but had even assisted to bring it about. The King was young, handsome and gallant; she was, besides, very young; she was naturally modest, and had a very good heart. She was very much grieved when she was made a Duchess, and her children legitimated; before that she thought no one knew she had had children. There was an inexpressible charm in her countenance, her figure was elegant, her eyes were always in my opinion much finer than Montespan's, and her whole deportment was unassuming. She was slightly lame, but not so much as to impair her appearance.

When I first arrived in France she had not retired to the convent, but was still in the Court. We became and continued very intimate until she took the veil. I was deeply affected when this charming person took that resolution; and, at the moment when the funeral pall was thrown over her, I shed so many tears that I could see no more. She visited me after the ceremony, and told me that I should rather congratulate than weep for her, for that from that moment her happiness was to begin: she added that she should never forget the kindness and friendship I had displayed towards her, and which was so much more than she deserved. A short time afterwards I went to see her. I was curious to know why she had remained so long in the character of an attendant to Montespan. She told me that God had touched her heart, and made her sensible of her crimes; that she felt she ought to perform a penitence, and suffer that which would be most painful to her, which was to love the King, and to be despised by him; that for the three years after the King had ceased to love her she had suffered the torments of the damned, and that she offered her sorrows to Heaven as the expiation of her sins; and as her sins had been public, so should be her repentance. She said she knew very well that she had been taken for a fool, who was not sensible of anything; but that at the very period she alluded to she suffered most, and continued to do so until God inspired her with the resolution to abandon everything, and to serve Him alone, which she had since put into execution; but that now she considered herself unworthy, on account of her past life, to live in the society of persons as pure and pious as the Carmelite Sisters. All this evidently came from the heart.

From the time she became professed, she was entirely devoted to Heaven. I often told her that she had only transposed her love, and had given to God that which had formerly been the King's. She has said frequently that if the King should come into the convent she would refuse to see him, and would hide herself so that he could not find her. She was, however, spared this pain, for the King not only never went, but seemed to have forgotten her, as if he had never known her.

To accuse La Valliere of loving any one besides the King was wicked to the last degree, but falsehoods cost Montespan but little. The Comte de Vermandois was a good sort of young man, and loved me as if I had been his mother. When his irregularities were first discovered,—[A more particular account of these will be found hereafter.]—I was very angry with him; and I had caused him to be told very seriously that if he had behaved ill I should cease to have any regard for him. This grieved him to the heart; he sent to me daily, and begged permission to say only a few words to me. I was firm during four weeks; at length I permitted him to come, when he threw himself at my feet, begged my pardon, promising to amend his conduct, and beseeching me to restore him my friendship (without which he said he could not exist), and to assist him again with my advice. He told me the whole history of his follies, and convinced me that he had been most grossly deluded.

When the Dauphine lay in of the Duke of Burgundy, I said to the King, "I hope your Majesty will not upon this occasion refuse a humble request I have to make to you."

He smiled and said, "What have you to ask, then?"

I replied, "The pardon, Monsieur, of the poor Comte de Vermandois."

He smiled once more, and said, "You are a very good friend; but as for M. Vermandois, he has not been sufficiently punished for his crimes."

"The poor lad," I rejoined, "is so very penitent for his offence."

The King replied, "I do not yet feel myself inclined to see him; I am too angry with him still."

Several months elapsed before the King would see him; but the young man was very grateful to me for having spoken in his behalf; and my own children could not be more attached to me than he was. He was well made, but his appearance, though not disagreeable, was not remarkably good; he squinted a little.

SECTION V.—MADAME DE MONTESPAN

The King at first could not bear Madame de Montespan,—[Daughter of Gabriel de Roche Chouart, first Duc de Mortemart.]—and blamed Monsieur and even the Queen for associating with her; yet, eventually, he fell deeply in love with her himself.

She was more of an ambitious than a libertine woman, but as wicked as the devil himself. Nothing could stand between her and the gratification of her ambition, to which she would have made any sacrifice. Her figure was ugly and clumsy, but her eyes bespoke great intelligence, though they were somewhat too bright. Her mouth was very pretty and her smile uncommonly agreeable. Her complexion was fairer than La Valliere's, her look was more bold, and her general appearance denoted her intriguing temper. She had very beautiful light hair, fine arms, and pretty hands, which La Valliere had not. But the latter was always very neat, and Montespan was filthy to the last degree. She was very amusing in conversation, and it was impossible to be tired in talking with her.

The King did not regret Montespan more than he did La Fontange. The Duc d'Antin, her only legitimate child, was also the only one who wept at her death. When the King had the others legitimated, the mother's name was not mentioned, so that it might appear Madame de Montespan was not their mother.

[Madame de Montespan had eight children by Louis XIV. The Duc du   Maine; Comte Vegin; Mademoiselle de Nantes, married to the Duc de   Bourbon; Mademoiselle de Tours, married to the Regent Duc d'Orleans;   the Comte de Toulouse, and two other sons who died young.]

She was once present at a review, and as she passed before the German soldiers they called out:

"Konigs Hure! Hure!" When the King asked her in the evening how she liked the review, she said: "Very well, but only those German soldiers are so simple as not to call things by their proper names, for I had their shouts explained to me."

Madame de Montespan and her eldest daughter could drink a large quantity of wine without being affected by it. I have seen them drink six bumpers of the strong Turin Rosa Solis, besides the wine which they had taken before. I expected to see them fall under the table, but, on the contrary, it affected them no more than a draught of water.

It was Madame de Montespan who invented the 'robes battantes' for the purpose of concealing her pregnancy, because it was impossible to discover the shape in those robes. But when she wore them, it was precisely as if she had publicly announced that which she affected to conceal, for everybody at the Court used to say, "Madame de Montespan has put on her robe battante, therefore she must be pregnant." I believe she did it on purpose, hoping that it commanded more attention for her at Court, as it really did.

It is quite true that she always had a Royal bodyguard, and it was fit that she should, because the King was always in her apartments by day and night. He transacted business there with his Ministers, but, as there were several chambers, the lady was, nevertheless, quite at liberty to do as she pleased, and the Marshal de Noailles, though a devout person, was still a man. When she went out in a carriage, she had guards, lest her husband should, as he had threatened, offer her some insult.

She caused the Queen great vexation, and it is quite true that she used to ridicule her; but then she did the same to everybody besides. She, however, never ventured upon any direct or remarkable impertinence to Her Majesty, for the King would not have suffered it.

She had married one of her cousins, M. de Montpipeau, to Mademoiselle Aubry, the daughter of a private citizen who was exceedingly rich. To convince her that she had made a good match, Madame de Montespan had her brought into her own small private room. The young lady was not accustomed to very refined society, and the first time she went she seated herself upon the table, and, crossing her legs, sat swinging there as if she had been in her own chamber. The laugh which this excited cannot be conceived, nor the comical manner in which Madame de Montespan turned it to the King's amusement. The young lady thought that her new relation was inclined to be favourable to her, and loaded her with compliments. In general, Montespan had the skill of representing things so humourously that it was impossible not to laugh at her.

According to the law of the land, all her children were supposed to be Monsieur de Montespan's. When her husband was dangerously ill, Madame de Montespan, who in some degree affected devotion, sent to ask him if he would allow her to nurse him in his sickness. He replied that he would very willingly, provided she would bring all his children home with her, but if she left one behind he would not receive her. After this answer, she took care not to go, for her husband was a great brute, and would have said whatever he pleased as soon as she presented herself to him.

With the exception of the Comte de Toulouse, all the children she had by the King are marked. The Duc du Maine is paralytic, Madame d'Orleans is crooked, and Madame la Duchesse is lame.

M. de Montespan was not a very estimable person; he did nothing but play. He was a very sordid man, and I believe if the King had chosen to give him a good round sum he would have been very quiet. It was amusing enough to see him and his son, d'Antin, playing with Madame d'Orleans and Madame la Duchesse, and presenting the cards very politely, and kissing his hand to the Princesses, who were called his own daughters. He thought it a joke himself, and always turned aside a little to laugh in his sleeve.

SECTION VI.—MADAME DE MAINTENON.

The marriage of Louis XIV. with old Maintenon proves how impossible it is to escape one's fate. The King said one day to the Duc de Crequi and to M. de La Rochefoucauld, long before he knew Mistress Scarron, "I am convinced that astrology is false. I had my nativity cast in Italy, and I was told that, after living to an advanced age, I should be in love with an old ——- to the last moment of my existence. I do not think there is any great likelihood of that." He laughed most heartily as he said this; and yet the thing has taken place.

The history of Theodora, in Procopius, bears a singular resemblance to that of Maintenon. In the history of Sweden, too, there is a similar character in the person of Sigbritta, a Dutch woman, who lived during the reign of Christian IL, King of Denmark, Sweden and Norway, who bears so great a likeness to Maintenon that I was struck with it as soon as I read it. I cannot imagine how they came to permit its publication. It is fortunate for the Abbe Vertot, who is the author, that the King does not love reading, otherwise he would certainly have been sent to the Bastille. Several persons thought that the Abbe had invented it by way of a joke, but he swears by all that is good that he found it in the annals of Sweden. The old woman cannot have read it either, for she is too much occupied in reading the letters written to her from Paris, relating all that is going on there and at the Court. Sometimes the packets have consisted of twenty or thirty sheets; she kept them or showed them to the King, according as she liked or disliked the persons.

She was not deficient in wit, and could talk very well whenever she chose. She did not like to be called La Marquise, but preferred the simpler and shorter title of Madame de Maintenon.

She did not scruple to display openly the hatred she had for me. For example, when the Queen of England came to Marly, and went out on foot or in the carriage with the King, on their return the Queen, the Dauphine, the Princess of England, and all the Princesses, went into the King's room; I alone was excluded.

It was with great regret that I gave up my Maids of Honour. I had four, sometimes five of them, with their governess and sub-governess; they amused me very much, for they were all very gay. The old woman feared there might be some among them to whom the King might take a fancy, as he had done to Ludre and Fontange. I only kept my Maids of Honour a year after the death of Monsieur. The King was always fond of the sex, and if the old woman had not watched him very narrowly he would have slipped through her fingers in spite of all his devotion.

She hated the Dauphine because the latter would not let her treat her like a child, but wished to keep a Court and live as became her rank. This the old woman could not and would not endure. She loved to set all things in confusion, as she did afterwards with the second Dauphine, in the hope of compelling the King to recognize and proclaim her as Queen; but this the King never would do, notwithstanding all her artifices.—

[Other writers including Madame de Montespan put it just the opposite way that the King wished to proclaim Maintenon Queen and she refused. D.W.]

Nobody at Court used perfumery except that old woman; her gloves were always scented with jessamine. The King could not bear scent on any other person, and only endured it in her because she made him believe that it was somebody else who was perfumed.

If Madame des Ursins had not been protected by Madame de Maintenon, she would have been ruined at Court long before the Queen of Spain dismissed her, for in his heart the King disliked her excessively; but all those who were supported by Madame de Maintenon were sure to triumph.

The old woman took great pains to conceal from the King all that could give him pain; but she did not scruple to torment him incessantly about the Constitution and those illegitimate children, whom she wished to raise higher than the King desired. She teased him also with her hatred of my son and myself, for he had no dislike to us.

Neither the Queen nor the first Dauphine nor myself ever received a farthing; but this old Maintenon took money on all sides, and taught the second Dauphine to do the same. Her example was followed by all the others.

In the time of the Queen and the first Dauphine, everything at Court was conducted with modesty and dignity. Those persons who indulged in secret debaucheries at least kept up a respect for appearances; but from the time that Maintenon's reign began, and the King's illegitimate children were made a part of the Royal Family, all was turned topsy-turvy.

When she once conceived a hatred against any person it was for life, and she never ceased secretly to persecute them, as I have personally experienced. She has laid many snares for me, which by the help of Providence I have always avoided. She was terribly annoyed by her first husband, who kept her always shut up in his chamber. Many people say, too, that she hastened the passage of poor Mansart into the other world. It is quite certain that he was poisoned by means of green peas, and that he died within three hours of eating them. She had learnt that on the same day M. de Torcy was going to show the King certain papers containing an account of the money which she had received from the post unknown to His Majesty. The King never knew anything of this adventure nor of that of Louvois, because, as people had no fancy for being poisoned, they held their tongues.

Before she got into power, the Church of France was very reasonable; but she spoiled everything by encouraging such follies and superstitions as the rosaries and other things. When any reasonable men appeared, the old woman and the Confessor had them banished or imprisoned. These two persons were the causes of all the persecutions which the Lutherans and those of the reformed religion underwent in France. Pere La Chaise, with his long ears, began this worthy enterprise, and Pere Letellier completed it; France was thus ruined in every way.

The Duchesse de Bourbon was taught by her mother and her aunt, Mesdames de Montespan and De Thiange, to ridicule everybody, under the pretext of diverting the King. The children, who were always present, learnt nothing else; and this practice was the universal dread of all persons in the Court; but not more so than that of the gouvernante of the children (Madame de Maintenon). Her habit was to treat things very seriously, and without the least appearance of jesting. She used to speak ill of persons to the King through charity and piety, for the sole purpose of correcting the faults of her neighbours; and under this pretext she filled the King with a bad opinion of the whole Court, solely that he might have no desire for any other company than that of herself and her creatures, who were alone perfect and without the slightest defect. What rendered her disclosures the more dangerous was that they were frequently followed by banishment, by 'lettres-de-cachet', and by imprisonment. When Montespan was in power, at least there was nothing of this sort. Provided she could amuse herself at the expense of all around her, she was content.

I have often heard Madame de Maintenon say, jestingly, "I have always been either too far from, or too near to, greatness, to know exactly what it is."

She could not forgive the King for not having proclaimed her Queen. She put on such an appearance of humility and piety to the Queen of England that she passed for a saint with her. The old woman knew very well that I was a right German, and that I never could endure unequal alliances. She fancied, therefore, that it was on my account the King was reluctant to acknowledge his marriage with her, and this it was that made her hate me so profoundly. From the time of the King's death and our departure from Versailles my son has never once seen her.

She would never allow me to meddle with anything, because she feared it would give me an opportunity of talking to the King. It was not that she was jealous lest he should be fond of me, but she feared that, in speaking according to my usual custom, freely and without restraint, I should open the King's eyes and point out to him the folly of the life he was leading. I had, however, no such intention.

All the mistresses the King had did not tarnish his reputation so much as the old woman he married; from her proceeded all the calamities which have since befallen France. It was she who excited the persecution against the Protestants, invented the heavy taxes which raised the price of grain so high, and caused the scarcity. She helped the Ministers to rob the King; by means of the Constitution she hastened his death; she brought about my son's marriage; she wanted to place bastards upon the throne; in short, she ruined and confused everything.

Formerly the Court never went into mourning for children younger than six years of age; but the Duc du Maine having lost a daughter only one year old, the old woman persuaded the King to order a mourning, and since that time it has been always worn for children of a year old.

The King always hated or loved as she chose to direct; it was not, therefore, surprising that he could not bear Montespan, for all her failings were displayed to him by the old woman, who was materially assisted in this office by Montespan's eldest son, the Duc du Maine. In her latter years she enjoyed a splendour which she could never have dreamed of before; the Court looked upon her as a sort of divinity.

The old lady never failed to manifest her hatred of my son on all occasions. She liked my husband no better than myself; and my son and my daughter and her husband were equally objects of her detestation. She told a lady once that her greatest fault was that of being attached to me. Neither my son nor I had ever done her any injury. If Monsieur thought fit to tell his niece, the Duchess of Burgundy, a part of Maintenon's history, in the vexation he felt at her having estranged the Princess from him, and not choosing that she should behave affectionately to her great-uncle, that was not our fault. She was as jealous of the Dauphine as a lover is of his mistress.

She was in the habit of saying, "I perceive there is a sort of vertigo at present affecting the whole world." When she perceived that the harvest had failed, she bought up all the corn she could get in the markets, and gained by this means an enormous sum of money, while the poor people were dying of famine. Not having a sufficient number of granaries, a large quantity of this corn became rotten in the boats loaded with it, and it was necessary to throw it into the river. The people said this was a just judgment from Heaven.

My son made me laugh the other day. I asked him how Madame de Maintenon was.

"Wonderfully well," he replied.

"That is surprising at her age," I said.

"Yes," he rejoined, "but do you not know that God has, by way, of punishing the devil, doomed him to exist a certain number of years in that ugly body?"

Montespan was the cause of the King's love for old Maintenon. In the first place, when she wished to have her near her children, she shut her ears to the stories which were told of the irregular life which the hussy had been leading; she made everybody who spoke to the King about her, praise her; her virtue and piety were cried up until the King was made to think that all he had heard of her light conduct were lies, and in the end he most firmly believed it. In the second place, Montespan was a creature full of caprice, who had no control over herself, was passionately fond of amusement, was tired whenever she was alone with the King, whom she loved only, for the purposes of her own interest or ambition, caring very little for him personally. To occupy him, and to prevent him from observing her fondness for play and dissipation, she brought Maintenon. The King was fond of a retired life, and would willingly have passed his time alone with Montespan; he often reproached her with not loving him sufficiently, and they quarrelled a great deal occasionally. Goody Scarron then appeared, restored peace between them, and consoled the King. She, however, made him remark more and more the bitter temper of Montespan; and, affecting great devotion, she told the King that his affliction was sent him by Heaven, as a punishment for the sins he had committed with Montespan. She was eloquent, and had very fine eyes; by degrees the King became accustomed to her, and thought she would effect his salvation. He then made a proposal to her; but she remained firm, and gave him to understand that, although he was very agreeable to her, she would not for the whole world offend Heaven. This excited in the King so great an admiration for her, and such a disgust to Madame de Montespan, that he began to think of being converted. The old woman then employed her creature, the Duc du Maine, to insinuate to his mother that, since the King had taken other mistresses, for example, Ludres and Fontange, she had lost her authority, and would become an object of contempt at Court. This irritated her, and she was in a very bad humour when the King came. In the meantime, Maintenon was incessantly censuring the King; she told him that he would be damned if he did not live on better terms with the Queen. Louis XIV. repeated this to his wife, who considered herself much obliged to Madame de Maintenon: she treated her with marks of distinction, and consented to her being appointed second dame d'atour to the Dauphine of Bavaria; so that she had now nothing to do with Montespan. The latter became furious, and related to the King all the particulars of the life of Dame Scarron. But the King, knowing her to be an arrant fiend, who would spare no one in her passion, would not believe anything she said to him. The Duc du Maine persuaded his mother to retire from Court for a short time in order that the King might recall her. Being fond of her son, and believing him to be honest in the advice he gave her, she went to Paris, and wrote to the King that she would never come back. The Duc du Maine immediately sent off all her packages after her without her knowledge; he even had her furniture thrown out of the window, so that she could not come back to Versailles. She had treated the King so ill and so unkindly that he was delighted at being rid of her, and he did not care by what means. If she had remained longer, the King, teased as he was, would hardly have been secure against the transports of her passion. The Queen was extremely grateful to Maintenon for having been the means of driving away Montespan and bringing back the King to the marriage-bed; an arrangement to which, like an honest Spanish lady, she had no sort of objection. With that goodness of heart which was so remarkable in her, she thought she was bound to do something for Madame de Maintenon, and therefore consented to her being appointed dame d'atour. It was not until shortly before her death that she learnt she had been deceived by her. After the Queen's death, Louis XIV. thought he had gained a triumph over the very personification of virtue in overcoming the old lady's scruples; he used to visit her every afternoon, and she gained such an influence over him as to induce him to marry.

Madame la Marechale de Schomberg had a niece, Mademoiselle d'Aumale, whom her parents had placed at St. Cyr during the King's life. She was ugly, but possessed great wit, and succeeded in amusing the King so well that the old Maintenon became disturbed at it. She picked a quarrel with her, and wanted to send her again to the convent. But the King opposed this, and made the old lady bring her back. When the King died, Mademoiselle d'Aumale would not stay any longer with Madame de Maintenon.

When the Dauphine first arrived, she did not know a soul. Her household was formed before she came. She did not know who Maintenon was; and when Monsieur explained it to her a year or two afterwards, it was too late to resist. The Dauphin used at first to laugh at the old woman, but as he was amorous of one of the Dauphine's Maids of Honour, and consequently was acquainted with the gouvernante of the Maids of Honour, Montchevreuil, a creature of Maintenon's, that old fool set her out in very fair colours. Madame de Maintenon did not scruple to estrange the Dauphin from the Dauphine, and very piously to sell him first Rambure and afterwards La Force.

18th April, 1719—To-day I will begin my letter with the story of Madame de Ponikau, in Saxony. One day during her lying-in, as she was quite alone, a little woman dressed in the ancient French fashion came into the room and begged her to permit a party to celebrate a wedding, promising that they would take care it should be when she was alone. Madame de Ponikau having consented, one day a company of dwarfs of both sexes entered her chamber. They brought with them a little table, upon which a good dinner, consisting of a great number of dishes, was placed, and round which all the wedding guests took their seats. In the midst of the banquet, one of the little waiting-maids ran in, crying,

"Thank Heaven, we have escaped great perplexity. The old —— is dead."

It is the same here, the old is dead. She quitted this world at St. Cyr, on Saturday last, the 15th day of April, between four and five o'clock in the evening. The news of the Duc du Maine and his wife being arrested made her faint, and was probably the cause of her death, for from that time she had not a moment's repose or content. Her rage, and the annihilation of her hopes of reigning with him, turned her blood. She fell sick of the measles, and was for twenty days in great fever. The disorder then took an unfavourable turn, and she died. She had concealed two years of her age, for she pretended to be only eighty-four, while she was really eighty-six years old. I believe that what grieved her most in dying was to quit the world, and leave me and my son behind her in good health. When her approaching death was announced to her, she said, "To die is the least event of my life." The sums which her nephew and niece De Noailles inherited from her were immense; but the amount cannot be ascertained, because she had concealed a large part of her wealth.

A cousin of hers, the Archbishop of Rouen, who created so much trouble with respect to the Constitution, followed his dear cousin into the other world exactly a week afterwards, on the same day, and at the same hour.

Nobody, knows what the King said to Maintenon on his death bed. She had retired to St. Cyr before he died. They fetched her back, but she did not stay, to the end. I think the King repented of his folly in having married her, and, indeed, notwithstanding all her contrivances, she could not persuade him to declare their marriage. She wept for the King's death, but was not so deeply afflicted as she ought to have been. She always flattered herself with the hope of reigning together with the Duc du Maine.

From the beginning to the end of their connection, the King's society was always irksome to her, and she did not scruple to say so to her own relations. She had before been much accustomed to the company of men, but afterwards dared see none but the King, whom she never loved, and his Ministers. This made her ill-tempered, and she did not fail to make those persons who were within her power feel its effects. My son and I have had our share of it. She thought only of two things, her ambition and her amusement. The old sorceress never loved any one but her favourite, the Duc du Maine. Perceiving that the

Dauphine was desirous of acting for herself and profiting by the king's favour, that she ridiculed her to her attendants, and seemed not disposed to yield to her domination, she withdrew her attention from her; and if the Dauphine had not possessed great influence with the King, Maintenon would have turned round upon her former favourite; she was therefore very soon consoled for this Princess's death. She thought to have the King entirely at her disposal through the Duc du Maine, and it was for this reason that she relied so much upon him, and was so deeply afflicted at his imprisonment.

She was not always so malicious, but her wickedness increased with her years. For us it had been well that she had died twenty years before, but for the honour of the late King that event ought to have taken place thirty-three years back, for, if I do not mistake, she was married to the King two years after the Queen's death, which happened five-and-thirty years ago.

If she had not been so outrageously inveterate against me, she could have done me much more injury with the King, but she set about it too violently; this caused the King to perceive that it was mere malice, and therefore it had no effect. There were three reasons why she hated me horribly. The first was, that the King treated me favourably. I was twenty-five years of age when she came into power; she saw that, instead of suffering myself to be governed by her, I would have my own way, and, as the King was kind to me, that I should undeceive him and counsel him not to suffer himself to be blindly led by so worthless a person. The second reason was that, knowing how much I must disapprove of her marriage with the King, she imagined I should always be an obstacle to her being proclaimed Queen; and the third was, that I had always taken the Dauphine's part whenever Maintenon had mortified her. The poor Dauphine did not know what to do with Maintenon, who possessed the King's heart, and was acquainted with all his intentions. Notwithstanding all the favour she enjoyed, the old lady was somewhat timid. If the Dauphine could have summoned courage to threaten Maintenon, as I advised her, to hint that her previous life was well known, and that unless she behaved better to the Dauphine the latter would expose her to the King, but that if, on the contrary, she would live quietly and on good terms, silence should be kept, then Maintenon would have pursued a very different conduct. That wicked Bessola always prevented this, because then she would have had no more tales to tell.

One day I found the Dauphine in the greatest distress and drowned in tears, because the old woman had threatened to make her miserable, to have Madame du Maine preferred to her, to make her odious to the whole Court and to the King besides. I laughed when she told me all this.

"Is it possible," I said, "with so much sense and courage as you possess that you will suffer this old hag to frighten you thus? You can have nothing to fear: you are the Dauphine, the first person in the kingdom; no one can do you any mischief without the most serious cause. When, therefore, they threaten you, answer boldly: 'I do not fear pour menaces; Madame de Maintenon is too much beneath me, and the King is too just to condemn without hearing me. If you compel me I will speak to him myself, and we shall see whether he will protect me or not.'"

The Dauphine was not backward in repeating this word for word. The old woman immediately said, "This is not your own speech; this proceeds from Madame's bad advice; you have not courage enough to think thus for yourself; however, we shall see whether Madame's friendship will be profitable to you or not." But from that time forth she never threatened the Princess. She had introduced the name of the Duchesse du Maine adroitly enough in her threats to the Dauphine, because, having educated the Duke, she thought her power at Court unlimited, and wished to chew that she could prefer the last Princess of the blood before the first person in France, and that therefore it was expedient to submit to her and obey her. But Bessola, who was jealous of me, and could not bear that the Dauphine should confide in me, had been bought over by the old woman, to whom she betrayed us, and told her all that I had said to console the Princess; she was commissioned, besides, to torment and intimidate her mistress as much as possible, and acquitted herself to a miracle, terrifying her to death, and at the same time seeming to act only from attachment, and to be entirely devoted to her. The poor Dauphine never distrusted this woman, who had been educated with her, and had accompanied her to France; she did not imagine that falsehood and perfidy existed to such an extent as this infernal creature carried them. I was perfectly amazed at it. I opposed Bessola, and did all I could to console the Dauphine and to alleviate her vexation. She told me when she was dying that I had prolonged her life by two years by inspiring her with courage. My exertions, however, procured for me Maintenon's cordial hatred, which lasted to the end of her life. Although the Dauphine might have something to reproach herself with, she was not to be taken to task for it by that old woman, for who had ever led a less circumspect life than she? In public, or when we were together, she never said anything unpleasant to me, for she knew that I would not have failed to answer her properly, as I knew her whole life. Villarceaux had told me more of her than I desired to know.

When the King was talking to me on his death-bed she turned as red as fire.

"Go away, Madame," said she; "the King is too much affected while he talks to you; it may do him harm. Pray go away."

As I went out she followed me and said, "Do not think, Madame, that I have ever done you an ill turn with the King."

I answered her with tears, for I thought I should choke with grief: "Madame, do not let us talk upon that subject," and so quitted her.

That humpbacked old Fagon, her favourite, used to say that he disliked Christianity because it would not allow him to build a temple to Maintenon and an altar to worship her.

The only trait in her character that I can find to praise is her conduct to Montchevreuil; although she was a wicked old devil, Maintenon had reason to love her and be kind to her, for she had fed and clothed her when Maintenon was in great want.

I believe the old woman would not procure for Madame de Dangeau the privilege of the tabouret, only because she was a German and of good family. She once had two young girls from Strasbourg brought to Court, and made them pass for Countesses Palatine, placing them in the office of attendants upon her nieces. I did not know a word of it until the Dauphine came to tell it me with tears in her eyes.

I said to her, "Do not disturb yourself, leave me alone to act; when I have a good reason for what I do, I despise the old witch."

When I saw from my window the niece walking with these German girls, I went into the garden and met them. I called one of them, and asked her who she was. She told me, boldly, that she was a Countess Palatine of Lutzelstein.

"By the left hand?" I asked.

"No," she replied, "I am not illegitimate; the young Count Palatine married my mother, who is of the house of Gehlen."

"In that case," I said, "you cannot be Countess Palatine; for we never allow such unequal marriages to hold good. I will tell you, moreover, that you lie when you say that the Count Palatine married your mother; she is a ———, and the Count has married her no more than a hundred others have done; I know her lawful husband is a hautboy-player. If you presume, in future, to pass yourself off as a Countess Palatine I will have you stripped; let me never again hear anything of this; but if you will follow my advice, and take your proper name, I shall not reproach you. And now you see what you have to choose between."

The girl took this so much to heart that she died some days afterwards. As for the second, she was sent to a boarding-house in Paris, where she became as bad as her mother; but as she changed her name I did not trouble myself any further about her.

I told the Dauphine what I had done, who was very much obliged to me, and confessed she should not have had courage enough to do it herself. She feared that the King would be displeased with me; but he only said to me, jestingly, "One must not play tricks with you about your family, for it seems to be a matter of life or death with you."

I replied, "I hate lies."

There was a troop of Italian players who had got up a comedy called "The Pretended Prude." When I learnt they were going to represent it, I sent for them and told them not to do so. It was in vain; they played it, and got a great deal of money by it; but they were afterwards sent away in consequence. They then came to me and wanted me to intercede for them; but I said, "Why did you not take my advice?" It was said they hit off the character of Maintenon with the most amusing fidelity. I should have liked to see it, but I would not go lest the old woman should have told the King that I had planned it out of ill-will to her.

SECTION VII.—THE QUEEN—CONSORT OF LOUIS XIV.

Our Queen was excessively ignorant, but the kindest and most virtuous woman in the world; she had a certain greatness in her manner, and knew how to hold a Court extremely well. She believed everything the King told her, good or bad. Her teeth were very ugly, being black and broken. It was said that this proceeded from her being in the constant habit of taking chocolate; she also frequently ate garlic. She was short and fat, and her skin was very white. When she was not walking or dancing she seemed much taller. She ate frequently and for a long time; but her food was always cut in pieces as small as if they were for a singing bird. She could not forget her country, and her manners were always remarkably Spanish. She was very fond of play; she played basset, reversis, ombre, and sometimes a little primero; but she never won because she did not know how to play.

She had such as affection for the King that she used to watch his eyes to do whatever might be agreeable to him; if he only looked at her kindly she was in good spirits for the rest of the day. She was very glad when the King quitted his mistresses for her, and displayed so much satisfaction that it was commonly remarked. She had no objection to being joked upon this subject, and upon such occasions used to laugh and wink and rub her little hands.

One day the Queen, after having conversed for half-an-hour with the Prince Egon de Furstemberg,—[Cardinal Furstemberg, Bishop of Strasbourg.]—took me aside and said to me, "Did you know what M. de Strasbourg has been saying? I have not understood him at all."

A few minutes afterwards the Bishop said to me, "Did your Royal Highness hear what the Queen said to me? I have not comprehended a single word."

"Then," said I, "why did you answer her."

"I thought," he replied, "that it would have been indecorous to have appeared not to understand Her Majesty."

This made me laugh so much that I was obliged precipitately to quit the Chamber.

The Queen died of an abscess under her arm. Instead of making it burst, Fagon, who was unfortunately then her physician, had her blooded; this drove in the abscess, the disorder attacked her internally, and an emetic, which was administered after her bleeding, had the effect of killing the Queen.

The surgeon who blooded her said, "Have you considered this well, Sir? It will be the death of my Mistress!"

Fagon replied, "Do as I bid you."

Gervais, the surgeon, wept, and said to Fagon, "You have resolved, then, that my Mistress shall die by my hand!"

Fagon had her blooded at eleven o'clock; at noon he gave her an emetic, and three hours afterwards she was dead. It may be truly said that with her died all the happiness of France. The King was deeply grieved by this event, which that old villain Fagon brought about expressly for the purpose of confirming that mischievous old woman's fortune.

After the Queen's death I also happened to have an abscess. Fagon did all he could to make the King recommend me to be blooded; but I said to him, in His Majesty's presence, "No, I shall do no such thing. I shall treat myself according to my own method; and if you had done the same to the Queen she would have been alive now. I shall suffer the abscess to gather, and then I shall have it opened." I did so, and soon got well.

The King said very kindly to me, "Madame, I am afraid you will kill yourself."

I replied, laughing, "Your Majesty is too good to me, but I am quite satisfied with not having followed my physician's advice, and you will soon see that I shall do very well."

After my convalescence I said at table, in presence of my two doctors, Daguin, who was then first physician, and Fagon, who succeeded him upon his being disgraced, "Your Majesty sees that I was right to have my own way; for I am quite well, notwithstanding all the wise sayings and arguments of these gentlemen."

They were a little confused, but put it off with a laugh; and Fagon said to me,—

"When folks are as robust as you, Madame, they may venture to risk somewhat."

I replied, "If I am robust, it is because I never take medicine but on urgent occasions."

BOOK 2.

Philippe I., Duc d'Orleans Philippe II., Duc d'Orleans, Regent of France The Affairs of the Regency The Duchesse d'Orleans, Consort of the Regent The Dauphine, Princess of Bavaria. Adelaide of Savoy, the Second Dauphine The First Dauphin The Duke of Burgundy, the Second Dauphin Petite Madame

SECTION VIII.—PHILIPPE I., DUC D'ORLEANS.

Cardinal Mazarin perceiving that the King had less readiness than his brother, was apprehensive lest the latter should become too learned; he therefore enjoined the preceptor to let him play, and not to suffer him to apply to his studies.

"What can you be thinking of, M. la Mothe le Vayer," said the Cardinal; "would you try to make the King's brother a clever man? If he should be more wise than his brother, he would not be qualified for implicit obedience."

Never were two brothers more totally different in their appearance than the King and Monsieur. The King was tall, with light hair; his mien was good and his deportment manly. Monsieur, without having a vulgar air, was very small; his hair and eye-brows were quite black, his eyes were dark, his face long and narrow, his nose large, his mouth small, and his teeth very bad; he was fond of play, of holding drawing-rooms, of eating, dancing and dress; in short, of all that women are fond of. The King loved the chase, music and the theatre; my husband rather affected large parties and masquerades: his brother was a man of great gallantry, and I do not believe my husband was ever in love during his life. He danced well, but in a feminine manner; he could not dance like a man because his shoes were too high-heeled. Excepting when he was with the army, he would never get on horseback. The soldiers used to say that he was more afraid of being sun-burnt and of the blackness of the powder than of the musket-balls; and it was very true. He was very fond of building. Before he had the Palais Royal completed, and particularly the grand apartment, the place was, in my opinion, perfectly horrible, although in the Queen-mother's time it had been very much admired. He was so fond of the ringing of bells that he used to go to Paris on All Souls' Day for the purpose of hearing the bells, which are rung during the whole of the vigils on that day he liked no other music, and was often laughed at for it by his friends. He would join in the joke, and confess that a peal of bells delighted him beyond all expression. He liked Paris better than any other place, because his secretary was there, and he lived under less restraint than at Versailles. He wrote so badly that he was often puzzled to read his own letters, and would bring them to me to decipher them.

"Here, Madame," he used to say, laughing, "you are accustomed to my writing; be so good as to read me this, for I really cannot tell what I have been writing." We have often laughed at it.

He was of a good disposition enough, and if he had not yielded so entirely to the bad advice of his favourites, he would have been the best master in the world. I loved him, although he had caused me a great deal of pain; but during the last three years of his life that was totally altered. I had brought him to laugh at his own weakness, and even to take jokes without caring for them. From the period that I had been calumniated and accused, he would suffer no one again to annoy me; he had the most perfect confidence in me, and took my part so decidedly, that his favourites dared not practise against me. But before that I had suffered terribly. I was just about to be happy, when Providence thought fit to deprive me of my poor husband. For thirty years I had been labouring to gain him to myself, and, just as my design seemed to be accomplished, he died. He had been so much importuned upon the subject of my affection for him that he begged me for Heaven's sake not to love him any longer, because it was so troublesome. I never suffered him to go alone anywhere without his express orders.

The King often complained that he had not been allowed to converse sufficiently with people in his youth; but taciturnity was a part of his character, for Monsieur, who was brought up with him, conversed with everybody. The King often laughed, and said that Monsieur's chattering had put him out of conceit with talking. We used to joke Monsieur upon his once asking questions of a person who came to see him.

"I suppose, Monsieur," said he, "you come from the army?"

"No, Monsieur," replied the visitor, "I have never joined it."

"You arrive here, then, from your country house?"

"Monsieur, I have no country house."

"In that case, I imagine you are living at Paris with your family?"

"Monsieur, I am not married."

Everybody present at this burst into a laugh, and Monsieur in some confusion had nothing more to say. It is true that Monsieur was more generally liked at Paris than the King, on account of his affability. When the King, however, wished to make himself agreeable to any person, his manners were the most engaging possible, and he won people's hearts much more readily than my husband; for the latter, as well as my son, was too generally civil. He did not distinguish people sufficiently, and behaved very well only to those who were attached to the Chevalier de Lorraine and his favourites.

Monsieur was not of a temper to feel any sorrow very deeply. He loved his children too well even to reprove them when they deserved it; and if he had occasion to make complaints of them, he used to come to me with them.

"But, Monsieur," I have said, "they are your children as well as mine, why do you not correct them?"

He replied, "I do not know how to scold, and besides they would not care for me if I did; they fear no one but you."

By always threatening the children with me, he kept them in constant fear of me. He estranged them from me as much as possible, but he left me to exercise more authority over my elder daughter and over the Queen of Sicily than over my son; he could not, however, prevent my occasionally telling them what I thought. My daughter never gave me any cause to complain of her. Monsieur was always jealous of the children, and was afraid they would love me better than him: it was for this reason that he made them believe I disapproved of almost all they did. I generally pretended not to see this contrivance.

Without being really fond of any woman, Monsieur used to amuse himself all day in the company of old and young ladies to please the King: in order not to be out of the Court fashion, he even pretended to be amorous; but he could not keep up a deception so contrary to his natural inclination. Madame de Fiennes said to him one day, "You are in much more danger from the ladies you visit, than they are from you." It was even said that Madame de Monaco had attempted to give him some violent proofs of her affection. He pretended to be in love with Madame de Grancey; but if she had had no other lover than Monsieur she might have preserved her reputation. Nothing culpable ever passed between them; and he always endeavoured to avoid being alone with her. She herself said that whenever they happened to be alone he was in the greatest terror, and pretended to have the toothache or the headache. They told a story of the lady asking him to touch her, and that he put on his gloves before doing so. I have often heard him rallied about this anecdote, and have often laughed at it.

Madame de Grancey was one of the most foolish women in the world. She was very handsome at the time of my arrival in France, and her figure was as good as her face; besides, she was not so much disregarded by others as by my husband; for, before the Chevalier de Lorraine became her lover, she had had a child. I knew well that nothing had passed between Monsieur and Grancey, and I was never jealous of them; but I could not endure that she should derive a profit from my household, and that no person could purchase an employment in it without paying a douceur to her. I was also often indignant at her insolence to me, and at her frequently embroiling me with Monsieur. It was for these reasons, and not from jealousy, as was fancied by those who knew nothing about it, that I sometimes sharply reprimanded her. The Chevalier de Lorraine, upon his return from Rome, became her declared lover. It was through his contrivances, and those of D'Effiat, that she was brought into the house of Monsieur, who really cared nothing about her. Her continued solicitations and the behaviour of the Chevalier de Lorraine had so much disgusted Monsieur, that if he had lived he would have got rid of them both.

He had become tired of the Chevalier de Lorraine because he had found out that his attachment to him proceeded from interested motives. When Monsieur, misled by his favourites, did something which was neither just nor expedient, I used to say to him, "Out of complaisance to the Chevalier de Lorraine, you put your good sense into your pocket, and button it up so tight that it cannot be seen."

After my husband's death I saw Grancey only once; I met her in the garden. When she ceased to be handsome, she fell into utter despair; and so great a change took place in her appearance that no one would have known her. Her nose, before so beautiful, grew long and large, and was covered with pimples, over each of which she put a patch; this had a very singular effect; the red and white paint, too, did not adhere to her face. Her eyes were hollow and sunken, and the alteration which this had caused in her face cannot be imagined. In Spain they, lock up all the ladies at night, even to the septuagenary femmes de chambre. When Grancey followed our Queen to Spain as dame d'atour, she was locked up in the evening, and was in great grief about it.

When she was dying, she cried, "Ah, mon Dieu, must I die, who have never once thought of death?"

She had never done anything but sit at play with her lovers until five or six o'clock in the morning, feast, and smoke tobacco, and follow uncontrolled her natural inclinations.

When she reached her climacteric, she said, in despair, "Alas, I am growing old, I shall have no more children."

This was exceedingly amusing; and her friends, as well as her enemies, laughed at it. She once had a high dispute with Madame de Bouillon. One evening, Grancey chose to hide herself in one of the recesses formed by the windows in the chamber of the former lady, who, not thinking she was heard, conversed very freely with the Marquise d'Allure, respecting the libertine life of Grancey; in the course of which she said several strange things respecting the treatment which her lovers had experienced from her. Grancey at length rushed out, and fell to abusing Madame de Bouillon like a Billingsgate. The latter was not silent, and some exceedingly elegant discourse passed between them. Madame de Bouillon made a complaint against Grancey; in the first place, for having listened to her conversation; and in the second, for having insulted her in her own house. Monsieur reproved Grancey; told her that she had brought this inconvenience upon herself by her own indiscretion, and ordered her to be reconciled with her adversary.

"How can I," said Grancey, "be reconciled to Madame de Bouillon, after all the wicked things she has said about me?" But after a moment's reflection she added, "Yes, I can, for she did not say I was ugly."

They afterwards embraced, and made it up.

....

Monsieur was taken ill at ten o'clock at night, but he did not die until the next day at noon. I can never think of this night without horror. I remained with him from ten at night until five the next morning, when he lost all consciousness.—[The Duc d'Orleans died of apoplexy on the 9th June, 1701]

The Electors of Germany would not permit Monsieur to write to them in the same style as the King did.

SECTION IX.—PHILIPPE II., DUC D' ORLEANS, REGENT OF FRANCE.

From the age of fourteen to that of fifteen years, my son was not ugly; but after that time he became very much sun-burnt in Italy and Spain. Now, however, he is too ruddy; he is fat, but not tall, and yet he does not seem disagreeable to me. The weakness of his eyes causes him sometimes to squint. When he dances or is on horseback he looks very well, but he walks horridly ill. In his childhood he was so delicate that he could not even kneel without falling, through weakness; by degrees, however, his strength improved. He loads his stomach too much at table; he has a notion that it is good to make only one meal; instead of dinner, he takes only one cup of chocolate, so that by supper he is extremely hungry and thirsty. In answer to whatever objections are made to this regimen, he says he cannot do business after eating. When he gets tipsy, it is not with strong potations, but with Champagne or Tokay. He is not very fond of the chase. The weakness of his sight arose from an accident which befell him at the age of four years, and which was something like an apoplexy. He sees well enough near, and can read the smallest writing; but at the distance of half the room he cannot distinguish persons without a glass. He had an application of a powder to that eye which is worst, and, although it had caused intolerable pain to every other person who had used it, it seemed to have no effect upon him, for he laughed and chatted as usual. He found some benefit from this; but W. Gendron was too severe for him. That physician forbade the petits-soupers and the amusements which usually followed them; this was not agreeable to my son, and those who used to frequent them to their own advantage; they therefore persuaded him to adopt some other remedies which almost deprived him of sight. For the last forty years (1719), that is to say since the accident happened, the month of October has never elapsed without his health and eyesight being affected towards the 21st in some way or other.

He was only seventeen years old when he was married. If he had not been threatened with imprisonment in the old castle of Villers-Cotterets, and if hopes had not been given him of seeing the Duchesse de Bourbon as he wished, they could not have induced him to form this accursed marriage. It is my son's unlucky destiny to have for a wife a woman who is desirous of ruling everything with her brothers. It is commonly said, that where one sins there one suffers; and thus it has happened to my son with respect to his wife and his brothers-in-law. If he had not inflicted upon me the deepest vexation by uniting himself with this low race, he might now speak to them boldly. I never quarrelled with my son; but he was angry with me about this marriage, which he had contracted against my inclination.

As I sincerely love him, I have forgotten it; and I do not believe that we shall ever quarrel in future. When I have anything to say about his conduct, I say it openly, and there is an end of it. He behaves to me very respectfully. I did all in my power to prevent his marriage; but since it did take place, and with his consent, though without mine, I wish now only for his tranquillity. His wife fancies that she has done him an honour in marrying him, because he is only the son of the brother of a king, while she is the daughter of a king; but she will not perceive that she is also the daughter of a ———. He was obliged to put down all his feelings of nobility; and if I had a hundred crowns for as many times as he has since repented it, I could almost buy France for the King, and pay his debts. My son visits his wife every day, and when she is in good humour he stays with her a long time; but when she is ill-tempered, which, unfortunately, happens too often, he goes away without saying anything. I have every reason to be satisfied with him; he lives on very good terms with me, and I have no right to complain of his conduct; but I see that he does not repose much confidence in me, and I know many persons to whom he is more communicative.

I love my son with all my heart; but I cannot see how any one else can, for his manners are little calculated to inspire love. In the first place, he is incapable of the passion, or of being attached to any one for a long time; in the second, he is not sufficiently polished and gallant to make love, but sets about it rudely and coarsely; in the third, he is very indiscreet, and tells plainly all that he has done.

I have said to him a hundred times, "I wonder how any woman can run after you, whom they ought rather to fly from."

He would reply, laughing, "Ah! you do not know the libertine women of the present day; provided they are talked of, they are satisfied."

There was an affair of gallantry, but a perfectly honourable one, between him and the Queen of Spain. I do not know whether he had the good fortune to be agreeable to her, but I know he was not at all in love with her. He thought her mien and figure good, but neither her manners nor her face were agreeable to him.

He was not in any degree romantic, and, not knowing how to conduct himself in this affair, he said to the Duc de Grammont, "You understand the manner of Spanish gallantry; pray tell me a little what I ought to say and do."

He could not, however, suit the fancy of the Queen, who was for pure gallantry; those who were less delicate he was better suited for, and for this reason it was said that libertine women used to run after him.

....

He never denied that he was indiscreet and inconstant. Being one day with me at the theatre, and hearing Valere say he was tired of his mistress, "That has been my case often," he cried. I told him he never was in love in his life, and that what he called love was mere debauchery.

He replied, "It is very true that I am not a hero of romance, and that I do not make love like a Celadon, but I love in my way."

"Your way," I said, "is an extremely gross one." . . . This made him laugh.

He likes the business of his gallantry to be conducted with beat of drum, without the least refinement. He reminds me of the old Patriarchs, who were surrounded by women.

....

All women do not please him alike. He does not like fine airs so well as profligate manners: the opera-house dancers are his favourites. The women run after him from mere interest, for he pays them well. A pleasant enough adventure happened last winter:

A young and pretty woman visited my son in his cabinet; he presented her with a diamond of the value of 2,000 Louis and a box worth 200. This woman had a jealous husband, but she had effrontery enough to shew him the jewels which she said had been offered to her a great bargain by persons who wanted the money, and she begged him not to let such an opportunity slip. The credulous husband gave her the money she asked for. She thanked him, put the box in her dressing-case and the diamond on her finger, and displayed it in the best company.

When she was asked where she got the ring and the bog, "M. de Parabere gave them to me," she said; and he, who happened to be present, added, "Yes, I gave them to her; can one do less when one has for a wife a lady of quality who loves none but her husband?"

This caused some mirth; for other people were not so simple as the husband, and knew very well where the presents came from. If my son has a queen-sultana, it is this Madame de Parabere. Her mother, Madame de la Vieuville, was dame d'atour to the Duchesse de Berri.—[Marie-Madeline de la Vieuville, Comtesse de la Parabere; it was she whom the Regent used to call "his little black crow."]—It was there that my son first became acquainted with the daughter, who is now a widow: she is of a slight figure, dark complexion, and never paints; her eyes and mouth are pretty; she is not very sensible, but is a desirable little person. My son says he likes her because she thinks of nothing but amusing herself, and never interferes with other affairs. That would be very well if she were not a drunkard, and if she did not make my son eat and drink so much, and take him to a farm which she has at Anieres, and where he sometimes sups with her and the country folks. It is said that he becomes a little jealous of Parabere, in which case he must love her more than he has done yet. I often tell him that, if he really loved, he would not suffer his mistresses to run after others, and to commit such frequent infidelities. He replied that there was no such thing as love except in romances. He broke with Seri, because, as he said, she wanted him to love her like an Arcadian. He has often made me laugh at his complaining of this seriously, and with an air of great affliction.

"Why do you disturb yourself?" I have said to him; "if that is not agreeable to you, leave her alone. You are not obliged to feign a love which you do not feel."

This convinces me, however, that my son is incapable of love. He willingly eats, drinks, sings, and amuses himself with his mistresses, but to love one of them more than another is not his way. He is not afraid of application; but when he has been actively engaged from morning till night he is glad to divert himself at supper with such persons. It is for this reason that Parabere, who is said to be a great fool, is so agreeable to him. She eats and drinks astonishingly, and plays absurd tricks, which divert him and make him forget his labour.

My son, it must be allowed, possesses some great qualities. He has good sense, understands several languages, is fond of reading, speaks well, has studied much, is learned and acquainted with most of the arts, however difficult. He is a musician, and does not compose badly; he paints well, he understands chemistry, is well versed in history, and is quick of comprehension. He soon, however, gets tired of everything. He has an excellent memory, is expert in war, and fears nothing in the world; his intentions are always just and fair, and if his actions are ever otherwise, it is the fault of others. His only faults are that he is too kind, not sufficiently reserved, and apt to believe people who have less sense than himself; he is, therefore, often deceived, for the knaves who know his easiness of temper will run all risks with him. All the misfortunes and inconveniences which befall him spring from that cause. His other fault is one not common to Frenchmen, the easiness with which women can persuade him, and this often brings him into domestic quarrels. He can refuse them nothing, and even carries his complaisance so far as to give them marks of affection without really liking them. When I tell him that he is too good, he says, "Is it not better to be good than bad?"

He was always extremely weak, too, with respect to lovers, who chose to make him their confidant.

The Duc de Saint Simon was one day exceedingly annoyed at this weakness of my son, and said to him, angrily, "Ah! there you are; since the days of Louis le Debonnaire there has been nobody so debonnaire as yourself."

My son was much amused at it.

When he is under the necessity of saying anything harsh, he is much more pained at it than the person who experiences the disgrace.

He is not fond of the country, but prefers living in town. He is in this respect like Madame de Longueville, who was tired to death of being in Normandy, where her husband was.

[The Duc de Longueville was Governor of Normandy; and after the reduction of Bordeaux, in 1652, the Duchesse de Longueville received an order from the Court to repair to her husband.]

Those who were about her said, "Mon Dieu, Madame, you are eaten up with ennui; will you not take some amusement? There are dogs and a beautiful forest; will you hunt?"

"No," she replied, "I don't like hunting."

"Will you work?"

"No, I don't like work."

"Will you take a walk, or play at some game?"

"No, I like neither the one nor the other."

"What will you do, then?" they asked.

"What can I do?" she said; "I hate innocent pleasures."

My son understands music well, as all the musicians agree. He has composed two or three operas, which are pretty. La Fare, his Captain of the guards, wrote the words. He had them played in his palace, but never would permit them to be represented on the public stage.

When he had nothing to do he painted for one of the Duchess's cabinets all the pastoral romance of "Daphnis and Chloe."

[The designs for the romance of "Daphnis and Chloe" were composed by the Regent, with the advice, and probably the assistance, of Claude Audran, a distinguished painter, whom Lebrun often employed to help him with his large pictures. He painted a part of the battles of Alexander. These designs were engraved by Benoit Audran; they embellish what is called "the Regent's edition" of the Pastoral of Longus, which was printed under his inspection in the year 1718. It is somewhat surprising that Madame should speak so disdainfully of so eminent an artist as Benoit Audran.]

With the exception of the first, he invented and painted all the subjects. They have been engraved by one Audran. The Duchess thought them so pretty that she had them worked in a larger size in tapestry; and these, I think, are better than the engravings.

My son's learning has not the least tinge of pedantry. He knows a quantity of facetious stories, which he learnt in Italy and in Spain. He does not tell them badly, but I like him better in his more serious moods, because they are more natural to him. When he talks upon learned topics it is easy to see that they are rather troublesome to him than otherwise. I often blamed him for this; but he used to reply that it was not his fault, that he was ready enough to learn anything, but that when he once knew it he no longer took pleasure in it.

He is eloquent enough, and when he chooses he can talk with dignity. He has a Jesuit for his confessor, but he does not suffer himself to be ruled by him. He pretends that his daughter has no influence over him. He was delighted when he obtained the command of the Spanish army, and was pleased with everything in that country; this procured him the hatred of the Princesse des Ursins, who feared that my son would diminish her authority and gain more of the confidence of the Spaniards than she possessed.

He learned to cook during his stay with the army in Spain.

I cannot tell where he learned so much patience; I am sure it was neither from Monsieur nor from me.

When he acted from himself I always found him reasonable; but he too often confided in rogues, who had not half his sense, and then all went wrong.

My son is like all the rest of his family; when they had become accustomed to a thing they suffered it to go its own way. It was for this reason he could not persuade himself to shake off the Abbe Dubois, although he knew him to be a rascal. This Abbe had the impudence to try to persuade even me that the marriage he had brought about was an excellent one.

"But the honour which is lost in it," said I, "how will you repair that?"

Old Maintenon had made immense promises to him, as well as to my son; but, thank God, she kept neither the one nor the other.

It is intolerable that my son will go about day and night with that wicked and impertinent Noce I hate that Noce as I hate the devil. He and Brogue run all risks, because they are thus enabled to sponge upon my son. It is said that Noce is jealous of Parabere, who has fallen in love with some one else. This proves that my son is not jealous. The person with whom she has fallen in love has long been a sort of adventurer: it is Clermont, a captain in my son's Swiss Guard; the same who preferred Chouin to the great Princesse de Conti. It is said that Noce utters whatever comes into his head, and about any persons; this makes my son laugh, and amuses him, for Noce has wit and can do this pleasantly, enough. His father was under-governor to my son, who has thus been accustomed from his infancy to this wicked rascal, and who is very fond of him. I do not know for what reason, for he is a person who fears neither God nor man, and has not a single good point about him; he is green, black, and deep yellow; he is ten years older than my son; it is incredible how many, millions this mercenary rogue has drawn from him. Madame de Berri has told me that Broglie's jokes consist only in saying openly, the most horrible things. The Broglii are of Italian extraction, but have been long settled in France. There were three brothers, the elder of whom died in the army; the second was an Abbe, but he cast aside his gown, and he is the knave of whom I have been speaking. The third is still serving in the army, and, according to common report, is one of the best gentlemen in the world. My son does not like him so well as his good-for-nothing brother, because he is too serious, and would not become his buffoon. My son excuses himself by saying that when he quits business he wants something to make him laugh, and that young Broglie is not old enough for this; that if he had a confidential business, or a warlike expedition to perform, he would prefer him; but that for laughing and dissipation of all sorts, his elder brother is more fit.

My son has three natural children, two boys and a girl, of whom only one has been legitimated; that is his son by Mademoiselle de Seri,

[N. de Seri de la Boissiere; the father had been ambassador in Holland. Mademoiselle de Seri was the Regent's first mistress; he gave her the title of Comtesse d'Argenton. Her son, the Chevalier d'Orleans, was Grand-Prieur of France.]

who was my Maid of Honour; she was genteel and gay, but not pretty nor of a good figure. This son was called the Chevalier d'Orleans. The other, who is now a lad of eighteen years, is the Abbe de Saint Albin; he had this child by Florence, an opera dancer, of a very neat figure, but a fool; although to look at her pretty face one would not have thought so. She is since dead. The third of my son's illegitimate children is a girl of fourteen years old, whom he had by Desmarets, an actress, who is still on the stage. This child has been educated at a convent at Saint Denis, but has not much inclination for a monastic life. When my son sent for her she did not know who she was.

Desmarets wanted to lay another child to my son's account; but he replied, "No, that child is too much of a harlequin."

When some one asked him what he meant, he said it was of so many different pieces, and therefore he renounced it.

I do not know whether the mother did not afterwards give it to the Elector of Bavaria, who had some share in it, and who sacrificed to her the most beautiful snuff-box that ever was seen; it was covered with large diamonds.

My first son was called the Duc de Valois; but as this name was one of evil omen, Monsieur would not suffer my other son to be called so; he took, therefore, the title of Duc de Chartres. After Monsieur's death my son took the name of Orleans, and his son that of Chartres.

[Alesandre-Louis d'Orleans, Duc de Valois, died an infant on the 16th of March, 1676; the Regent was born on the 4th of August, 1674. It is unnecessary to mention the unhappy ends of Henri III. and of the three Kings, his sons, who all died without issue.]

My son is too much prejudiced in favour of his nation; and although he sees daily that his countrymen are false and treacherous, he believes there is no nation comparable to them. He is not very lavish of his praise; and when he does approve of anything his sincerity gives it an additional value.

As he is now in his forty-second year the people of Paris do not forgive him for running about at balls, like a young fool, for the amusement of women, when he has the cares of the kingdom upon his shoulders. When the late King ascended the throne he had reason to take his diversion; it is not so now. Night and day it is necessary to labour in order to repair the mischief which the late King, or rather his Ministers, did to the country.

When my son gently reproached that old Maintenon for having maligned him, and asked her to put her hand upon her heart, and say whether her calumnies were true, she replied, "I said it because I believed it."

My son replied, "You could not believe it, because you knew the contrary."

She said arrogantly, and yet my son kept his temper, "Is not the Dauphine dead?"

"Is it my fault," he rejoined, "that she is dead? Was she immortal?"

"Well," she replied, "I was so much distressed at the loss that I could not help detesting him whom I was told was the cause of it."

"But, Madame," said my son, "you know, from the report which has been made to the King, that I was not the cause, and that the Dauphine was not poisoned."

"I do know it," she replied, "and I will say nothing more about it."

SECTION X.—THE AFFAIRS OF THE REGENCY.

The old Maintenon wished to have the Duc du Maine made Regent; but my son's harangue to the Parliament frustrated her intention.

He was very angry with Lord Stair because he believed that he had done him an ill office with the King of England, and prevented the latter from entering into the alliance with France and Holland. If that alliance had taken place my son could have prevented the Pretender from beginning his journey; but as England refused to do so, the Regent was obliged to do nothing but what was stipulated for by the treaty of peace: that is to say, not to succour the Pretender with money nor arms, which he faithfully performed. He sent wherever Lord Stair requested.

[The Duc d'Orleans ordered, in Lord Stair's presence, Contades, Major of the Guard, to arrest the Pretender on his passage through Chateau-Thierry; but, adds Duclos, Contades was an intelligent man, and well acquainted with the Regent's secret intentions, and so he set out resolved not to find what he went in search of.]

He believed that the English people would not be well pleased to see their King allied to the Crown of France.

1717

The Baron Goertz thought to entrap my son, who, however, did not trust him; he would not permit him to purchase a single ship, and it was upon this that the Baron had built all his hopes of success.

That tall Goertz, whom I have seen, has an unlucky physiognomy; I do not believe that he will die a fair death.

The Memoir of the thirty noblemen has so much angered my son that he will hasten to pronounce sentence.

[Goertz was the Swedish minister, and had been sent into Holland and France to favour the cause of the Pretender. He was arrested in Holland in 1717, and remained in prison for several months. He was a very cunning person, and a great political intriguer. On the death of Charles XII. he was taken before an extraordinary tribunal, and condemned in an unjust and arbitrary manner to be beheaded, which sentence was executed in, May, 1719.]

1718

The whole of the Parliament was influenced against him. He made a remonstrance against this, which was certainly effected at the instigation of the eldest bastard and his wife.—[The Duc and Duchesse du Maine.]—If any one spoke ill of my son, and seemed dissatisfied, the Duchesse du Maine: invited them to Sceaux, and pitied and caressed them to hear them abuse my son. I wondered at his patience. He has great courage, and went steadily on without disturbing himself about anything. Although the Parliament of Paris sent to all the other parliaments in the kingdom to solicit them to unite with it, none of them did so, but all remained faithful to my son. The libels which were dispersed for the purpose of exciting the people against him had scarcely any effect. I believe the plot would have succeeded better if the bastard and his wife had not engaged in it, for they were extraordinarily hated at Paris. My son told the Parliament they had nothing to do with the coinage; that he would maintain the royal authority, and deliver it to the King when he should be of age in the same state as he had found it on his becoming Regent.

The Marechale d'Uxelles hated my son mortally, but after the King's death he played the fawning dog so completely that my son forgave him and took him into favour again. In the latter affair he was disposed once more to follow his natural inclination, but my son, having little value for whatever he could do, said, "Well, if he will not sign he may let it alone."

When the Marshal saw my son was serious and did not care at all for his bravadoes, he became submissive and did what my son desired.

The wife of the cripple, the Duchesse du Maine, resolved to have an explanation with my son. She made a sententious speech, just as if she had been on the stage; she asked how he could think that the answer to Fitz-Morris's book should have proceeded from her, or that a Princess of the blood would degrade herself by composing libels? She told him, too, that the Cardinal de Polignac was engaged in affairs of too much importance to busy himself in trifles like this, and M. de Malezieux was too much a philosopher to think of anything but the sciences. For her own part, she said she had sufficient employment in educating her children as became that royal dignity of which she had been wrongfully deprived. My son only replied to her thus:—

"I have reason to believe that these libels have been got up at your house, and by you, because that fact has been attested by persons who have been in your service, and who have seen them in progress; beyond this no one makes me believe or disbelieve anything."

He made no reply to her last observation, and so she went away. She afterwards boasted everywhere of the firmness with which she had spoken to my son.

My son this day (26th of August) assembled the Council of the Regency. He had summoned the Parliament by a 'lettre-de-cachet': they repaired to the Tuileries in a procession on foot, dressed in scarlet robes, hoping by this display to excite the people in their favour; but the mob only called out, "Where are these lobsters going?" The King had caused the Keeper of the Seals to make a remonstrance to the Parliament for having infringed upon his authority in publishing decrees without his sanction. He commanded them to quash the decree, which was done; and to confirm the authority of the Keeper of the Seals, which they did also. He then ordered them with some sternness not to interfere with the affairs of the Government beyond their province; and as the Duc du Maine had excited the Parliament against the King, he was deprived of the care of His Majesty's education, and he with his brothers were degraded from the rank of Princes of the blood, which had been granted to them. They will in future have no other rank than that of their respective peerages; but the Duc du Maine alone, for the fidelity he has always manifested towards the King, will retain his rank for his life, although his issue, if he should have any, will not inherit it.

[Saint-Simon reports that it was the Comte de Toulouse who was allowed to retain his rank.—See The Memoirs of Saint-Simon, Chapter XCIII.—D.W.]

Madame d'Orleans was in the greatest despair, and came to Paris in such a condition as moved my pity for her. Madame du Maine is reported to have said, three weeks ago, at a grand dinner, "I am accused of having caused the Parliament to revolt against the Duc d'Orleans, but I despise him too much to take so noble a vengeance; I will be revenged in another manner."

The Parliament had very notable projects in hand. If my son had delayed four-and-twenty hours longer in removing the Duc du Maine from the King it would have been decided to declare His Majesty of full age; but my son frustrated this by dismissing the Duke, and degrading him at the same time. The Chief President is said to have been so frightened that he remained motionless, as if he had been petrified by a gaze at the head of Medusa. That celebrated personage of antiquity could not have been more a fury than Madame du Maine; she threatened dreadfully, and did not scruple to say, in the presence of her household, that she would yet find means to give the Regent such a blow as should make him bite the dust. That old Maintenon and her pupil have also had a finger in the pie.

The Parliament asked pardon of my son, which proves that the Duc and Duchesse du Maine were the mainsprings of the plot.

There is reason to believe that the old woman and the former Chancellor were also implicated in it. The Chancellor, who would have betrayed my son in so shameful a manner, was under the heaviest obligations to him. What has happened is a great mortification to Maintenon, and yet she has not given up all hopes. This makes me very anxious, for I know how expertly she can manage poison. My son, instead of being cautious, goes about the town at night in strange carriages, sometimes supping with one or another of his people, none of whom are worthy of being trusted, and who, excepting their wit, have not one good quality.

Different reports respecting the Duchesse du Maine are abroad; some say she has beaten her husband and broken the glasses and everything brittle in her room. Others say she has not spoken a word, and has done nothing but weep. The Duc de Bourbon has undertaken the King's education. He said that, not being himself of age, he did not demand this office before, but that being so now he should solicit it, and it was immediately given to him.

One president and two counsellors have been arrested. Before the close of the session, the Parliament implored my son to use his good offices with the King for the release of their members, and promised that they should, if found culpable, be punished by the Parliament itself. My son replied that they could not doubt he should always advise the King to the most lenient measures; that His Majesty would not only be gracious to them as a body, while they merited it, but also to each individual; that, as to the prisoners, they would in good time be released.

That old Maintenon has fallen sick of grief that her project for the Duc du Maine has miscarried.

The Duke and the Parliament had resolved to have a bed of justice held, where my son should be dismissed, and the Regency be committed to the Duke, while at the same time the King's household should be under arms. The Duke and the Prince de Conti had long been urging my son without knowing all the particulars. The Duc du Maine has not been banished to the country, but has permission to go with his family wherever he pleases; he will not, however, remain at Paris, because he no longer enjoys his rank; he chooses rather to live at Sceaux, where he has an elegant mansion and a fine park.

The little dwarf (the Duchesse du Maine) says she has more courage than her husband, her son, and her brother-in-law put together; and that, like another Jael, she would kill my son with her own hand, and would drive a nail into his head. When I implored my son to be on his guard against her, and told him this, he laughed at my fears and shook his head incredulously.

I do not believe that the Devil, in his own person, is more wicked than that old Maintenon, the Duc du Maine, and the Duchess. The latter said openly that her husband and her brother-in-law were no better than cowards; that, woman as she was, she was ready to demand an audience of my son and to plunge a dagger in his heart. Let any one judge whether I have not reason to fear such persons, and particularly, when they, have so strong a party. Their cabal is very considerable; there are a dozen persons of consideration, all great noblemen at Court. The richest part of the people favour the Spanish pretensions, as well as the Duc and Duchesse du Maine; they wish to call in the King of Spain. My brother has too much sense for them; they want a person who will suffer himself to be led as they, please; the King of Spain is their man; and, for this reason, they are trying all means to induce him to come. It is for these reasons that I think my son is in so great danger.

My son has not yet released the three rogues of the Parliament, although their liberation has been twice petitioned for.

The Duc du Maine and the cabal have made his sister believe that if my son should die they would make her Regent, and would aid her with their counsel to enable her to become one of the greatest persons in the world. They say they mean no violence towards my son, who cannot live long on account of his irregularities; that he must soon die or lose his sight; and in the latter event he would consent to her becoming Regent. I know a person to whom the Duc du Maine said so. This put an end to one's astonishment, that she should have wished to force her daughter to marry the Duc du Maine.

All this gave me great anxiety. I foresaw it all and said to my son, "You are committing a folly, for which I shall have to suffer all my life."

He has made great changes; instead of a great number of Councils he has appointed Secretaries of State. M. d'Armenouville is Secretary of State for the Navy; M. le Blanc, for the Army; M. de la Vrilliere, for the Home Department; the Abbe Dubois, for Foreign Affairs; M. de Maurepas, for the Royal Household; and a Bishop for the Church Benefices.

Malezieux and the Cardinal de Polignac had probably as great a share in the answer to Fitz-Morris as the Duchesse du Maine.

The Duc de Bourbon and the Prince de Conti assisted very zealously in the disgrace of the Duc du Maine. My son could not bring himself to resolve upon it until the treachery had been clearly demonstrated to him, and he saw that he should lend himself to his own dishonour if he did not prevent the blow.

My son is very fond of the Comte de Toulouse, whom he finds a sensible person on all occasions: if the latter had followed the advice of the Duc du Maine he would have shared his fate; but he despised his brother's advice and followed that of his wife.

My son believes as firmly in predestination as if he had been, like me, a Calvinist, for nineteen years. I do not know how he learnt the affair of the Duc du Maine; he has always kept it a great secret. But what appears the most singular to me is that he does not hate his brother-in-law, who has endeavoured to procure his death and dishonour. I do not believe his like was ever seen: he has no gall in his composition; I never knew him to hate any one.

He says he will take as much care as he can; but that if God has ordained that he shall perish by the hands of his enemies he cannot change his destiny, and that therefore he shall go on tranquilly.

He has earnestly requested Lord Stair to speak to the King of England on your account.—[This passage is addressed to the Princess of Wales.]—He says no one can be more desirous than he is that you should be reinstated in your father's affection, and that he will neglect no opportunity of bringing it about, being persuaded that it is to the advantage of the King of England, as well as of yourself, that you should be reconciled.

M. Law must be praised for his talent, but there is an astonishing number of persons who envy him in this country. My son is delighted with his cleverness in business.

He has been compelled to arrest the Spanish Ambassador, the Prince of Cellamara, because letters were found upon his courier, the Abbe Porto Carero, who was his nephew, and who has also been arrested, containing evidence of a plot against the King and against my son. The Ambassador was arrested by two Counsellors of State. It was time that this treachery should be made public. A valet of the Abbe Porto Carero having a bad horse, and not being able to get on so quick as his master, stayed two relays behind, and met on his way the ordinary courier from Poitiers. The valet asked him, "What news?"

"I don't know any," replied the postilion, "except that they have arrested at Poitiers an English bankrupt and a Spanish Abbe who was carrying a packet."

When the valet heard this he instantly took a fresh horse, and, instead of following his master, he came back full gallop to Paris. So great was his speed, that he fell sick upon his arrival in consequence of the exertion. He outstripped my son's courier by twelve hours, and so had time to apprise the Prince of Cellamara twelve hours before his arrest, which gave him time to burn his most important letters and papers. My son's enemies pretend to treat this affair as insignificant to the last degree; but I cannot see anything insignificant in an Ambassador's attempting to cause a revolt in a whole kingdom, and among the Parliament, against my son, and meditating his assassination as well as that of his son and daughter. I alone was to have been let live.

That Des Ursins must have the devil in her to have stirred up Pompadour against my son. He is not any very great personage; but his wife is a daughter of the Duc de Navailles, who was my son's governor. Madame de Pompadour was the governess of the young Duc d'Alencon, the son of Madame de Berri. As to the Abbe Brigaut, I know him very well. Madame de Ventadour was his godmother, and he was baptized at the same time with the first Dauphin, when he received the name of Tillio. He has talent, but he is an intriguer and a knave. He pretended at first to be very devout, and was appointed Pere de l'Oratoire; but, getting tired of this life, he took up the trade of catering for the vices of the Court, and afterwards became the secretary and factotum of Madame du Maine, for whom he used to assist in all the libels and pasquinades which were written against my son. It would be difficult to say which prated most, he or Pompadour.

Madame d'Orleans has great influence over my son. He loves all his children, but particularly his eldest daughter. While still a child, she fell dangerously ill, and was given over by her physicians. My son was in deep affliction at this, and resolved to attempt her cure by treating her in his own way, which succeeded so well that he saved her life, and from that moment has loved her better than all his other children.

....

The Abbe Dubois has an insinuating manner towards every one; but more particularly towards those of whom he had the care in their childhood.

Two Germans were implicated in the conspiracy; but I am only surprised at one of them, the Brigadier Sandrazky, who was with me daily, and in whose behalf I have often spoken, because his father served my brother as commandant at Frankendahl; he died in the present year. The other is the Count Schlieben, who has only one arm. I am not astonished at him; for, in the first place, I know how he lost his arm; and, in the second, he is a friend and servant of the Princesse des Ursins: they expect to take him at Lyons. Sandrazky was at my toilette the day before yesterday; as he looked melancholy, I asked him what was the matter? He replied, "I am ill with vexation: I love my wife, who is an Englishwoman, very tenderly, and she is no less fond of me; but, as we have not the means of keeping up an establishment, she must go into a convent. This distresses me so much that I am really very unwell."

I was grieved to hear this, and resolved to solicit my son for him.

My son sometimes does as is said in Atys,—[The opera of Atys, act ii., scene 3.]— "Vous pourriez aimer et descendre moins bas;" for when Jolis was his rival, he became attached to one of his daughter's 'filles de chambre', who hoped to marry Jolis because he was rich; for this reason she received him better than my son, who, however, at last gained her favour. He afterwards took her away from his daughter, and had her taught to sing, for she had a fine voice.

The printed letters of Cellamara disclose the whole of the conspiracy. The Abbe Brigaut, too, it is said, begins to chatter about it. This affair has given me so much anxiety that I only sleep through mere exhaustion. My heart beats incessantly; but my son has not the least care about it. I beseech him, for God's sake, not to go about in coaches at night, and he promises me he will not; but he will no more keep that promise than he did when he made it to me before.

It is now eight days since the Duc du Maine and his wife were arrested (29th December). She was at Paris, and her husband at Sceaux in his chateau. One of the four captains of the King's Guard arrested the Duchess, the Duke was arrested only by a lieutenant of the Body Guard. The Duchess was immediately taken to Dijon and her husband to the fortress of Doullens. I found Madame d'Orleans much more calm than I had expected. She was much grieved, and wept bitterly; but she said that, since her brother was convicted, she must confess he had done wrong; that he was, with his wife, the cause of his own misfortune, but that it was no less painful to her to know that her own brother had thus been plotting against her husband. His guilt was proved upon three points: first, in a paper under the hand of the Spanish Ambassador, the Prince of Cellamara, in which he imparted to Alberoni that the Duchesse and the Duc du Maine were at the head of the conspiracy; he tells him how many times he has seen them, by whose means, and in what place; then he says that he has given money to the Duc du Maine to bribe certain persons, and he mentions the sum. There are already two men in the Bastille who confess to have received money, and others who have voluntarily stated that they conducted the Ambassador to the Duke and Duchess, and negotiated everything between the parties. The greater part of their servants have been sent to the Bastille. The Princess is deeply afflicted; and, although the clearest proofs are given of her children's crime, she throws all the blame upon the Duke, her grandson, who, she says, has accused them falsely, because he hates them, and she has refused to see him. The Duchess is more moderate in her grief. The little Princesse de Conti heartily pities her sister and weeps copiously, but the elder Princess does not trouble herself about her uncle and aunt.

The Cardinals cannot be arrested, but they may be exiled; therefore the Cardinal de Polignac has been ordered to retire to one of his abbeys and to remain there. It was love that turned his head. He was formerly a great friend of my son's, and he did not change until he became attached to that little hussy.

Magni

[Foucault de Magni, introducteur des ambassadeurs, and son of a   Counsellor of State. Duclos says he was a silly fellow, who never   did but, one wise thing, which was to run away.]

has not yet been taken; he flies from one convent to another. He stayed with the Jesuits a long time.

1719

They say that the Duchesse du Maine used all her persuasions to induce her husband to fly; but that he replied, as neither of them had written anything with their own hands, nothing could be proved against them; while, by flying, they would confess their guilt. They did not consider that M. de Pompadour could say enough to cause their arrest.

The Duchess's fraternal affection is a much stronger passion than her love for her children.

A letter of Alberoni's to the lame bastard has been intercepted, in which is the following passage: "As soon as you declare war in France spring all your mines at once."

What enrages me is that Madame d'Orleans and the Princess would still make one believe that the Duc and Duchesse du Maine are totally innocent, although proofs of their guilt are daily appearing. The Duchess came to me to beg I would procure an order for her daughter's people, that is, her dames d'honneur, her femmes de chambre, and her hairdresser, to be sent to her. I could not help laughing, and I said, "Mademoiselle de Launay is an intriguer and one of the persons by whom the whole affair was conducted."

But she replied, "The Princess is at the Bastille."—"I know it," I said; "and well she has deserved it." This almost offended the Princess.

The Duchesse du Maine said openly that she should never be happy until she had made an end of my son. When her mother reproached her with it, she did not deny it, but only replied, "One says things in a passion which one does not mean to do."

Although the plot has been discovered, the conspirators have not yet been all taken. My son says, jokingly, "I have hold of the monster's head and tail, but I have not yet got his body."

I can guess how it happened that the mercantile letters stated my son to have been arrested; it is because the conspirators intended to have done so, and two days later it would have taken place. It must have been persons of this party, therefore, who wrote to England.

When Schlieben was seized, he said, "If Monsieur the Regent does not take pity upon me, I am ruined."

He was for a long time at the Spanish Court, where he was protected by the Princesse des Ursins. He has some wit, can chatter well, and is an excellent spy for such a lady. The persons who had arrested him took him to Paris by the diligence, without saying a word. On reaching Paris the diligence was ordered to the Bastille; the poor travellers not knowing why, were in a great fright, and expected all to be locked up, but were not a little pleased at being set free. Sandrazky is not very clever; he is a Silesian. He married an Englishwoman, whose fortune he soon dissipated, for he is a great gambler.

The Duchesse du Maine has fallen sick with rage, and that old Maintenon is said to be afflicted by the affair more than any other person. It was by her fault that they fell into this scrape, for she put it into their heads that it was unjust they should not reign, and that the kingdom belonged as much to them as King Solomon's did to him.

Madame d'Orleans weeps for her brother by day and night.

They tried to arrest the Duc de Saint-Aignan at Pampeluna; but he effected his escape with his wife, and in disguise.

When they carried away the Duc du Maine, he said, "I shall soon return, for my innocence will be speedily manifested; but I only speak for myself, my wife may not come back quite so soon."

Madame d'Orleans cannot believe that her brother has been engaged in a conspiracy; she says it must have been his wife who acted in his name. The Princess, on the other hand, believes that her daughter is innocent, and that the Duc du Maine alone has carried on the plot.

The factum is not badly drawn up. Our priest can write well enough when he likes; he drew it up, and my son corrected it.

The more the affair is examined, the more clearly does the guilt of the Duke and Duchess appear; for three days ago, Malezieux, who is in the Bastille, gave up his writing-desk. The first thing that was found in it was a projet, which Malezieux had written at the Duchess's bedside, and which Cardinal de Polignac had corrected with his own hand. Malezieux pretends that it is a Spanish letter, addressed to the Duchess, and that he had translated it for her, with the assistance of the Cardinal de Polignac; and yet the letters of Alberoni to the Prince de Cellamara refer so directly to this projet that it is easy to see that they spring from the same source.

The Duchesse du Maine has made the Princess believe that the Duke (of Bourbon) was the cause of all this business, so that now he dare not appear before the latter, although he has always behaved with great respect and friendship towards her; while the Duc and Duchesse du Maine, on the contrary, have been engaged in a law-suit against her for five years. It was not until after the Princess had inherited the property of Monsieur de Vendome, that this worthy couple insinuated themselves into her good graces.

The Parliament is reconciled to my son, and has pronounced its decree, which is favourable to him, and which is another proof that the Duc du Maine had excited it against him.

The Jesuits have probably been also against my son; for all those who have declared against the Constitution cannot be friendly to him; they have, however, kept so quiet that nothing can be brought against them. They are cunning old fellows.

Madame d'Orleans begins to recover her spirits and to laugh again, particularly since I learn she has consulted the Premier President and other persons, to know whether, upon my son's death, she would become the Regent. They told her that could not be, but that the office would fall upon the Duke. This answer is said to have been very unpalatable to her.

If my son would have paid a price high enough to the Cardinal de Polignac, he would have betrayed them all. He is now consoling himself in his Abbey with translating Lucretius.

The King of Spain's manifesto, instead of injuring my son, has been useful to him, because it was too violent and partial. Alberoni must needs be a brutal and an intemperate person. But how could a journeyman gardener know the language which ought to be addressed to crowned heads? Several thousand copies of this manifesto have been transmitted to Paris, addressed to all the persons in the Court, to all the Bishops, in short, to everybody; even to the Parliament, which has taken the affair up very properly, from Paris to Bordeaux, as the decree shows. I thought it would have been better to burn this manifesto in the post-office instead of suffering it to be spread about; but my son said they should all be delivered, for the express purpose of discovering the feelings of the parties to whom they were addressed, and a register of them was kept at the post-office. Those who were honest brought them of their own accord; the others kept them, and they are marked, without the public knowing anything about it. The manifesto is the work of Malezieux and the Cardinal de Polignac.

A pamphlet has been cried about the streets, entitled, "Un arret contre les poules d'Inde." Upon looking at it, however, it seems to be a decree against the Jesuits, who had lost a cause respecting a priory, of which they had taken possession. Everybody bought it except the partisans of the Constitution and of the Spanish faction.

My son is more fond of his daughters, legitimate and illegitimate, than his son.

The Duc and Duchesse du Maine rely upon nothing having been found in their writing; but Mademoiselle de Montauban and Malezieux have written. in their name; and is not what Pompadour has acknowledged voluntarily quite as satisfactory a proof as even their own writing?

They have got the pieces of all the mischievous Spanish letters written by the same hand, and corrected by that of the Cardinal de Polignac, so that there can be no doubt of his having composed them.

A manifesto, too, has been found in Malezieux's papers. It is well written, but not improved by the translation. Malezieux pretends that he only translated it before it was sent hence to Spain.

Mademoiselle de Montauban and Mademoiselle de Launay, a person of some wit, who has kept up a correspondence with Fontenelle, and who was 'femme de chambre' to the Duchesse du Maine, have both been sent to the Bastille.

The Duc du Maine now repents that he followed his wife's advice; but it seems that he only followed the worst part of it.

The Duchesse d'Orleans has been for some days past persuading my son to go masked to a ball. She says that his daughter, the Duchesse de Berri, and I, make him pass for a coward by preventing him from going to balls and running about the town by night as he used to do before; and that he ought not to manifest the least symptom of fear. He replied that he knew he should give me great pain by doing so, and that the least he could do was to tranquillize my mind by living prudently. She then said that the Duchesse de Berri filled me with unfounded fears in order that she might have more frequent opportunities of being with him, and of governing him entirely. Can the Devil himself be worse than this bastard? It teaches me, however, that my son is not secure with her. I must do violence to myself that my suspicions may not be apparent.

My son has not kept his word; he went to this ball, although he denies it.

Although it is well known that Maintenon has had a hand in all these affairs, nothing can be said to her, for her name does not appear in any way.

When my son is told of persons who hate him and who seek his life, he laughs and says, "They dare not; I am not so weak that I cannot defend myself." This makes me very angry.

If the proofs against Malezieux are not manifest, and if they do not put the rogue upon his trial, it will be because his crime is so closely connected with that of the Duchesse du Maine that, in order to convict him before the Parliament, he must be confronted with her. Besides, as the Parliament is better disposed towards the Duc and Duchesse du Maine than to my son, they might be acquitted and taken out of his hands, which would make them worse than they are now. For this reason it is that they are looking for proofs so clear that the Parliament cannot refuse to pronounce upon them.

The Duc du Maine writes thus to his sister:

"They ought not to have put me in prison; but they ought to have stripped me and put me into petticoats for having been thus led by my wife;" and he wrote to Madame de Langeron that he enjoyed perfect repose, for which he thanked God; that he was glad to be no longer exposed to the contempt of his family; and that his sons ought to be happy to be no longer with him.

The King of Spain and Alberoni have a personal hatred against my son, which is the work of the Princesse des Ursins.

My son is naturally brave, and fears nothing: death is not at all terrible to him.

On the 29th of March the young Duc de Richelieu was taken to the Bastille: this caused a great number of tears to be shed, for he is universally loved. He had kept up a correspondence with Alberoni, and had got his regiment placed at Bayonne, together with that of his friend, M. de Saillant, for the purpose of delivering the town to the Spaniards. He went on Wednesday last to the Marquis de Biron, and urged him to despatch him as promptly as possible to join his regiment at Bayonne, and so prove the zeal which attached him to my son. His comrade, who passes for a coward and a sharper at play, has also been shut up in the Bastille.

[On the day that they were arrested, the Regent said he had that in his pocket which would cut off four heads, if the Duke had so many. —Memoires de Duclos.]

The Duc de Richelieu had the portraits of his mistresses painted in all sorts of monastic habits: Mademoiselle de Charolais as a Recollette nun, and it is said to be very like her. The Marechales de Villars and d'Estrees are, it is said, painted as Capuchin nuns.

When the Duc de Richelieu was shown his letter to Alberoni, he confessed all that concerned himself, but would not disclose his accomplices.

Nothing but billets-doux were found in his writing-case. Alberoni in this affair trusted a man who had formerly been in his service, but who is now a spy of my son's. He brought Alberoni's letter to the Regent; who opened it, read it, had a copy made, resealed it, and sent it on to its destination. The young Duc de Richelieu answered it, but my son can make no use of this reply because the words in which it is written have a concealed sense.

The Princess has strongly urged my son to permit the Duchesse du Maine to quit Dijon, under the pretext that the air was unwholesome for her. My son consented upon condition that she should be conducted in her own carriage, but under the escort of the King's Guard, from Dijon to Chalons-sur-Saone.

Here she thought she should enjoy comparative liberty, and that the town would be her prison: she was much astonished to find that she was as closely confined at Chalons as at Dijon. When she asked the reason for this rigour she was told that all was discovered, and that the prisoners had disclosed the particulars of the conspiracy. She was immediately struck with this; but recovering her self-possession, she said, "The Duc de Orleans thinks that I hate him; but if he would take my advice, I would counsel him better than any other person." My son's wife remains very tranquil.

On the 17th of April a rascal was brought in who was near surprising my son in the Bois de Boulogne a year ago. He is a dismissed colonel; his name is La Jonquiere. He had written to my son demanding enormous pensions and rewards; but meeting with a refusal, he went into Spain, where he promised Alberoni to carry off my son, and deliver him into his hands, dead or alive. He brought one hundred men with him, whom he put in ambuscade near Paris. He missed my son only by a quarter of an hour in the Bois de Boulogne, which the latter had passed through in his way to La Muette, where he went to dine with his daughter. La Jonquiere having thus failed, retired in great vexation to the Low Countries, where he boasted that, although he had missed this once, he would take his measures so much better in future that people should soon hear of a great blow being struck. This was luckily repeated to my son, who had him arrested at Liege. He sent a clever fellow to him, who caught him, and leading him out of the house where they were, he clapped a pistol to his throat, and threatened to shoot him on the spot if he did not go with him and without speaking a word. The rascal, overcome with terror, suffered himself to be taken to the boat, but when he saw that they were approaching the French territory he did not wish to go any further; he said he was ruined, and should be drawn and quartered. They bound him and carried him to the Bastille.

I have exhorted my son to take care of himself, and not to go out but in a carriage. He has promised that he will not, but I cannot trust him.

The late Monsieur was desirous that his son's wife should not be a coquette. This was not the particular which I so much disapproved of; but I wished the husband not to be informed of it, or that it should get abroad, which would have had no other effect than that of convincing my son that his wife had dishonoured him.

I must never talk to my son about the conspiracy in the presence of Madame d'Orleans; it would be wounding her in the tenderest place; for all that concerns her brother is to her the law and the prophets.

My son has so satisfactorily disproved the accusations of that old Maintenon and the Duc du Maine, that the King has believed him, and, after a minute examination, has done my son justice. But Madame d'Orleans has not conducted herself well in this affair; she has spread by means of her creatures many calumnies against my son, and has even said that he wanted to poison her. By such means she has made her peace with old Maintenon, who could not endure her before. I have often admired the patience with which my son suffers all this, when he knows it just as well as I do. If things had remained as Madame de Maintenon had arranged them at the death of the King, my son would only have been nominally Regent, and the Duc du Maine would actually have enjoyed all the power. She thought because my son was in the habit of running after women a little that he would be afraid of the labour, and that he would be contented with the title and a large pension, leaving her and the Duc du Maine to have their own way. This was her plan, and she fancied that her calumnies had so far succeeded in making my son generally despised that no person would be found to espouse his cause. But my son was not so unwise as to suffer all this; he pleaded his cause so well to the Parliament that the Government was entrusted to him, and yet the old woman did not relinquish her hopes until my son had the Duc du Maine arrested; then she fainted.

The Pope's nuncio thrusts his nose into all the plots against my son; he may be a good priest, but he is nevertheless a wicked devil.

On the 25th of April M. de Laval, the Duchesse de Roquelaure's brother, was arrested.

M. de Pompadour has accused the Duc de Laval of acting in concert with the Prince de Cellamara, to whom, upon one occasion, he acted as coachman, and drove him to the Duchesse du Maine at the Arsenal. This Comte de Laval is always sick and covered with wounds; he wears a plaster which reaches from ear to ear; he is lame, and often has his arm in a sling; nevertheless, he is full of intrigue, and is engaged night and day in writing against my son.

Madame de Maintenon is said to have sent large sums of money into the provinces for the purpose of stirring up the people against my son; but, thank God, her plan has not succeeded.

The old woman has spread about the report that my son poisoned all the members of the Royal Family who have died lately. She hired one of the King's physicians first to spread this report. If Marechal, the King's surgeon, who was present at the opening of the bodies, had not stated that there was no appearance of poison, and confirmed that statement to the King, this infamous creature would have plunged my innocent son into a most deplorable situation.

Mademoiselle de Charolais says that the affair of Bayonne cannot be true, for that the Duc de Richelieu did not tell her of it, and he never concealed anything from her. She says, too, that she will not see my son, for his having put the Duke into the Bastille.

The Duke walks about on the top of the terrace at the Bastille, with his hair dressed, and in an embroidered coat. All the ladies who pass stop their carriages to look at the pretty fellow.

[This young man, says Duclos, thought himself of some consequence when he was made a State prisoner, and endured his confinement with the same levity which he had always displayed in love, in business, or in war. The Regent was much amused with him, and suffered him to have all he wanted-his valet de chambre, two footmen, music, cards, etc.; so that, although he was deprived of his liberty, he might be as licentious as ever.]

Madame d'Orleans has been so little disposed to undertake her husband's defence in public, that she has pretended to believe the charges against him, although no person in the world knows better than she does that the whole is a lie. She sent to her brothers for a counter-poison, so that my son should not take her off by those means; and thus she reconciled Maintenon, who was at enmity with her. I learnt this story during the year, and I do not know whether my son is aware of it. I would not say anything to him about it, for I did not wish to embroil man and wife.

The Abbe Dubois—[Madame probably means the Duc du Maine]—seems to think that we do not know how many times he went by night to Madame de Maintenon's, to help this fine affair.

My son has been dissuaded from issuing the manifesto.

Madame d'Orleans has at length quite regained her husband; and, following her advice, he goes about by night in a coach. On Wednesday night he set off for Anieres, where Parabere has a house. He supped there, and, getting into his carriage again, after midnight, he put his foot into a hole and sprained it.

I am very much afraid my son will be attacked by the small-pox. He eats heavy suppers; he is short and fat, and just one of those persons whom the disease generally attacks.

The Cardinal de Noailles has been pestering my son in favour of the Duc de Richelieu; and as it cannot be positively proved that he addressed the letter to Alberoni, they can do no more to him than banish him to Conflans, after six months' imprisonment. Mademoiselle de Charolais procured some one to ask my son secretly by what means she could see the Duc de Richelieu, and speak with him, before he set off for Conflans.

[This must have been a joke of Mademoiselle de Charolais; for she had already, together with Mademoiselle Valois, paid the Duke several visits in the Bastille. When the Duke was sent to Conflans to the Cardinal de Noailles, he used to escape almost every night, and come to see his mistresses. It was this that determined the Regent to send him to Saint-Germain en Laye; but, soon afterwards, Mademoiselle de Valois obtained from her father a pardon for her lover.—-Memoirs de Richelieu, tome iii., p. 171]

My son replied, "that she had better speak to the Cardinal de Noailles; for as he was to conduct the Duke to Conflans, and keep him in his own house, he would know better than any other person how he might be spoken with." When she learnt that the Duke had arrived at Saint-Germain, she hastened thither immediately.

I never doubted for a moment that my son's marriage was in every respect unfortunate; but my advice was not listened to. If the union had been a good one, that old Maintenon would not have insisted on it.

Nothing less than millions are talked of on all sides: my sun has made me also richer by adding 130,000 livres to my pension.

By what we hear daily of the insurrection in Bretagne, it seems that my son's enemies are more inveterate against him than ever. I do not know whether it is true, as has been said, that there was a conspiracy at Rochelle, and that the governor intended to give up the place to the Spaniards, but has fled; that ten officers were engaged in the plot, some of whom have been arrested, and the others have fled to Spain.

I always took the Bishop of Soissons for an honest man. I knew him when he was only an Abbe, and the Duchess of Burgundy's almoner; but the desire to obtain a Cardinal's hat drives most of the Bishops mad. There is not one of them who does not believe that the more impertinently he behaves to my son about the Constitution, the more he will improve his credit with the Court of Rome, and the sooner become a Cardinal.

My son, although he is Regent, never comes to see me, and never quits me, without kissing my hand before he embraces me; and he will not even take a chair if I hand it to him. He is not, however, at all timid, but chats familiarly with me, and we laugh and talk together like good friends.

While the Dauphin was alive La Chouin behaved very ill to my son; she embroiled him with the Dauphin, and would neither speak to nor see him; in short, she was constantly opposed to him. And yet, when he learnt that she had fallen into poverty, he sent her money, and secured her a pension sufficient to live upon.

My son gave me actions to the amount of two millions, which I distributed among my household. The King also took several millions for his own, household; all the Royal Family have had them; all the enfans and petits enfans de France, and the Princes of the blood.

[This may be stock the M. Law floated in the Mississippi Company. D.W.]

The old Court is doing its utmost to put people, out of conceit with Law's bank.

I do not think that Lord Stair praises my son so much as he used to do, for they do not seem to be very good friends. After having received all kinds of civilities from my son, who has made him richer than ever he expected to be in his life, he has turned his back upon him, caused him numerous little troubles, and annoys him so much that my son would gladly be rid of him.

My son was obliged to make a speech at the Bank, which was applauded.

1720

They have been obliged to adopt severe measures in Bretagne; four persons of quality have been beheaded. One of them, who might have escaped by flying to Spain, would not go. When he was asked why, he said it had been predicted that he should die by sea (de la mer). Just before he was executed he asked the headsman what his name was.

"My name is Sea (La Mer)," replied the man.

"Then," said the nobleman, "I am undone."

All Paris has been mourning at the cursed decree which Law has persuaded my son to make. I have received anonymous letters, stating that I have nothing to fear on my own account, but that my son shall be pursued with fire and sword; that the plan is laid and the affair determined on. From another quarter I have learnt that knives are sharpening for my son's assassination. The most dreadful news is daily reaching me. Nothing could appease the discontent until, the Parliament having assembled, two of its members were deputed to wait upon my son, who received them graciously, and, following their advice, annulled the decree, and so restored things to their former condition. This proceeding has not only quieted all Paris, but has reconciled my son (thank God) to the Parliament.

My son wished by sending an embassy to give a public proof how much he wished for a reconciliation between the members of the Royal Family of England, but it was declined.

The goldsmiths will work no longer, for they charge their goods at three times more than they are worth, on account of the bank-notes. I have often wished those bank-notes were in the depths of the infernal regions; they have given my son much more trouble than relief. I know not how many inconveniences they have caused him. Nobody in France has a penny; but, saving your presence, and to speak in plain palatine, there is plenty of paper.

....

It is singular enough that my son should only become so firmly attached to his black Parabere, when she had preferred another and had formally dismissed him.

Excepting the affair with Parabere, my son lives upon very good terms with his wife, who for her part cares very little about it; nothing is so near to her heart as her brother, the Duc du Maine. In a recent quarrel which she had with my son on this subject, she said she would retire to Rambouillet or Montmartre. "Wherever you please," he replied; "or wherever you think you will be most comfortable." This vexed her so much that she wept day and night about it.

On the 17th of June, while I was at the Carmelites, Madame de Chateau-Thiers came to see me, and said to me, "M. de Simiane is come from the Palais Royal; and he thinks it fit you should know that on your return you will find all the courts filled with the people who, although they do not say anything, will not disperse. At six o'clock this morning they brought in three dead bodies which M. Le Blanc has had removed. M. Law has taken refuge in the Palais Royal: they have done him no harm; but his coach man was stoned as he returned, and the carriage broken to pieces. It was the coachman's fault, who told them 'they were a rabble, and ought to be hanged.'" I saw at once that it would not do to seem to be intimidated, so I ordered the coach to be driven to the Palais Royal. There was such a press of carriages that I was obliged to wait a full hour before I reached the rue Saint-Honore; then I heard the people talking: they did not say anything against my son; they gave me several benedictions, and demanded that Law should be hanged. When I reached the Palais Royal all was calm again. My son came to me, and in the midst of my anxiety he was perfectly tranquil, and even made me laugh.

M. Le Blanc went with great boldness into the midst of the irritated populace and harangued them. He had the bodies of the men who had been crushed to death in the crowd brought away, and succeeded in quieting them.

My son is incapable of being serious and acting like a father with his children; he lives with them more like a brother than a father.

The Parliament not only opposed the edict, and would not allow it to pass, but also refused to give any opinion, and rejected the affair altogether. For this reason my son had a company of the footguard placed on Sunday morning at the entrance of the palace to prevent their assembling; and, at the same time, he addressed a letter to the Premier-President, and to the Parliament a 'lettre-de-cachet', ordering them to repair to Pontoise to hold their sittings. The next day, when the musketeers had relieved the guards, the young fellows, not knowing what to do to amuse themselves, resolved to play at a parliament. They elected a chief and other presidents, the King's ministers, and the advocates. These things being settled, and having received a sausage and a pie for breakfast, they pronounced a sentence, in which they condemned the sausage to be cooked and the pie to be cut up.

All these things make me tremble for my son. I receive frequently anonymous letters full of dreadful menaces against him, assuring me that two hundred bottles of wine have been poisoned for him, and, if this should fail, that they will make use of a new artificial fire to burn him alive in the Palais Royal.

It is too true that Madame d'Orleans loves her brother better than her husband.

The Duc du Maine says that if, by his assistance, the King should obtain the direction of his own affairs, he would govern him entirely, and would be more a monarch than the King, and that after my son's death he would reign with his sister.

A week ago I received letters in which they threatened to burn my son at the Palais Royal and me at Saint Cloud. Lampoons are circulated in Paris.

My son has already slept several times at the Tuileries, but I fear that the King will not be able to accustom himself to his ways, for my son could never in his life play with children: he does not like them.

He was once beloved, but since the arrival of that cursed Law he is hated more and more. Not a week passes without my receiving by the post letters filled with frightful threats, in which my son is spoken of as a bad man and a tyrant.

I have just now received a letter in which he is threatened with poison. When I showed it to him he did nothing but laugh, and said the Persian poison could not be given to him, and that all that was said about it was a fable.

To-morrow the Parliament will return to Paris, which will delight the Parisians as much as the departure of Law.

That old Maintenon has sent the Duc du Maine about to tell the members of the Royal Family that my son poisoned the Dauphin, the Dauphine, and the Duc de Berri. The old woman has even done more she has hinted to the Duchess that she is not secure in her husband's house, and that she should ask her brother for a counter-poison, as she herself was obliged to do during the latter days of the King's life.

The old woman lives very retired. No one can say that any imprudent expressions have escaped her. This makes me believe that she has some plan in her head, but I cannot guess what it is.

SECTION XI.—THE DUCHESSE D'ORLEANS, WIFE OF THE REGENT.

If, by shedding my own blood, I could have prevented my son's marriage, I would willingly have done so; but since the thing was done, I have had no other wish than to preserve harmony. Monsieur behaved to her with great attention during the first month, but as soon as he suspected that she looked with too favourable an eye upon the Chevalier du Roye,

[Bartholemi de La Rochefoucauld, at first Chevalier de Roye, but afterwards better known by the title of Marquis de La Rochefoucauld. He was Captain of the Duchesse de Berri's Body-Guards, and he died in 1721.]

he hated her as the Devil. To prevent an explosion, I was obliged daily to represent to him that he would dishonour himself, as well as his son, by exposing her conduct, and would infallibly bring upon himself the King's displeasure. As no person had been less favourable to this marriage than I, he could not suspect but that I was moved, not from any love for my daughter-in-law, but from the wish to avoid scandal and out of affection to my son and the whole family. While all eclat was avoided, the public were at least in doubt about the matter; by an opposite proceeding their suspicions would have been confirmed.

Madame d'Orleans looks older than she is; for she paints beyond all measure, so that she is often quite red. We frequently joke her on this subject, and she even laughs at it herself. Her nose and cheeks are somewhat pendant, and her head shakes like an old woman: this is in consequence of the small-pox. She is often ill, and always has a fictitious malady in reserve. She has a true and a false spleen; whenever she complains, my son and I frequently rally her about it. I believe that all the indispositions and weaknesses she has proceed from her always lying in bed or on a sofa; she eats and drinks reclining, through mere idleness; she has not worn stays since the King's death; she never could bring herself to eat with the late King, her own father, still less would she with me. It would then be necessary for her to sit upon a stool, and she likes better to loll upon a sofa or sit in an arm-chair at a small table with her favourite, the Duchess of Sforza. She admits her son, and sometimes Mademoiselle d'Orleans. She is so indolent that she will not stir; she would like larks ready roasted to drop into her mouth; she eats and walks slowly, but eats enormously. It is impossible to be more idle than she is: she admits this herself; but she does not attempt to correct it: she goes to bed early that she may lie the longer. She never reads herself, but when she has the spleen she makes her women read her to sleep. Her complexion is good, but less so than her second daughter's. She walks a little on one side, which Madame de Ratzenhausen calls walking by ear. She does not think that there is her equal in the world for beauty, wit, and perfection of all kinds. I always compare her to Narcissus, who died of self-admiration. She is so vain as to think she has more sense than her husband, who has a great deal; while her notions are not in the slightest degree elevated. She lives much in the femme-de-chambre style; and, indeed, loves this society better than that of persons of birth. The ladies are often a week together without seeing her; for without being summoned they cannot approach her. She does not know how to live as the wife of a prince should, having been educated like the daughter of a citizen. A long time had elapsed before she and her younger brother were legitimated by the King; I do not know for what reason.

[This legitimation presented great difficulties during the life of the Marquis de Montespan. M. Achille de Harlai, Procureur-General du Parliament, helped to remove them by having the Chevalier de Longueville, son of the Duke of that name and of the Marechale de la Feste, recognized without naming his mother. This once done, the children of the King and of Madame de Montespan were legitimated in the same manner.]

When they arrived at Court their conversation was exactly like that of the common people.

In my opinion my son's wife has no charms at all; her physiognomy does not please me. I don't know whether my son loves her much, but I know she does what she pleases with him. The populace and the femmes de chambre are fond of her; but she is not liked elsewhere. She often goes to the Salut at the Quinze Vingts; and her women are ordered to say that. she is a saint, who suffers my son to be surrounded by mistresses without complaining. This secures the pity of the populace and makes her pass for one of the best of wives, while, in fact; she is, like her elder brother, full of artifice.

She is very superstitious. Some years ago a nun of Fontevrault, called Madame de Boitar, died. Whenever Madame d'Orleans loses anything she promises to this nun prayers for the redemption of her soul from purgatory, and then does not doubt that she shall find what she has lost. She piques herself upon being extremely pious; but does not consider lying and deceit are the works of the Devil and not of God. Ambition, pride and selfishness have entirely spoilt her. I fear she will not make a good end. That I may live in peace I seem to shut my eyes to these things. My son often, in allusion to her pride, calls her Madame Lucifer. She is not backward in believing everything complimentary that is said to her. Montespan, old Maintenon, and all the femmes de chambre have made her believe that she did my son honour in marrying him; and she is so vain of her own birth and that of her brothers and sisters that she will not hear a word said against them; she will not see any difference between legitimate and illegitimate children.

She wishes to reign; but she knows nothing of true grandeur, having been educated in too low a manner. She might live well as a simple duchess; but not as one of the Royal Family of France. It is too true that she has always been ambitious of possessing, not my son's heart, but his power; she is always in fear lest some one else should govern him. Her establishment is well regulated; my son has always let her be mistress in this particular. As to her children, I let them go on in their own way; they were brought here without my consent, and it is for others to take care of them. Sometimes she displays more affection for her brother than even for her children. An ambitious woman as she is, having it put into her head by her brother that she ought to be the Regent, can love none but him. She would like to see him Regent better than her husband, because he has persuaded her that she shall reign with him; she believes it firmly, although every one else knows that his own wife is too ambitious to permit any one but herself to reign. Besides her ambition she has a great deal of ill-temper. She will never pardon either the nun of Chelles or Mademoiselle de Valois, because they did not like her nephew with the long lips. Her anger is extremely bitter, and she will never forgive. She loves only her relations on the maternal side. Madame de Sforza, her favourite, is the daughter of Madame de Thianges, Madame de Montespan's sister, and therefore a cousin of Madame d'Orleans, who hates her sister and her nephew worse than the Devil.

I could forgive her all if she were not so treacherous. She flatters me when I am present, but behind my back she does all in her power to set the Duchesse de Berri against me; she tells her not to believe that I love her, but that I wish to have her sister with me. Madame d'Orleans believes that her daughter, Madame de Berri, loves her less than her father. It is true that the daughter has not a very warm attachment to her mother, but she does her duty to her; and yet the more they are full of mutual civilities the more they quarrel. On the 4th of October, 1718, Madame de Berri having invited her father to go and sleep at La Muette, to see the vintage feast and dance which were to be held on the next day. Madame d'Orleans wrote to Madame de Berri, and asked her if she thought it consistent with the piety of the Carmelites that she should ask her father to sleep in her house. Madame de Berri replied that it had never been thought otherwise than pious that a parent should sleep in his daughter's house. The mother did this only to annoy her husband and daughter, and when she chooses she has a very cutting way. It may be imagined how this letter was received by the father and daughter. I arrived at La Muette just as it had come. My son dare not complain to me, for as often as he does, I say to him, "George Dandin, you would have it so:"—[Moliere]—he therefore only laughed and said nothing. I did not wish to add to the bitterness which this had occasioned, for that would have been to blow a fire already too hot; I confined myself, therefore, to observing that when she wrote it she probably had the spleen.

She is not very fond of her children, and, as I think, she carries her indifference too far; for the children see she does not love them, and this makes them fond of being with me. This angers the mother, and she reproaches them for it, which only makes them like her less.

Although she loves her son, she does not in general care so much for her children as for her brothers, and all who belong to the House of Mortemart.

I was the unintentional cause of making a quarrel between her and the nun of Chelles. At the commencement of the affair of the Duc du Maine, I received a letter from my daughter addressed to Madame d'Orleans; and not thinking that it was for the Abbess, who bears the same title with her mother, I sent it to the latter. This letter happened, unluckily, to be an answer to one of our Nun's, in which she had very plainly said what she thought of the

Duc and Duchesse du Maine, and ended by pitying her father for being the Duke's brother-in-law, and for having contracted an alliance so absurd and injurious. It may be guessed whether my daughter's answer was palatable to my daughter-in-law. I am very sorry that I made the mistake; but what right had she to read a letter which was not meant for her?

The new Abbess of Chelles has had a great difference with her mother, who says she will never forgive her for having agreed with her father to embrace the religious profession without her knowledge. The daughter said that, as her mother had always taken the side of the former Abbess against her, she had not confided this secret to her, from a conviction that she would oppose it to please the Abbess. This threw the mother into a paroxysm of grief. She said she was very unhappy both in her husband and her children; that her husband was the most unjust person in the world, for that he kept her brother-in-law in prison, who was one of the best and most pious of men—in short, a perfect saint; and that God would punish such wickedness. The daughter replied it was respect for her mother that kept her silent; and the latter became quite furious. This shows that she hates us like the very Devil, and that she loves none but her lame brother, and those who love him or are nearly connected with him.

She thinks there never was so perfect a being in the world as her mother. She cannot quite persuade herself that she was ever Queen, because she knew the Queen too well, who always called her daughter, and treated her better than her sisters; I cannot tell why, because she was not the most amiable of them.

It is quite true that there is little sympathy between my son's wife and me; but we live together as politely as possible. Her singular conduct shall never prevent me from keeping that promise which I made to the late King in his last moments. He gave some good Christian exhortations to Madame d'Orleans; but, as the proverb says, it is useless to preach to those who have no heart to act.

In the spring of this year (1718) her brothers and relations said that but for the antidotes which had been administered to Madame d'Orleans, without the knowledge of me or my son, she must have perished.

I had resolved not to interfere with anything respecting this affair; but had the satisfaction of speaking my mind a little to Madame du Maine. I said to her: "Niece" (by which appellation I always addressed her), "I beg you will let me know who told you that Madame d'Orleans had taken a counterpoison unknown to us. It is the greatest falsehood that ever was uttered, and you may say so from me to whoever told it you."

She looked red, and said, "I never said it was so."

"I am very glad of it, niece," I replied; "for it would be very disgraceful to you to have said so, and you ought not to allow people to bring you such tales." When she heard this she went off very quickly.

Madame d'Orleans is a little inconstant in her friendship. She is very fond of jewels, and once wept for four-and-twenty hours because my son gave a pair of beautiful pendants to Madame de Berri.

My son has this year (1719) increased his wife's income by 160,000 livres, the arrears of which have been paid to her from 1716, so that she received at once the sum of 480,000 livres. I do not envy her this money, but I cannot bear the idea that she is thus paid for her infidelity. One must, however, be silent.

SECTION XII.—MARIE-ANNE CHRISTINE VICTOIRE OF BAVARIA, THE FIRST DAUPHINE.

She was ugly, but her extreme politeness made her very agreeable. She loved the Dauphin more like a son than a husband. Although he loved her very well, he wished to live with her in an unceremonious manner, and she agreed to it to please him. I used often to laugh at her superstitious devotion, and undeceived her upon many of her strange opinions. She spoke Italian very well, but her German was that of the peasants of the country. At first, when she and Bessola were talking together, I could not understand a word.

She always manifested the greatest friendship and confidence in me to the end of her days. She was not haughty, but as it had become the custom to blame everything she did, she was somewhat disdainful. She had a favourite called Bessola—a false creature, who had sold her to Maintenon. But for the infatuated liking she had for this woman, the Dauphine would have been much happier. Through her, however, she was made one of the most wretched women in the world.

This Bessola could not bear that the Dauphine should speak to any person but herself: she was mercenary and jealous, and feared that the friendship of the Dauphine for any one else would discredit her with Maintenon, and that her mistress's liberality to others would diminish that which she hoped to experience herself. I told this person the truth once, as she deserved to be told, in the presence of the Dauphine; from which period she has neither done nor said anything troublesome to me. I told the Dauphine in plain German that it was a shame that she should submit to be governed by Bessola to such a degree that she could not speak to whom she chose. I said this was not friendship, but a slavery, which was the derision of the Court.

Instead of being vexed at this, she laughed, and said, "Has not everybody some weakness? Bessola is mine."

This wench often put me in an ill-humour: at last I lost all patience, and could no longer restrain myself. I would often have told her what I thought, but that I saw it would really distress the poor Dauphine: I therefore restrained myself, and said to her, "Out of complaisance to you, I will be silent; but give such orders that Bessola may not again rouse me, otherwise I cannot promise but that I may say something she will not like."

The Dauphine thanked me affectionately, and thus more than ever engaged my silence.

When the Dauphine arrived from Bavaria, the fine Court of France was on the decline: it was at the commencement of Maintenon's reign, which spoilt and degraded everything. It was not, therefore, surprising that the poor Dauphine should regret her own country. Maintenon annoyed her immediately after her marriage in such a manner as must have excited pity. The Dauphine had made her own marriage; she had hoped to be uncontrolled, and to become her own mistress; but she was placed in that Maintenon's hands, who wanted to govern her like a child of seven years old, although she was nineteen. That old Maintenon, piqued at the Dauphine for wishing to hold a Court, as she should have done, turned the King against her. Bessola finished this work by betraying and selling her; and thus was the Dauphine's misery accomplished! By selecting me for her friend, she filled up the cup of Maintenon's hatred, who was paying Bessola; because she knew she was jealous of me, and that I had advised the Dauphine not to keep her, for I was quite aware that she had secret interviews with Maintenon.

That lady had also another creature in the Dauphine's household: this was Madame de Montchevreuil, the gouvernante of the Dauphine's filles d'honneur. Madame de Maintenon had engaged her to place the Dauphin upon good terms with the filles d'honneur, and she finished by estranging him altogether from his wife. During her pregnancy, which, as well as her lying-in, was extremely painful, the Dauphine could not go out; and this Montchevreuil took advantage of the opportunity thus afforded her to introduce the filles d'honneur to the Dauphin to hunt and game with him. He became fond, in his way, of the sister of La Force, who was afterwards compelled to marry young Du Roure. The attachment continued, notwithstanding this marriage; and she procured the Dauphin's written promise to marry her in case of the death of the Dauphine and her husband. I do not know how the late King became acquainted with this fact; but it is certain that he was seriously angered at it, and that he banished Du Roure to Gascony, his native country. The Dauphin had an affair of gallantry with another of his wife's filles d'honneur called Rambures. He did not affect any dissimulation with his wife; a great uproar ensued; and that wicked Bessola, following the directions of old Maintenon, who planned everything, detached the Dauphin from his wife more and more. The latter was not very fond of him; but what displeased her in his amours was that they exposed her to be openly and constantly ridiculed and insulted. Montchevreuil made her pay attention to all that passed, and Bessola kept up her anger against her husband.

Maintenon had caused it to be reported among the people by her agents that the Dauphine hated France, and that she urged the imposition of new taxes.

The Dauphine was so ill-treated in her accouchement of the Duc de Berri that she became quite deformed, although previous to this her figure had been remarkably good. On the evening before she died, as the little Duke was sitting on her bed, she said to him, "My dear Berri, I love you very much, but I have paid dearly for you." The Dauphin was not grieved at her death; old Montchevreuil had told him so many lies of his wife that he could not love her. That old Maintenon hoped, when this event happened, that she should be able to govern the Duke by means of his mistresses, which could not have been if he had continued to be attached to his wife. This old woman had conceived so violent a hatred against the poor Princess, that I do believe she prevailed on Clement, the accoucheur, to treat her ill in her confinement; and what confirms me in this is that she almost killed her by visiting her at that time in perfumed gloves. She said it was I who wore them, which was untrue. I would not swear that the Dauphine did not love Bessola better than her husband; she deserved no such attachment. I often apprised her mistress of her perfidy, but she would not believe me.

The Dauphine used to say, "We are two unhappy persons, but there is this difference between us: you endeavoured, as much as you could, to avoid coming here; while I resolved to do so at all events. I have therefore deserved my misery more than you."

They wanted to make her pass for crazy, because she was always complaining. Some hours before her death she said to me, "I shall convince them to-day that I was not mad in complaining of my sufferings." She died calmly and easily; but she was as much put to death as if she had been killed by a pistol-shot.

When her funeral service was performed I carried the taper (nota bene) and some pieces of gold to the Bishop who performed the grand mass, and who was sitting in an armchair near the altar. The prelate intended to have given them to his assistants, the priests of the King's chapel; but the monks of Saint Denis ran to him with great eagerness, exclaiming that the taper and the gold belonged to them. They threw themselves upon the Bishop, whose chair began to totter, and made his mitre fall from his head. If I had stayed there a moment longer the Bishop, with all the monks, would have fallen upon me. I descended the four steps of the altar in great haste, for I was nimble enough at that time, and looked on the battle at a distance, which appeared so comical that I could not but laugh, and everybody present did the same.

That wicked Bessola, who had tormented the Dauphine day and night, and had made her distrust every one who approached her, and thus separated her from all the world, returned home a year after her mistress's death. Before her departure she played another trick by having a box made with a double bottom, in which she concealed jewels and ready money to the amount of 100,000 francs; and all this time she went about weeping and complaining that, after so many years of faithful service, she was dismissed as poor as a beggar. She did not know that her contrivance had been discovered at the Customhouse and that the King had been apprised of it. He ordered her to be sent for, showed her the things which she had prepared to carry away, and said he thought she had little reason to complain of the Dauphine's parsimony. It may be imagined how foolish she looked. The King added that, although he might withhold them from her, yet to show her that she had done wrong in acting clandestinely, and in complaining as she had done, he chose to restore her the whole.

SECTION XIII.—ADELAIDE OF SAVOY, THE SECOND DAUPHINE.

The Queen of Spain stayed longer with her mother than our Dauphine, and therefore was better educated. Maintenon, who understood nothing about education, permitted her to do whatever she pleased, that she might gain her affections and keep her to herself. This young lady had been well brought up by her virtuous mother; she was genteel and humorous, and could joke very pleasantly: when she had a colour she did not look ugly. No one can imagine what mad-headed people were about this Princess, and among the number was the Marechale d'Estrees. Maintenon was very properly recompensed for having given her these companions; for the consequence was that the Dauphine no longer liked her society. Maintenon was very desirous to know the reason of this, and teased the Princess to tell her. At length she did; and said that the Marechale d'Estrees was continually asking her, "What are you always doing with that old woman? Why do you not associate with folks who would amuse you more than that old skeleton?" and that she said many other uncivil things of her. Maintenon told me this herself, since the death of the Dauphine, to prove that it was only the Marechale's fault that the Dauphine had been on such bad terms with me. This may be partly true; but it is no less certain that Maintenon had strongly prepossessed her against me. Almost all the foolish people who were about her were relations or friends of the old woman; and it was by her order that they endeavoured to amuse her and employ her, so that she might want no other society.

The young Dauphine was full of pantomime tricks. * * * * She was fond, too, of collecting a quantity of young persons about her for the King's amusement, who liked to see their sports; they, however, took care never to display any but innocent diversions before him: he did not learn the rest until after her death. The Dauphine used to call old Maintenon her aunt, but only in jest; the fines d'honneur called her their gouvernante, and the Marechale de La Mothe, mamma; if the Dauphine had also called the old woman her mamma, it would have been regarded as a declaration of the King's marriage; for this reason she only called her aunt.

It is not surprising that the Dauphine, even when she was Duchess of Burgundy, should have been a coquette. One of Maintenon's maxims was that there was no harm in coquetry, but that a grande passion only was a sin. In the second place, she never took care that the Duchess of Burgundy behaved conformably to her rank; she was often left quite alone in her chateau with the exception of her people; she was permitted to run about arm-in-arm with one of her young ladies, without esquires, or dames d'honneur or d'atour. At Marly and Versailles she was obliged to go to chapel on foot and without her stays, and seat herself near the femmes de chambre. At Madame de Maintenon's there was no observance of ranks; every one sat down there promiscuously; she did this for the purpose of avoiding all discussion respecting her own rank. At Marly the Dauphine used to run about the garden at night with the young people until two or three o'clock in the morning. The King knew nothing of these nocturnal sports. Maintenon had forbidden the Duchesse de Lude to tease the Duchess of Burgundy, or to put her out of temper, because then she would not be able to divert the King. Maintenon had threatened, too, with her eternal vengeance whoever should be bold enough to complain of the Dauphine to the King. It was for this reason that no one dared tell the King what the whole Court and even strangers were perfectly well acquainted with. The Dauphine liked to be dragged along the ground by valets, who held her feet. These servants were in the habit of saying to each other, "Come, shall we go and play with the Duchess of Burgundy?" for so she was at this time. She was dreadfully nasty,

....

She made the Dauphin believe whatever she chose, and he was so fond of her that one of her glances would throw him into an ecstacy and make him forget everything. When the King intended to scold her she would put on an air of such deep dejection that he was obliged to console her instead; the aunt, too, used to affect similar sorrow, so that the King had enough to do with consoling them both. Then, for quietness' sake, he used to lean upon the old aunt, and think nothing more about the matter.

The Dauphine never cared for the Duc de Richelieu, although he boasted of the contrary, and was sent to the Bastille for it. She was a coquette, and chatted with all the young men; but if she loved any of them it was Nangis, who commanded the King's regiment. She had commanded him to pretend to be in love with little La Vrilliere, who, though not so pretty nor with so good a presence as the Dauphine, had a better figure and was a great coquette. This badinage, it is said, afterwards became reality. The good Dauphin was like the husbands of all frail wives, the last to perceive it. The Duke of Burgundy never imagined that his wife thought of Nangis, although it was visible to all the world besides that she did. As he was very much attached to Nangis, he believed firmly that his wife only behaved civilly to him on his account; and he was besides convinced that his favourite had at the same time an affair of gallantry with Madame la Vrilliere.

The Dauphin had good sense, but he suffered his wife to govern him; he loved only such persons as she loved, and he hated all who were disagreeable to her. It was for this reason that Nangia enjoyed so much of his favour, that he, with all his sense, became so perfectly ridiculous.

The Dauphine of Burgundy was the person whom the King loved above all others, and whom Maintenon had taught to do whatever was agreeable to him. Her natural wit made her soon learn and practise everything. The King was inconsolable for her death; and when La Maintenon saw that all she could say had no effect upon his grief, it is said that she told the King all that she had before concealed with respect to the Dauphine's life, and by this means dissipated his great affliction.

[This young lady, so fascinating and so dear to the King, betrayed, nevertheless, the secrets of the State by informing her father, then Duke of Savoy, and our enemy, of all the military projects which she found means to read. The King had the proofs of this by the letters which were found in the Princess's writing case after her death. "That little slut," said he to Madame Maintenon, "has deceived us." Memoires de Duclos, tome i.]

Three years before her death, however, the Dauphine changed greatly for the better; she played no more foolish tricks, and left off drinking to excess. Instead of that untameable manner which she had before, she became polite and sensible, kept up her dignity, and did not permit the younger ladies to be too familiar with her, by dipping their fingers into her dish, rolling upon the bed, and other similar elegancies. She used to converse with people, and could talk very well. It was the marriage of Madame de Berri that effected this surprising change in the Dauphine. Seeing that young lady did not make herself beloved, and began things in the wrong way, she was desirous to make herself more liked and esteemed than she was. She therefore changed her behaviour entirely; she became reserved and reasonable, and, having sense enough to discover her defects, she set about correcting them, in which she succeeded so as to excite general surprise. Thus she continued until her death, and often expressed regret that she had led so irregular a life. She used to excuse herself by saying it was mere childishness, and that she had little to thank those young ladies for who had given her such bad advice and set her such bad examples. She publicly manifested her contempt for them, and prevailed on the King not to invite them to Marly in future. By this conduct she gained everybody's affection.

She was delicate and of rather a weak constitution. Dr. Chirac said in her last illness that she would recover; and so she probably would have done if they had not permitted her to get up when the measles had broken out upon her, and she was in a copious perspiration. Had they not blooded her in the foot she might have been alive now (1716). Immediately after the bleeding, her skin, before as red as fire, changed to the paleness of death, and she became very ill. When they were lifting her out of bed I told them it was better to let the perspiration subside before they blooded her. Chirac and Fagon, however, were obstinate and laughed at me.

Old Maintenon said to me angrily, "Do you think you know better than all these medical men?"

"No, Madame," I replied; "and one need not know much to be sure that the inclination of nature ought to be followed; and since that has displayed itself it would be better to let it have way, than to make a sick person get up in the midst of a perspiration to be blooded."

She shrugged up her shoulders ironically. I went to the other side and said nothing.

SECTION XIV.—THE FIRST DAUPHIN.

All that was good in the first Dauphin came from his preceptor; all that was bad from himself. He never either loved or hated any one much, and yet he was very wicked. His greatest pleasure was to do something to vex a person; and immediately afterwards, if he could do something very pleasing to the same person, he would set about it with great willingness. In every respect he was of the strangest temper possible: when one thought he was good-humoured, he was angry; and when one supposed him to be ill-humoured, he was in an amiable mood. No one could ever guess him rightly, and I do not believe that his like ever was or ever will be born. It cannot be said that he had much wit; but still less was he a fool. Nobody was ever more prompt to seize the ridiculous points of anything in himself or in others; he told stories agreeably; he was a keen observer, and dreaded nothing so much as to be one day King: not so much from affection for his father, as from a dread of the trouble of reigning, for he was so extremely idle that he neglected all things; and he would have preferred his ease to all the kingdoms and empires of the earth. He could remain for a whole day, sitting on a sofa or in an arm-chair, beating his cane against his shoes, without saying a word; he never gave an opinion upon any subject; but when once, in the course of the year, he did speak, he could express himself in terms sufficiently noble. Sometimes when he spoke one would say he was stupidity itself; at another time he would deliver himself with astonishing sense. At one time you would think he was the best Prince in the world; at another he would do all he could to give people pain. Nobody seemed to be so ill with him but he would take the trouble of making them laugh at the expense of those most dear to him. His maxim was, never to seem to like one man in the Court better than another. He had a perfect horror of favourites, and yet he sought favour himself as much as the commonest courtier could do. He did not pride himself upon his politeness, and was enraged when any one penetrated his intentions. As I had known him from his infancy I could sometimes guess his meaning, which angered him excessively. He was not very fond of being treated respectfully; he liked better not to be put to any trouble. He was rather partial than just, as may be shown by the regulations he made as to the rank of my son's daughter. He never liked or hated any Minister. He laughed often and heartily. He was a very obedient son, and never opposed the King's will in any way, and was more submissive to Maintenon than any other person. Those who say that he would have retired, if the King had declared his marriage with that old woman, did not know him; had he not an old mistress of his own, to whom he was believed to be privately married? What prevented Maintenon from being declared Queen was the wise reasons which the Archbishop of Cambray, M. de Fenelon, urged to the King, and for which she persecuted that worthy man to the day of his death.

If the Dauphin had chosen, he might have enjoyed greater credit with his father. The King had offered him permission to go to the Royal Treasury to bestow what favours he chose upon the persons of his own Court; and at the Treasury orders were given that he should have whatever he asked for. The Dauphin replied that it would give him so much trouble. He would never know anything about State affairs lest he should be obliged to attend the Privy Councils, and have no more time to hunt. Some persons thought he did this from motives of policy and to make the King believe he had no ambition; but I am persuaded it was from nothing but indolence and laziness; he loved to live a slothful life, and to interfere with nothing.

At the King of Spain's departure our King wept a good deal; the Dauphin also wept much, although he had never before manifested the least affection for his children. They were never seen in his apartment morning and evening. When he was not at the chase the Dauphin passed his time with the great Princesse de Conti, and latterly with the Duchess. One must have guessed that the children belonged to him, for he lived like a stranger among them. He never called them his sons, but the Duke of Burgundy, the Duc d'Anjou, the Duc de Berri; and they, in turn, always called him Monseigneur.

I lived upon a very good understanding with him for more than twenty years, and he had great confidence in me until the Duchess got possession of him; then everything with regard to me was changed: and as, after my husband's death, I never went to the chase with the Dauphin, I had no further relation with him, and he behaved as if he had never seen or known me. If he had been wise he would have preferred the society of the Princesse de Conti to that of the Duchess, because the first, having a good heart, loved him for himself; while the other loved nothing in the world, and listened to nothing but her taste for pleasure, her interest, and her ambition. So that, provided she attained her ends, she cared little for the Dauphin, who by his condescension for this Princess gave a great proof of weakness.

In general, his heart was not correct enough to discern what real friendship was; he loved only those who afforded him amusement, and despised all others. The Duchess was very agreeable and had some pleasant notions; she was fond of eating, which was the very thing for the Dauphin, because he found a good breakfast at her house every morning and a collation in the afternoon. The Duchess's daughters were of the same character as their mother; so that the Dauphin might be all the day in the company of gay people.

He was strongly attached to his son's wife; but when she quarrelled with the Duchess her father-in-law changed his opinion of her. What displeased him besides was that the Duchess of Burgundy married his younger son, the Duc de Berri, against his inclination. He was not wrong in that, because, although the marriage was to our advantage, I must confess that the Dauphin was not even treated with decency in the business.

Neither of the two Dauphins or the Dauphines ever interested themselves much about their children. The King had them educated without consulting them, appointed all their servants, and was even displeased if they interfered with them in any way. The Dauphin knows nothing of good breeding; he and his sons are perfect clowns.

The women of La Halle had a real passion for the first Dauphin; they had been made to believe that he would take the part of the people of Paris, in which there was not a word of truth. The people believed that he was better hearted than he was. He would not, in fact, have been wicked if the Marechal d'Uxelles, La Chouin and Montespan, with whom he was in his youth, as well as the Duchess, had not spoiled him, and made him believe that malice was a proof of wit.

He did not grieve more than a quarter of an hour at the death of his mother or of his wife; and when he wrapped himself up in his long mourning cloak he was ready to choke with laughter.

He had followed his father's example in taking an ugly, nasty mistress, who had been fille d'honneur to the elder Princess de Conti: her name is Mademoiselle de Chouin, and she is still living at Paris (1719). It was generally believed that he had married her clandestinely; but I would lay a wager he never did. She had the figure of a duenna; was of very small stature; had very short legs; large rolling eyes; a round face; a short turned-up nose; a large mouth filled with decayed teeth, which made her breath so bad that the room in which she sat could hardly be endured.

....

And yet this short, fat woman had a great deal of wit; and I believe the Dauphin accustomed himself to take snuff that he might not be annoyed by her bad teeth. He was very civil to the Marechal d'Uxelles, because he pretended to be the intimate with this lady; but as soon as the Dauphin was caught, the Marechal ceased to see her, and never once set foot in her house, although before that he had been in the habit of visiting her daily.

The Dauphin had a daughter by Raisin the actress, but he would never acknowledge her, and after his death the Princess Conti took care of her, and married her to a gentleman of Vaugourg. The Dauphin was so tired of the Duc du Maine that he had sworn never to acknowledge any of his illegitimate children. This Raisin must have had very peculiar charms to make an impression upon a heart so thick as that of the Dauphin, who really loved her. One day he sent for her to Choisy, and hid her in a mill without anything to eat or drink; for it was a fast day, and the Dauphin thought there was no greater sin than to eat meat on a fast day. After the Court had departed, all that he gave her for supper was some salad and toast with oil. Raisin laughed at this very much herself, and told several persons of it. When I heard of it I asked the Dauphin what he meant by making his mistress fast in this manner.

"I had a mind," he said, "to commit one sin, but not two."

I cannot bear that any one should touch me behind; it makes me so angry that I do not know what I do. I was very near giving the Dauphin a blow one day, for he had a wicked trick of coming behind one for a joke, and putting his fist in the chair just where one was going to sit down. I begged him, for God's sake, to leave off this habit, which was so disagreeable to me that I would not answer for not one day giving him a sound blow, without thinking of what I was doing. From that time he left me alone.

The Dauphin was very much like the Queen; he was not tall, but good-looking enough. Our King was accustomed to say: "Monseigneur (for so he always called him) has the look of a German prince." He had, indeed, something of a German air; but it was only the air; for he had nothing German besides. He did not dance well. The Queen-Dowager of Spain flattered herself with the hope of marrying him.

He thought he should recommend himself to the King by not appearing to care what became of his brothers.

When the Dauphin was lying sick of the small-pox, I went on the Wednesday to the King.

He said to me, sarcastically, "You have been frightening us with the great pain which Monseigneur would have to endure when the suppuration commences; but I can tell you that he will not suffer at all, for the pustules have already begun to dry."

I was alarmed at this, and said, "So much the worse; if he is not in pain his state is the more dangerous, and he soon will be."

"What!" said the King, "do you know better than the doctors?"

"I know," I replied, "what the small-pox is by my own experience, which is better than all the doctors; but I hope from my heart that I may be mistaken."

On the same night, soon after midnight, the Dauphin died.

SECTION XV.—THE DUKE OF BURGUNDY, THE SECOND DAUPHIN.

He was quite humpbacked. I think this proceeded from his having been made to carry a bar of iron for the purpose of keeping himself upright, but the weight and inconvenience of which had had a contrary effect. I often said to the Duke de Beauvilliers he had very good parts, and was sincerely pious, but so weak as to let his wife rule him like a child. In spite of his good sense, she made him believe whatever she chose. She lived upon very good terms with him, but was not outrageously fond, and did not love him better than many other persons; for the good gentleman had a very disagreeable person, and his face was not the most beautiful. I believe, however, she was touched with his great affection for her; and indeed it would be impossible for a man to entertain a more fervent passion than he did for his wife. Her wit was agreeable, and she could be very pleasant when she chose: her gaiety dissipated the melancholy which sometimes seized upon the devout Dauphin. Like almost all humpbacked men, he had a great passion for women; but at the same time was so pious that he feared he committed a grievous sin in looking at any other than his own wife; and he was truly in love with her. I saw him once, when a lady had told him that he had good eyes, squint immediately that he might appear ugly. This was really an unnecessary trouble; for the good man was already sufficiently plain, having a very ill-looking mouth, a sickly appearance, small stature, and a hump at his back.

He had many good qualities: he was charitable, and had assisted several officers unknown to any one. He certainly died of grief for the loss of his wife, as he had predicted. A learned astrologer of Turin, having cast the nativity of the Dauphine, told her that she would die in her twenty-seventh year.

She often spoke of it, and said one day to her husband, "The time is approaching when I shall die; you cannot remain without a wife as well on account of your rank as your piety; tell me, then, I beg of you, whom you will marry?"

"I hope," he replied, "that God will not inflict so severe a punishment on me as to deprive me of you; but if this calamity should befall me, I shall not marry again, for I shall follow you to the grave in a week."

This happened exactly as he said it would; for, on the seventh day after his wife's death, he died also. This is not a fiction, but perfectly true.

While the Dauphine was in good health and spirits she often said, "I must enjoy myself now. I shall not be able to do so long, for I shall die this year."

I thought it was only a joke, but it turned out to be too true. When she fell sick she said she should never recover.

SECTION XVI.—PETITE MADAME.

A cautery which had been improperly made in the nape of the neck had drawn her mouth all on one side, so that it was almost entirely in her left cheek. For this reason talking was very painful to her, and she said very little. It was necessary to be accustomed to her way of speaking to understand her. Just when she was about to die her mouth resumed its proper place, and she did not seem at all ugly. I was present at her death. She did not say a word to her father, although a convulsion had restored her mouth. The King, who had a good heart and was very fond of his children, wept excessively and made me weep also. The Queen was not present, for, being pregnant, they would not let her come.

It is totally false that the Queen was delivered of a black child. The late Monsieur, who was present, said that the young Princess was ugly, but not black. The people cannot be persuaded that the child is not still alive, and say that it is in a convent at Moret, near Fontainebleau. It is, however, quite certain that the ugly child is dead, for all the Court saw it die.

BOOK 3.

Henrietta of England, Monsieur's First Consort The Due de Berri The Duchesse de Berri Mademoiselle d'Orleans, Louise-Adelaide de Chartres Mademoiselle de Valois, Consort of the Prince of Modena The Illegitimate Children of the Regent, Duc d'Orleans The Chevalier de Lorraine Philip V., King of Spain The Duchess, Consort of the Duc de Bourbon The Younger Duchess Duc Louis de Bourbon Francois-Louis, Prince de Conti La Grande Princesse de Conti The Princess Palatine, Consort of Prince Francois-Louis de Conti The Princesse de Conti, Louise-Elizabeth, Consort of Louis-Armand Louis-Armand, Prince de Conti The Abbe Dubois Mr. Law

SECTION XVII.—HENRIETTA OF ENGLAND, THE FIRST WIFE OF MONSIEUR, BROTHER OF LOUIS XIV.

It is true that the late Madame was extremely unhappy; she confided too much in people who betrayed her: she was more to be pitied than blamed, being connected with very wicked persons, about whom I could give some particulars. Young, pretty and gay, she was surrounded by some of the greatest coquettes in the world, the mistresses of her bitterest foes, and who sought only to thrust her into some unfortunate situation and to embroil her with Monsieur. Madame de Coetquen was the Chevalier de Lorraine's mistress, although Madame did not know it; and she contrived that the Marechal de Turenne should become attached to her. Madame having told the Marshal all her secrets respecting the negotiations with England, he repeated them to his mistress, Madame de Coetquen, whom he believed to be devoted to his mistress. This woman went every night to the Chevalier de Lorraine and betrayed them all. The Chevalier used this opportunity to stir up Monsieur's indignation against Madame, telling him that he passed with the King for a simpleton, who could not hold his tongue; that he would lose all confidence, and that his wife would have everything in her own hand. Monsieur wished to know all the particulars from Madame; but she refused to tell him her brother's secrets, and this widened the breach between them. She became enraged, and had the Chevalier de Lorraine and his brother driven away, which in the end cost her own life; she, however, died with the consciousness of never having done her husband any harm. She was the confidante of the King, to whom it had been hinted that it might be expedient to give some employment to Monsieur, who might otherwise make himself beloved in the Court and in the city. For this reason the King assisted Madame in her affairs of gallantry, in order to occupy his brother. I have this from the King himself. Madame was besides in great credit with her brother, Charles II. (of England). Louis XIV. wished to gain him over through his sister, wherefore it was necessary to take part with her, and she was always better treated than I have been. The late Monsieur never suspected his wife of infidelity with the King, her brother-in-law, he told me, all her life, and would not have been silent with respect to this intrigue if he had believed it. I think that with respect to this great injustice is done to Madame. It would have been too much to deceive at once the brother and the nephew, the father and the son.

The late Monsieur was very much disturbed at his wife's coquetry; but he dared not behave ill to her, because she was protected by the King.

The Queen-mother of England had not brought up her children well: she at first left them in the society of femmes de chambre, who gratified all their caprices; and having afterwards married them at a very early age, they followed the bad example of their mother. Both of them met with unhappy deaths; the one was poisoned, and the other died in child-birth.

Monsieur was himself the cause of Madame's intrigue with the Comte de Guiche. He was one of the favourites of the late Monsieur, and was said to have been handsome once. Monsieur earnestly requested Madame to shew some favour to the Comte de Guiche, and to permit him to wait upon her at all times. The Count, who was brutal to every one else, but full of vanity, took great pains to be agreeable to Madame, and to make her love him. In fact, he succeeded, being seconded by his aunt, Madame de Chaumont, who was the gouvernante of Madame's children. One day Madame went to this lady's chamber, under the pretence of seeing her children, but in fact to meet De Guiche, with whom she had an assignation. She had a valet de chambre named Launois, whom I have since seen in the service of Monsieur; he had orders to stand sentinel on the staircase, to give notice in case Monsieur should approach. This Launois suddenly ran into the room, saying, "Monsieur is coming downstairs."

The lovers were terrified to death. The Count could not escape by the antechamber on account of Monsieur's people who were there. Launois said, "I know a way, which I will put into practice immediately; hide yourself," he said to the Count, "behind the door." He then ran his head against Monsieur's nose as he was entering, and struck him so violently that he began to bleed. At the same moment he cried out, "I beg your pardon, Monsieur, I did not think you were so near, and I ran to open you the door."

Madame and Madame de Chaumont ran in great alarm to Monsieur, and covered his face with their handkerchiefs, so that the Comte de Guiche had time to get out of the room, and escape by the staircase. Monsieur saw some one run away, but he thought it was Launois, who was escaping through fear. He never learnt the truth.

What convinces me of the late Madame's innocence is that, after having received the last sacraments, she begged pardon of Monsieur for all disquiets she had occasioned, and said that she hoped to reach heaven because she had committed no crime against her husband.

I think M. de Monmouth was much worse than the Comte de Guiche; because, although a bastard, he was the son of Madame's own brother; and this incest doubled the crime. Madame de Thiange, sister of Madame de Montespan, conducted the intrigue between the Duke of Monmouth and Madame.

It is said here that Madame was not a beauty, but that she had so graceful a manner as to make all she did very agreeable. She never forgave. She would have the Chevalier de Lorraine dismissed; he was so, but he was amply revenged of her. He sent the poison by which she was destroyed from Italy by a nobleman of Provence, named Morel: this man was afterwards given to me as chief maitre d'hotel, and after he had sufficiently robbed me they made him sell his place at a high price. This Morel was very clever, but he was a man totally void of moral or religious principle; he confessed to me that he did not believe in anything. At the point of death he would not hear talk of God. He said, speaking of himself, "Let this carcass alone, it is now good for nothing." He would steal, lie and swear; he was an atheist and.....

....

It is too true that the late Madame was poisoned, but without the knowledge of Monsieur. While the villains were arranging the plan of poisoning the poor lady, they deliberated whether they should acquaint Monsieur with it or not. The Chevalier de Lorraine said "No, don't tell him, for he cannot hold his tongue. If he does not tell it the first year he may have us hanged ten years afterwards;" and it is well known that the wretches said, "Let us not tell Monsieur, for he would tell the King, who would certainly hang us all." They therefore made Monsieur believe that Madame had taken poison in Holland, which did not act until she arrived here.

[It is said that the King sent for the maitre d'hotel, and that, being satisfied that Monsieur had not been a party to the crime, he said, "Then I am relieved; you may retire." The Memoirs of the day state also that the King employed the Chevalier de Lorraine to persuade Monsieur to obey his brother's wishes.]

It appears, therefore, that the wicked Gourdon took no part in this affair; but she certainly accused Madame to Monsieur, and calumniated and disparaged her to everybody.

It was not Madame's endive-water that D'Effiat had poisoned; that report must have been a mere invention, for other persons might have tasted it had Madame alone drank from her own glass. A valet de chambre who was with Madame, and who afterwards was in my service (he is dead now), told me that in the morning, while Monsieur and Madame were at Mass, D'Effiat went to the sideboard and, taking the Queen's cup, rubbed the inside of it with a paper. The valet said to him, "Monsieur, what do you do in this room, and why do you touch Madame's cup?" He answered, "I am dying with thirst; I wanted something to drink, and the cup being dirty, I was wiping it with some paper." In the afternoon Madame asked for some endive-water; but no sooner had she swallowed it than she exclaimed she was poisoned. The persons present drank some of the same water, but not the same that was in the cup, for which reason they were not inconvenienced by it. It was found necessary to carry Madame to bed. She grew worse, and at two o'clock in the morning she died in great pain. When the cup was sought for it had disappeared, and was not found until long after. It seems it had been necessary to pass it through the fire before it could be cleaned.

A report prevailed at St. Cloud for several years that the ghost of the late Madame appeared near a fountain where she had been accustomed to sit during the great heats, for it was a very cool spot. One evening a servant of the Marquis de Clerambault, having gone thither to draw water from the fountain, saw something white sitting there without a head. The phantom immediately arose to double its height. The poor servant fled in great terror, and said when he entered the house that he had seen Madame. He fell sick and died. Then the captain of the Chateau, thinking there was something hidden beneath this affair, went to the fountain some days afterwards, and, seeing the phantom, he threatened it with a sound drubbing if it did not declare what it was.

The phantom immediately said, "Ah, M. de Lastera, do me no harm; I am poor old Philipinette."

This was an old woman in the village, seventy-seven years old, who had lost her teeth, had blear eyes, a great mouth and large nose; in short, was a very hideous figure. They were going to take her to prison, but I interceded for her. When she came to thank me I asked her what fancy it was that had induced her to go about playing the ghost instead of sleeping.

She laughed and said, "I cannot much repent what I have done. At my time of life one sleeps little; but one wants something to amuse one's mind. In all the sports of my youth nothing diverted me so much as to play the ghost. I was very sure that if I could not frighten folks with my white dress I could do so with my ugly face. The cowards made so many grimaces when they saw it that I was ready to die with laughing. This nightly amusement repaid me for the trouble of carrying a pannier by day."

If the late Madame was better treated than I was it was for the purpose of pleasing the King of England, who was very fond of his sister.

....

Madame de La Fayette, who has written the life of the late Madame, was her intimate friend; but she was still more intimately the friend of M. de La Rochefoucauld, who remained with her to the day of his death. It is said that these two friends wrote together the romance of the Princesse de Cloves.

SECTION XVIII.—THE DUC DE BERRI.

It is not surprising that the manners of the Duc de Berri were not very elegant, since he was educated by Madame de Maintenon and the Dauphine as a valet de chambre. He was obliged to wait upon the old woman at table, and at all other times upon the Dauphine's ladies, with whom he was by day and night. They made a mere servant of him, and used to talk to him in a tone of very improper familiarity, saying, "Berri, go and fetch me my work; bring me that table; give me my scissors."

Their manner of behaving to him was perfectly shameful. This had the effect of degrading his disposition, and of giving him base propensities; so that it is not surprising he should have been violently in love with an ugly femme de chambre. His good father was naturally of rather a coarse disposition.

But for that old Maintenon, the Duc de Berri would have been humpbacked, like the rest who had been made to carry iron crosses.

The Duc de Berri's character seemed to undergo a total change; it is said to be the ordinary lot of the children in Paris that, if they display any sense in their youth, they become stupid as they grow older.

It was in compliance with the King's will that he married. At first he was passionately fond of his wife; but at the end of three months he fell in love with a little, ugly, black femme de chambre. The Duchess, who had sufficient penetration, was not slow in discovering this, and told her husband immediately that, if he continued to live upon good terms with her, as he had done at first, she would say nothing about it, and act as if she were not acquainted with it; but if he behaved ill, she would tell the whole affair to the King, and have the femme de chambre sent away, so that he should never hear of her again. By this threat she held the Duke, who was a very simple man, so completely in check, that he lived very well with her up to his death, leaving her to do as she pleased, and dying himself as fond as ever of the femme de chambre. A year before his death he had her married, but upon condition that the husband should not exercise his marital rights. He left her pregnant as well as his wife, both of whom lay-in after his decease. Madame de Berri, who was not jealous, retained this woman, and took care of her and her child.

The Duke abridged his life by his extreme intemperance in eating and drinking. He had concealed, besides, that in falling from his horse he had burst a blood-vessel. He threatened to dismiss any of his servants who should say that he had lost blood. A number of plates were found in the ruelle of his bed after his death. When he disclosed the accident it was too late to remedy it. As far as could be judged his illness proceeded from gluttony, in consequence of which emetics were so frequently administered to him that they hastened his death.

He himself said to his confessor, the Pere de la Rue, "Ah, father, I am myself the cause of my death!"

He repented of it, but not until too late.

SECTION XIX.—THE DUCHESSE DE BERRI.

My son loves his eldest daughter better than all the rest of his children, because he has had the care of her since she was seven years old. She was at that time seized with an illness which the physicians did not know how to cure. My son resolved to treat her in his own way. He succeeded in restoring her to health, and from that moment his love seemed to increase with her years. She was very badly educated, having been always left with femmes de chambre. She is not very capricious, but she is haughty and absolute in all her wishes.

[Her pride led her into all sorts of follies. She once went through Paris preceded by trumpets and drama; and on another occasion she appeared at the theatre under a canopy. She received the Venetian Ambassador sitting in a chair elevated upon a sort of a platform. This haughtiness, however, did not prevent her from keeping very bad company, and she would sometimes lay aside her singularities and break up her orgies to pass some holy days at the Carmelites.]

From the age of eight years she has had entirely her own way, so that it is not surprising she should be like a headstrong horse. If she had been well brought up, she would have been a worthy character, for she has very good sense and a good natural disposition, and is not at all like her mother, to whom, although she was very severely treated, she always did her duty. During her mother's last illness, she watched her like a hired nurse. If Madame de Berri had been surrounded by honest people, who thought more of her honour than of their own interest, she would have been a very admirable person. She had excellent feelings; but as that old woman (Maintenon) once said, "bad company spoils good manners." To be pleasing she had only to speak, for she possessed natural eloquence, and could express herself very well.

Her complexion is very florid, for which she often lets blood, but without effect; she uses a great quantity of paint, I believe for the purpose of hiding the marks of the small-pox. She cannot dance, and hates it; but she is well-grounded in music. Her voice is neither strong nor agreeable, and yet she sings very correctly. She takes as much diversion as possible; one day she hunts, another day she goes out in a carriage, on a third she will go to a fair; at other times she frequents the rope-dancers, the plays, and the operas, and she goes everywhere 'en echarpe', and without stays. I often rally her, and say that she fancies she is fond of the chase, but in fact she only likes changing her place. She cares little about the result of the chase, but she likes boar-hunting better than stag-hunting, because the former furnishes her table with black puddings and boars' heads.

I do not reckon the Duchesse de Berri among my grandchildren. She is separated from me, we live like strangers to each other, she does not disturb herself about me, nor I about her. (7th January, 1716.)

Madame de Maintenon was so dreadfully afraid lest the King should take a fancy to the Duchesse de Berri while the Dauphine was expected, that she did her all sorts of ill offices. After the Dauphine's death she repaired the wrong; but then, to tell the truth, the King's inclination was not so strong.

If the Duchesse de Berri was not my daughter-in-law, I should have no reason to be dissatisfied with her; she behaves politely to me, which is all that I can say. (25th Sept., 1716.)

She often laughs at her own figure and shape. She has certainly good sense, and is not very punctilious. Her flesh is firm and healthy, her cheeks are as hard as stone. I should be ungrateful not to love her, for she does all sorts of civil things towards me, and displays so great a regard for me that I am often quite amazed at it. (12th April, 1718.)

She is magnificent in her expenditure; to be sure she can afford to be so, for her income amounts to 600,000 livres. Amboise was her jointure, but she preferred Meudon.

She fell sick on the 28th March, 1719. I went to see her last Sunday, the 23rd May, and found her in a sad state, suffering from pains in her toes and the soles of her feet until the tears came into her eyes. I went away because I saw that she refrained from crying out on my account. I thought she was in a bad way. A consultation was held by her three physicians, the result of which was that they determined to bleed her in the feet. They had some difficulty in persuading her to submit to it, because the pain in her feet was so great that she uttered the most piercing screams if the bedclothes only rubbed against them. The bleeding, however, succeeded, and she was in some degree relieved. It was the gout in both feet.

The feet are now covered with swellings filled with water, which cause her as much pain as if they were ulcers; she suffers day and night. Whatever they may say, there has been no other swelling of the feet since those blisters appeared. (13th June.)

The swelling has now entirely disappeared, but the pain is greater than before. All the toes are covered with transparent blisters; she cries out so that she may be heard three rooms off. The doctors now confess they do not know what the disorder is. (20th June.) The King's surgeon says it is rheumatic gout. (11th July.) I believe that frequent and excessive bathing and gluttony have undermined her health. She has two fits of fever daily, and the disease does not abate. She is not impatient nor peevish; the emetic given to her the day before yesterday causes her much pain; it seems that from time to time rheumatic pains have affected her shoulders without her taking much notice of them. From being very fat, as she was, she has become thin and meagre. Yesterday she confessed, and received the communion. (18th July.) She was bled thrice before she took the emetic. (Tuesday, 18th July.) She received the last Sacrament with a firmness which deeply affected her attendants. Between two and three o'clock this night (19th July) she died. Her end was a very easy one;

they say she died as if she had gone to sleep. My son remained with her until she lost all consciousness, which was about an hour before her death. She was his favourite daughter. The poor Duchesse de Berri was as much the cause of her own death as if she had blown her brains out, for she secretly ate melons, figs and milk; she herself confessed, and her doctor told me, that she had closed her room to him and to the other medical attendants for a fortnight that she might indulge in this way. Immediately after the storm she began to die. Yesterday evening she said to me: "Oh, Madame! that clap of thunder has done me great harm;" and it was evident that it had made her worse.

My son has not been able to sleep. The poor Duchesse de Berri could not have been saved; her brain was filled with water; she had an ulcer in the stomach and another in the groin; her liver was affected, and her spleen full of disease. She was taken by night to St. Denis, whither all her household accompanied her corse. They were so much embarrassed about her funeral oration that it was resolved ultimately not to pronounce one.

With all her wealth she has left my son 400,000 livres of debt to pay. This poor Princess was horribly robbed and pillaged. You may imagine what a race these favourites are; Mouchi, who enjoyed the greatest favour, did not grieve for her mistress a single moment; she was playing the flute at her window on the very day that the Princess was borne to St. Denis, and went to a large dinner party in Paris, where she ate and drank as if nothing had happened, at the same time talking in so impertinent a manner as disgusted all the guests. My son desired her and her husband to quit Paris.

My son's affliction is so much the greater since he perceives that, if he had been less complying with his beloved daughter, and if he had exercised somewhat more of a parent's authority, she would have been alive and well at this time.

That Mouchi and her lover Riom have been playing fine tricks; they had duplicate keys, and left the poor Duchess without a sou. I cannot conceive what there is to love in this Riom; he has neither face nor figure; he looks, with his green-and-yellow complexion, like a water fiend; his mouth, nose and eyes are like those of a Chinese. He is more like a baboon than a Gascon, which he is. He is a very dull person, without the least pretensions to wit; he has a large head, which is sunk between a pair of very broad shoulders, and his appearance is that of a low-minded person; in short, he is a very ugly rogue.

And yet the toad does not come of bad blood; he is related to some of the best families. The Duc de Lauzun is his uncle, and Biron his nephew. He is, nevertheless, unworthy of the honour which was conferred on him; for he was only a captain in the King's Guard. The women all ran after him; but, for my part, I find him extremely disagreeable; he has an unhealthy air and looks like one of the Indian figures upon a screen.

He was not here when Madame de Berri died, but was with the army, in the regiment which had been bought for him. When the news of the Duchess's death reached him the Prince de Conti went to seek Riom, and sang a ridiculous song, my son was a little vexed at this, but he did not take any notice of it.

There can be no doubt that the Duchess was secretly married to Riom; this has consoled me in some degree for her loss. I had heard it said before, and I made a representation upon the subject to my granddaughter.

She laughed, and replied: "Ah, Madame, I thought I had the honour of being so well known to you that you could not believe me guilty of so great a folly; I who am so much blamed for my pride."

This answer lulled my suspicions, and I no longer believed the story. The father and mother would never have consented to this marriage; and even if they had sanctioned such an impertinence I never would!

[The Duchess, with her usual violence, teased her father to have her marriage made public; this was also Riom's most ardent desire, who had married her solely from ambitious motives. The Regent had despatched Riom to the army for the purpose of gaining time. One daughter was the result of the connection between Riom and the Duchesse de Berri, who was afterwards sent into a convent at Pontoisse.]

The toad had made the Princess believe that he was a Prince of the House of Aragon, and that the King of Spain unjustly withheld from him his kingdom; but that if she would marry him he could sue for his claim through the treaties of peace. Mouchi used to talk

64

about this to the Duchess from morning to night; and it was for this reason that she was so greatly in favour.

That Mouchi is the granddaughter of Monsieur's late surgeon. Her mother, La Forcade, had been appointed by my son the gouvernante of his daughter and son, and thus the young Forcade was brought up with the Duchesse de Berri, who married her to Monsieur Mouchi, Master of the Wardrobe to the Duke, and gave her a large marriage-portion. While the King lived the Princess could not visit her much; and it was not until after his death that she became the favourite, and was appointed by the Duchess second dame d'atour.

SECTION XX.—MADEMOISELLE D'ORLEANS, LOUISE-ADELAIDE DE CHARTRES.

Mademoiselle de Chartres, Madame d'Orleans' second daughter, is well made, and is the handsomest of my granddaughters. She has a fine skin, a superb complexion, very white teeth, good eyes, and a faultless shape, but she stammers a little; her hands are extremely delicate, the red and white are beautifully and naturally mingled in her skin. I never saw finer teeth; they are like a row of pearls; and her gums are no less beautiful. A Prince of Auhalt who is here is very much in love with her; but the good gentleman is ugly enough, so that there is no danger. She dances well, and sings better; reads music at sight, and understands the accompaniment perfectly; and she sings without any grimace. She persists in her project of becoming a nun; but I think she would be better in the world, and do all in my power to change her determination: it seems, however, to be a folly which there is no eradicating. Her tastes are all masculine; she loves dogs, horses, and riding; all day long she is playing with gunpowder, making fusees and other artificial fireworks. She has a pair of pistols, which she is incessantly firing; she fears nothing in the world, and likes nothing which women in general like; she cares little about her person, and for this reason I think she will make a good nun.

She does not become a nun through jealousy of her sister, but from the fear of being tormented by her mother and sister, whom she loves very much, and in this she is right. She and her sister are not fond of their mother's favourites, and cannot endure to flatter them. They have no very reverent notions, either, of their mother's brother, and this is the cause of dissensions. I never saw my granddaughter in better spirits than on Sunday last; she was with her sister, on horseback, laughing, and apparently in great glee. At eight o'clock in the evening her mother arrived; we played until supper; I thought we were afterwards going to play again, but Madame d'Orleans begged me to go into the cabinet with her and Mademoiselle d'Orleans; the child there fell on her knees, and begged my permission, and her mother's, to go to Chelles to perform her devotions. I said she might do that anywhere, that the place mattered not, but that all depended upon her own heart, and the preparation which she made. She, however, persisted in her desire to go to Chelles. I said to her mother:

"You must decide whether your daughter shall go to Chelles or not."

She replied, "We cannot hinder her performing her devotions."

[In the Memoirs of the time it is said that Mademoiselle de Chartres, being at the Opera with her mother, exclaimed, while Caucherau was singing a very tender air, "Ah! my dear Caucherau!" and that her mother, thinking this rather too expressive, resolved to send her to a convent.]

So yesterday morning at seven o'clock she set off in a coach; she afterwards sent back the carriage, with a letter to her father, her mother, and myself, declaring that she will never more quit that accursed cloister. Her mother, who has a liking for convents, is not very deeply afflicted; she looks upon it as a great blessing to be a nun, but, for my part, I think it is one of the greatest misfortunes.

My son went yesterday to Chelles, and took with him the Cardinal de Noailles, to try for the last time to bring his daughter away from the convent. (20th July, 1718.)

My heart is full when I think that our poor Mademoiselle d'Orleans has made the profession of her vows. I said to her all I could, in the hope of diverting her from this diabolical project, but all has been useless. (23rd August, 1718.) I should not have restrained my tears if I had been present at the ceremony of her profession. My son dreaded it also. I cannot tell for what reason Mademoiselle d'Orleans resolved to become a nun. Mademoiselle de Valois wanted to do the same thing, but she could not prevail upon her mother. In the convent they assume the names of saints. My granddaughter has taken that of Sister Bathilde; she is of the Benedictine order.

Madame d'Orleans has long wished her daughter to take this step, and it was on her account that the former Abbess, Villars' sister, was prevailed upon to quit the convent. He is in the interest of the Duc du Maine. I do not see, however, that his sister has much to complain of, for they gave her a pension of 12,000 livres until the first abbey should become vacant. Madame d'Orleans is, however, vexed at the idea of Villars' sister being obliged to yield to my son's daughter, which is, nevertheless, as it should be.

Our Abbess is upon worse terms than ever with her mother. She complains that the latter never comes but to scold her. She does not envy her sister her marriage, for she finds herself very happy, and in this she displays great good sense.

SECTION XXI.—MADEMOISELLE DE VALOIS, CHARLOTTE-AGLAE, CONSORT OF THE PRINCE OF MODENA.

Mademoiselle de Valois is not, in my opinion, pretty, and yet occasionally she does not look ugly. She has something like charms, for her eyes, her colour and her skin are good. She has white teeth, a large, ill-looking nose, and one prominent tooth, which when she laughs has a bad effect. Her figure is drawn up, her head is sunk between her shoulders, and what, in my opinion, is the worst part of her appearance, is the ill grace with which she does everything. She walks like an old woman of eighty. If she were a person not very anxious to please, I should not be surprised at the negligence of her gait; but she likes to be thought pretty. She is fond of dress, and yet she does not understand that a good mien and graceful manners are the most becoming dress, and that where these are wanting all the ornaments in the world are good for nothing. She has a good deal of the Mortemart family in her, and is as much like the Duchess of Sforza, the sister of Montespan, as if she were her daughter; the falsehood of the Mortemarts displays itself in her eyes. Madame d'Orleans would be the most indolent woman in the world but for Madame de Valois, her daughter, who is worse than she. To me nothing is more disgusting than a young person so indolent. She cares little for me, or rather cannot bear me, and, for my part, I care as little for a person so educated.

She is not upon good terms with her mother, because she wanted to marry her to the Prince de Dombes, the Duc du Maine's eldest son. The mother says now reproachfully to her daughter that, if she had married her nephew, neither his father's nor his own misfortunes would have taken place. She cannot bear to have her daughter in her sight, and has begged me to keep her with me.

My son has agreed to give his daughter to the Prince of Modem, at which I very sincerely rejoice. On the day before yesterday (28th November, 1719) she came hither with her mother to tell me that the courier had arrived. Her eyes were swollen and red, and she looked very miserable. The Duchess of Hanover tells me that the intended husband fell in love with Mademoiselle de Valois at the mere sight of her portrait. I think her rather pretty than agreeable. Her hawk nose spoils all, in my opinion. Her legs are long, her body stout and short, and her gait shows that she has not learnt to dance; in fact, she never would learn. Still, if the interior was as good as the exterior, all might pass; but she has as much of the father as of the mother in her, and this it is that I dislike.

Our bride-elect is putting, as we say here, as good a face as she can upon a bad bargain; although her language is gay her eyes are swollen, and it is suspected that she has been weeping all night. The Grand Prior, who is also General of the Galleys, will escort his sister into Italy. The Grand Duchess of Tuscany says that she will not see Mademoiselle de Valois nor speak to her, knowing very well what Italy is, and believing that Mademoiselle de Valois will not be able to reconcile herself to it. She is afraid that if her niece should ever return to France they will say, "There is the second edition of the Grand Duchess;" and that for every folly she may commit towards her father-in-law and husband they will add, "Such are the instructions which her aunt, the Grand Duchess, has given her." For this reason she said she would not go to see her.

The present has come from Modena; it does not consist of many pieces; there is a large jewel for the bride, with some very fine diamonds, in the midst of which is the portrait of the Prince of Modena, but it is badly executed. This present is to be given on the day of the marriage and at the signature of the contract in the King's presence; this ceremony will take place on the 11th (of February, 1720). The nuptial benediction will be pronounced on Monday, and on Thursday she will set off. I never in my life saw a bride more sorrowful; for the last three days she has neither eaten nor drunk, and her eyes are filled with tears.

I have been the prophetess of evil, but I have prophesied too truly. When our Princess of Modena told me that she wished to go to Chelles to bid her sister farewell, I told her that the measles had been in the convent a short time before, that the Abbess herself had been attacked by this disease, which was contagious. She replied that she would seek it. I said such things are more easily found than anything good; you run a risk of your life, and I recommend you to take care. Notwithstanding my advice, she went on Sunday morning to Chelles, and passed the whole of the day with her sister. Soon afterwards she found herself unwell, and was laid up with the measles. Her consolation is that this illness retards her journey.

On the 12th of March (1720) my son brought his daughter to bid me farewell. She could not articulate a word. She took my hands, kissed and pressed them, and then clasped her own. My son was much affected when he brought her. They thought at first of marrying her to the Prince of Piedmont. Her father had given her some reason to hope for this union, but he afterwards retracted.

[According to Duclos it was Madame herself who prevented this marriage by writing to the Queen of Sicily that she was too much her friend to make her so worthless a present as Mademoiselle de Valois. Duclos adds that the Regent only laughed at this German blunder of his mother's.]

She would have preferred marrying the Duke or the Comte de Charolois, because then she would have remained with her friends. Her father has given her several jewels. The King's present is superb. It consists of fourteen very large and fine diamonds, to each of which are fastened round pearls of the first water, and together they form a necklace. The Grand Duchess advised her niece well in telling her not to follow her example, but to endeavour to please her husband and father-in-law.

[The same author (Duclos) says, on the contrary, that the Duchess had given her niece the following advice: "My dear, do as I have done. Have one or two children and try to get back to France; there is nothing good for us out of that country."]

The Prince of Modena will repair to Genoa incognito, because the Republic has declared that they will pay due honours to his bride as a Princess of the blood, but not as Princess of Modena. They have already begun to laugh here at the amusements of Modena. She has sent to her father from Lyons an harangue which was addressed to her by a curate. In spite of her father, she will visit the whole of Provence. She will go to Toulon, La Ste. Beaume, and I know not what. I believe she wishes to see everything or anything except her husband.

[She performed her journey so slowly that the Prince complained of it, and the Regent was obliged to order his daughter to go directly to the husband, who was expecting her.]

It may truly be said of this Princess that she has eaten her white bread first.

All goes well at Modena at present, but the too charming brother-in-law is not permitted to be at the petite soupers of his sister. The husband, it is said, is delighted with his wife; but she has told him that he must not be too fond of her, for that is not the fashion in France, and would seem ridiculous. This declaration has not, as might be guessed, given very great satisfaction in this country.

The Grand Duchess says, in the time of the Queen-mother's regency, when the Prince and his brother, the Prince de Conti, were taken to the Bastille, they were asked what books they would have to amuse themselves with? The Prince de Conti said he should like to have "The Imitation of Jesus Christ;" and the Prince de Condo said he would rather like "The Imitation of the Duc de Beaufort," who had then just left the Bastille.

"I think," added the Duchess, "that the Princess of Modena will soon be inclined to ask for 'The Imitation of the Grand Duchess.'"

[The Princess of Modena did, in fact, go back to France, and remained there for the rest of her life.]

Our Princess of Modena has found her husband handsomer and likes him better than she thought she should; she has even become so fond of him, that she has twice kissed his hands; a great condescension for a person so proud as she is, and who fancies that, there is not her equal on the earth.

The Duke of Modena is a very strange person in all matters. His son and his son's wife have requested him to get rid of Salvatico, who has been here in the quality of envoy. This silly person made on the journey a declaration in form of his love for the Princess, and threatened her with all sorts of misfortune if she did not accept his love. He began his declaration with,

"Ah! ah! ah! Madame, ah! ah! ah! Madame."

The Princess interrupted him: "What do you mean with your ah's?"

He replied, "Ah! the Prince of Modena is under great obligations; I have made him happy."

He had begun the same follies here, and was in the habit of entering the Princess's chamber at all times, and he even had the impudence to be jealous. The Princess complained of him to her husband, and he told his father of it, begging him to send the rogue away; but the father was so far from complying that he wanted to make Salvatico his major-domo. Upon the whole, I think that Salvatico's love for our Princess of Modena is fortunate for her; for, having learnt all that had passed here,

[Mademoiselle de Valois had an amorous intrigue with the Duc de Richelieu; and it is said that she only consented to marry the Prince of Modena upon condition that her father, the Regent, would set her husband at liberty. Madame had intimated to the Duc de Richelieu that, if he approached the places where her granddaughter was with her, his life would be in great peril.]

he might have made inconvenient reports: he would, however, perhaps have done it in vain, for the Prince would not have believed him. Salvatico is quite crazy. He is the declared favourite of the Duke of Modena, which verifies the German proverb, "Like will to like, as the devil said to the collier."

The Prince and Princess are very fond of each other; but it is said they join in ridiculing the old father (2nd August, 1720). The Princess goes about all day from room to room, crying, "How tired I am, how tiresome everything is here!" She, however, lives a little better with her husband than at the beginning.

SECTION XXII.—THE ILLEGITIMATE CHILDREN OF THE REGENT, DUC D'ORLEANS.

My son has three illegitimate children, two boys and a girl; but only one of them is legitimated, that is, his son by Mademoiselle de Seri, a lady of noble family, and who was my Maid of Honour. The younger Margrave of Anspach was also in love with her. This son is called the Chevalier d'Orleans. The other, who is now (1716) about eighteen years old, is an Abbe; he is the son of La Florence, a dancer at the Opera House. The daughter is by Desmarets, the actress. My son says that the Chevalier d'Orleans is more unquestionably his than any of the others; but, to tell the truth, I think the Abbe has a stronger family likeness to my son than the Chevalier, who is like none of them. I do not know where my son found him; he is a good sort of person, but he has neither elegance nor beauty. It is a great pity that the Abbe is illegitimate: he is well made; his features are not bad; he has very good talents, and has studied much.—[Duclos says that this 'eleve' of the Jesuits was, nevertheless, the most zealous ignoramus that ever their school produced.]—He is a good deal like the portraits of the late Monsieur in his youth, only that he is bigger. When he stands near Mademoiselle de Valois it is easy to see that they belong to the same father. My son purchased for the Chevalier d'Orleans the office of General of the Galleys from the Marechal de Tasse. He intends to make him a Knight of Malta, so that he may live unmarried, for my son does not wish to have the illegitimate branches of his family extended. The Chevalier does not want wit; but he is a little satirical, a habit which he takes from his mother.

My son will not recognize the Abbe Saint-Albin, on account of the irregular life which his mother, La Florence, has led. He fears being laughed at for acknowledging children so different. The Abbe Dubois was a chief cause, too, why my son would not acknowledge this son. It was because the Abbe, aspiring to the Cardinal's hat, was jealous of every one who might be a competitor with him. I love this Abbe Saint-Albin, in the first place, because he is attached to me, and, in the second, because he is really very clever; he has wit and sense, with none of the mummery of priests. My son does not esteem him half so much as he deserves, for he is one of the best persons in the world; he is pious and virtuous, learned in every point, and not vain. It is in vain for my son to deny him; any one may see of what race he comes, and I am sorry that he is not legitimated. My son is much more fond of Seri's Son.

The poor Abbe de Saint-Albin is grieved to death at not being acknowledged; while Fortune smiles upon his elder brother, he is forgotten, despised, and has no rank; he seeks only to be legitimated. I console him as well as I can; but why should I tease my son about the business?

[The Abbe de Saint-Albin was appointed Bishop of Laon, and, after Dubois' death, Archbishop of Cambrai. When he wished to become a member of the Parliament he could not give the names either of his father or mother; he had been baptized in the name of Cauche, the Regent's valet de chambre and purveyor.]

It would only put him in the way of greater inconveniences, for, as he has also several children by Parabere, she would be no less desirous that he should legitimate hers. This consideration ties my tongue.

The daughter of the actress Desmarets is somewhat like her mother, but she is like no one else. She was educated in a convent at Saint Denis, but had no liking for a nun's life. When my son had her first brought to him he did not know who she was. When my son told her he was her father, she was transported with joy, fancying that she was the daughter of Seri and sister to the Chevalier; she thought, too, that she would be legitimated immediately. When my son told her that could not be done, and that she was Desmarets' daughter, she wept excessively. Her mother had never been permitted to see her in the convent; the nuns would not have allowed it, and her presence would have been injurious to the child. From the time she was born, her mother had not seen her until the present year (1719), when she saw her in a box at the theatre, and wept for joy. My son married this girl to the Marquis de Segur.

An actress at the Opera House, called Mdlle. d'Usg, who is since dead, was in great favour with my son, but that did not last long. At her death it appeared that, although she had had several children, neither she nor her mother nor her grandmother had ever been married.

SECTION XXIII.—THE CHEVALIER DE LORRAINE.

The Chevalier de Lorraine looked very ill, but it was in consequence of his excessive debauchery, for he had once been a handsome man. He had a well-made person, and if the interior had answered to the exterior I should have had nothing to say against him. He was, however, a very bad man, and his friends were no better than he. Three or four years before my husband's death, and for his satisfaction, I was reconciled with the Chevalier, and from that time he did me no mischief. He was always before so much afraid of being sent away that he used to tell Monsieur he ought to know what I was saying and doing, that he might be apprised of any attempt that should be made against the Chevalier or his creatures.

He died so poor that his friends were obliged to bury him; yet he had 100,000 crowns of revenue, but he was so bad a manager that his people always robbed him. Provided they would supply him when he wanted them with a thousand pistoles for his pleasures or his play, he let them dispose of his property as they thought fit. That Grancey drew large sums from him. He met with a shocking death. He was standing near Madame de Mare, Grancey's sister, and telling her that he had been sitting up at some of his extravagant pleasures all night, and was uttering the most horrible expressions, when suddenly he was stricken with apoplexy, lost the power of speech, and shortly afterwards expired.

[He died suddenly in his own house, playing at ombre, as many of his family had done, and was regretted by no person except Mdlle. de Lillebonne, to whom he was believed to have been privately married. —Note to Dangeau's Journal. This man, who was suspected of having poisoned the King's sister-in-law, was nevertheless in possession of four abbeys, the revenues of which defrayed the expenses of his debaucheries.]

SECTION XXIV.—PHILIP V., KING OF SPAIN.

Louis XIV. wept much when his grandson set out for Spain. I could not help weeping, too. The King accompanied him as far as Sceaux. The tears and lamentations in the drawing-room were irresistible. The Dauphin was also deeply affected.

The King of Spain is very hunchbacked, and is not in other respects well made; but he is bigger than his brothers. He has the best mien, good features, and fine hair. What is somewhat singular, although his hair is very light, his eyes are quite black; his complexion is clear red and white; he has an Austrian mouth; his voice is deep, and he is singularly slow in speaking. He is a good and peaceable sort of a person, but a little obstinate when he takes it in his head. He loves his wife above all things, leaves all affairs to her, and never interferes in anything. He is very pious, and believes he should be damned if he committed any matrimonial infidelity. But for his devotion he would be a libertine, for he is addicted to women, and it is for this reason he is so fond of his wife. He has a very humble opinion of his own merit. He is very easily led, and for this reason the Queen will not lose sight of him. He receives as current truths whatever is told him by persons to whom he is accustomed, and never thinks of doubting. The good gentleman ought to be surrounded by competent persons, for his own wit would not carry him far; but he is of a good disposition, and is one of the quietest men in the world. He is a little melancholy, and there is nothing in Spain to make him gay.

He must know people before he will speak to them at all. If you desire him to talk you must tease him and rally him a little, or he will not open his mouth. I have seen Monsieur very impatient at his talking to me while he could not get a word from him. Monsieur did not take the trouble to talk to him before he was a King, and then he wished him to speak afterwards; that did not suit the King. He was not the same with me. In the apartment, at table, or at the play, he used to sit beside me. He was very fond of hearing tales, and I used to tell them to him for whole evenings: this made him well accustomed to me, and he had always something to ask me. I have often laughed at the answer he made me when I said to him, "Come, Monsieur, why do not you talk to your uncle, who is quite distressed that you never speak to him."

"What shall I say to him?" he replied, "I scarcely know him."

It is quite true that the Queen of Spain was at first very fond of the Princesse des Ursins, and that she grieved much when that Princess was dismissed for the first time. The story that is told of the Confessor is also very true; only one circumstance is wanting in it, that is, that the Duc de Grammont, then Ambassador, played the part of the Confessor, and it was for this reason he was recalled.

The Queen had one certain means of making the King do whatever she wished. The good gentleman was exceedingly fond of her, and this fondness she turned to good account. She had a small truckle-bed in her room, and when the King would not comply with any of her requests she used to make him sleep in this bed; but when she was pleased with him he was admitted to her own bed; which was the very summit of happiness to the poor King. After the Princesse des Ursins had departed, the King recalled the Confessor from Rome, and kept him near his own person (1718).

The King of Spain can never forgive, and Madame des Ursins has told him so many lies to my son's disadvantage that the King can never, while he lives, be reconciled to him.

Rebenac's—[Francois de Feuquieres, Called the Comte de Rebenac, Extraordinary Ambassador to Spain.]—passion for the late Queen of Spain was of no disadvantage to her; she only laughed at it, and did not care for him. It was the Comte de Mansfeld, the man with the pointed nose, who poisoned her. He bought over two of her French femmes de chambre to give her poison in raw oysters; and they afterwards withheld from her the antidote which had been entrusted to their care.

The Queen of Spain, daughter of the first Madame,—[Henrietta of England.]—died in precisely the same manner as she did, and at the same age, but in a much more painful manner, for the violence of the poison was such as to make her nails fall off.

SECTION XXV.—THE DUCHESSE LOUISE-FRANCISQUE, CONSORT OF LOUIS III., DUC DE BOURBON.

I knew a German gentleman who has now been dead a long time (1718), who has sworn to me positively that the Duchess is not the daughter of the King, but of Marechal de Noailles. He noted the time at which he saw the Marshal go into Montespan's apartment, and it was precisely nine months from that time that the Duchess came into the world. This German, whose name was Bettendorf, was a brigadier in the Body Guard; and he was on guard at Montespan's when the captain of the first company paid this visit to the King's mistress.

The Duchess is not prettier than her daughters, but she has more grace; her manners are more fascinating and agreeable; her wit shines in her eyes, but there is some malignity in them also. I always say she is like a very pretty cat, which, while you play with it, lets you feel it has claws. No person has a better carriage of the head. It is impossible to dance better than the Duchess and her daughters can; but the mother dances the best. I do not know how it is, but even her lameness is becoming to her. The Duchess has the talent of saying things in so pleasant a manner that one cannot help laughing. She is very amusing and uncommonly good company; her notions are so very comical. When she wishes to make herself agreeable to any one she is very insinuating, and can take all shapes; if she were not also treacherous, one might say truly that nobody is more amiable than the Duchess; she understands so well how to accommodate herself to people's peculiar habits that one would believe she takes a real interest in them; but there is nothing certain about her. Although her sense is good, her heart is not. Notwithstanding her ambition, she seems at first as if she thought only of amusing and diverting herself and others; and she can feign so skilfully that one would think she had been very agreeably entertained in the society of persons, whom immediately upon her return home she will ridicule in all possible ways.

La Mailly complained to her aunt, old Maintenon, that her husband was in love with the Duchess; but this husband, having afterwards been captivated by an actress named Bancour, gave up to her all the Duchess's letters, for which he was an impertinent rascal. The Duchess wrote a song upon Mailly, in which she reproached her, notwithstanding her airs of prudery, with an infidelity with Villeroi, a sergeant of the Guard.

In the Duchess's house malice passes for wit, and therefore they are under no restraint. The three sisters—the Duchess, the Princesse de Conti, and Madame d'Orleans—behave to each other as if they were not sisters.

The Princess is a very virtuous person, and is much displeased at her daughter-in-law's manner of life, for Lasso is with her by day and by night; at the play, at the Opera, in visits, everywhere Lasso is seen with her.

SECTION XXVI.—THE YOUNGER DUCHESS.

The Duke's wife is not an ill-looking person: she has good eyes, and would be very well if she had not a habit of stretching and poking out her neck. Her shape is horrible; she is quite crooked; her back is curved into the form of an S. I observed her one day, through curiosity, when the Dauphine was helping her to dress.

She is a wicked devil; treacherous in every way, and of a very dangerous temper. Upon the whole, she is not good for much. Her falsehood was the means of preventing the Duke from marrying one of my granddaughters. Being the intimate friend of Madame de Berri, who was very desirous that one of her sisters should marry the Duke and the other the Prince de Conti, she promised to bring about the marriage, provided Madame de Berri would say nothing of it to the King or to me. After having imposed this condition, she told the King that Madame de Berri and my son were planning a marriage without his sanction; in order to punish them she begged the King to marry the Duke to herself, which was actually done.

Thanks to her good sense, she lives upon tolerable terms with her husband, although he has not much affection for her. They follow each their own inclinations; they are not at all jealous of each other, and it is said they have separate beds.

She causes a great many troubles and embarrassments to her relation, the young Princesse de Conti, and perfectly understands tormenting folks.

The young Duchess died yesterday evening (22nd March, 1720). The Duke's joy at the death of his wife will be greatly diminished when he learns that she has bequeathed to her sister, Mademoiselle de la Roche-sur-Yon, all her property; and as the husband and wife lived according to the custom of Paris, 'en communaute', the Duke will be obliged to refund the half of all he gained by Law's bank.

After the death of the younger Duchess, the Princesse de Conti, her mother, wrote to a Chevalier named Du Challar, who was the lover of the deceased, to beg him to come and see her, as he was the only object left connected with her daughter, and assuring him that he might reckon upon her services in everything that depended upon her. It was the younger Duchess who was so fond of Lasse, and who had been so familiar with him at a masked ball.

I recognized only two good qualities in her: her respect and affection for her grandmother, the Princess, and the skill with which she concealed her faults. Beside this, she was good for nothing, in whatever way her character is regarded. That she was treacherous is quite certain; and she shortened her life by her improper conduct. She neither loved nor hated her husband, and they lived together more like brother and sister than husband and wife.

The Elector of Bavaria, during his stay at Paris, instead of visiting his nephews and nieces, passed all his time, by day and by night, with the Duchess and her daughters. As to me, he fled me as he would fly the plague, and never spoke to me but in the company of M. de Torcy. The Duchess had three of the handsomest daughters in the world: the one called Mademoiselle de Clermont is extremely beautiful; but I think her sister, the Princesse de Conti, more amiable. The Duchess can drink very copiously without being affected; her daughters would fain imitate her, but they soon get tipsy, and cannot control themselves as their mother can.

SECTION XXVII.—LOUIS III., DUC DE BOURBON.

It is said that the Duke has solid parts; he does everything with a certain nobility; he has a good person, but the loss of that eye, which the Duc de Berri struck out, disfigures him much. He is certainly very politic, and this quality he has from his mother. He is polite and well-bred; his mind is not very comprehensive, and he has been badly instructed. They say he is unfit for business for three reasons: first, on account of his ignorance; secondly, for his want of application; and, thirdly, for his impatience. I can see that in examining him narrowly one would find many defects in him; but he has also many praiseworthy qualities, and he possesses many friends. He has a greatness and nobility of soul, and a good deportment.

The Prince is in love with Madame de Polignac; but she is fond of the Duke, who cannot yet forget Madame de Nesle, although she has dismissed him to make room for that great calf, the Prince of Soubise. The latter person is reported to have said, "Why does the Duke complain? Have I not consented to share Madame de Nesle's favours with him whenever he chooses?"

Such is the delicacy which prevails here in affairs of love.

The Duke is very passionate. When Madame de Nesle dismissed him he almost died of vexation; he looked as if he was about to give up the ghost, and for six months he did not know what to do.

The Marquis de Villequier, the Duc d'Aumont's son, one day visited the Marquise de Nesle. She took it into her head to ask him if he was very fond of his wife. Villequier replied, "I am not in love with her; I see her very little; our humours differ greatly. She is serious, and for my part I like pleasure and gaiety. I feel for her a friendship founded on esteem, for she is one of the most virtuous women in France."

Madame de Nesle, of whom no man could say so much, took this for an insult, and complained of it to the Duke, who promised to avenge her. Some days afterwards he invited young Villequier to dine with him at the Marquis de Nesle's; there were, besides Madame de Nesle, the Marquis de Gevres, Madame de Coligny, and others. During dinner the Duke began thus:

"A great many men fancy they are sure of the fidelity of their wives, but it is a mistake. I thought to protect myself from this common fate by marrying a monster, but it served me nought; for a villain named Du Challar, who was more ugly than I am, played me false. As to the Marquis de Gevres, as he will never marry * * *, he will be exempt; but you, Monsieur de Nesle, you are so and so." Nesle, who did not believe it, although it was very true, only laughed. Then addressing himself to Villequier, he said, "And you, Villequier, don't you think you are so?" He was silent. The Duke continued, "Yes, you are befooled by the Chevalier de Pesay."

Villequier blushed, but at last said, "I confess that up to this moment I had no reason to believe it; but since you put me into such good company I have no right to complain."

I do not think Madame de Nesle was well revenged.

I remember that the Duke, who was terribly ill-made, said one day to the late Monsieur, who was a straight, well-formed person, that a mask had taken him for Monsieur. The latter, somewhat mortified at such a mistake, replied, "I lay that, with all other wrongs done to me, at the foot of the Cross."

Ever since the Duchess espoused the party of her son against her brother and his nephews, the Duke has displayed a great fondness for his mother, about whom he never disturbed himself before.

Mdlle. de Polignac made the Duke believe she was very fond of him. He entertained great suspicions of her, and had her watched, and learnt that she was carrying on a secret intrigue with the Chevalier of Bavaria. He reproached her with it, and she denied the accusation. The Duke cautioned her not to think that she could deceive him. She protested that he had been imposed upon. As soon, however, as she had quitted him she went to the Chevalier's house; and the Duke, who had had her dogged, knew whither she had gone. The next day he appointed her to visit him; she went directly to the bedroom, believing that his suspicions were entirely lulled. The Duke then opened the door wide, so that she might be seen from the cabinet, which was full of men; and calling the Chevalier of Bavaria, he said to him: "Here, Sir Chevalier, come and see your mistress, who will now have no occasion to go so far to find you."

Although the Duke and the Prince de Conti are brothers-in-law in two ways, they cannot bear each other.

The Duke is at this moment (1718) very strongly attached to Madame de Prie. She has already received a good beating on his account from her husband, but this does not deter her. She is said to have a good deal of sense; she entirely governs the Duke, who is solely occupied with making her unfaithful to M. de Prie. She has consoled the Duke for his dismissal from Madame de Nesle; but it is said that she is unfaithful to him, and that she has two other lovers. One is the Prince of Carignan, and the other Lior, the King's first maitre d'hotel, which latter is the handsomest of the three.

It is impossible that the Duke can now inspire any woman with affection for him. He is tall, thin as a lath; his legs are like those of a crane; his body is bent and short, and he has no calves to his legs; his eyes are so red that it is impossible to distinguish the bad eye from the good one; his cheeks are hollow; his chin so long that one would not suppose it belonged to the face; his lips uncommonly large: in short, I hardly ever saw a man before so ugly. It is said that the inconstancy of his mistress, Madame de Prie, afflicts him profoundly.

The Marchioness was extremely beautiful, and her whole person was very captivating. Possessing as many mental as personal charms, she concealed beneath an apparent simplicity the most dangerous treachery. Without the least conception of virtue, which, according to her ideas, was a word void of sense, she affected innocence in vice, was violent under an appearance of meekness, and libertine by constitution. She deceived her lover with perfect impunity, who would believe what she said even against the evidence of his own eyes. I could mention several instances of this, if they were not too indecent. It is, however, sufficient to say that she had one day to persuade him that he was the cause of a libertinism of which he was really the victim.—Memoires de Duclos, tome ii. It is well known that, after the Duke assumed the Regency, upon the death of the Regent, the Marchioness du Prie governed in his name; and that she was exiled, and died two years afterwards of ennui and vexation.

The Princess of Modena takes nothing by the death of the Duchess; the Duke has said that he never would have married that Princess, and that now he will not marry at all.

In order that Mademoiselle de la Roche-sur-Yon may enjoy the millions that belong to her of right, in consequence of her sister's death, it is necessary first for her to receive them; but the Duke, it is reported, as the good Duc de Crequi used to say, "Holds back as tight as the trigger of the Cognac cross-bow;" and in fact he has not only refused to give up to his sister what she should take under her sister's will, but he disputes her right to the bank-notes which she had given to the Duchess to take care of for her, when she herself was dangerously ill.

The Duke and his mother are said to have gained each two hundred and fifty millions.

The Duke, who is looked upon as Law's very good friend, has been ill-treated by the people, who have passed all kinds of insults upon him, calling him even a dog. His brother, the Marquis de Clermont, too, has fared little better; for they cried after him at the Port Royal, "Go along, dog! you are not much better than your brother." His tutor alighted for the purpose of haranguing the mob; but they picked up some stones, and he soon found it expedient to get into the carriage again, and make off with all speed.

SECTION XXVIII.—FRANCOIS-LOUIS, PRINCE DE CONTI.

The Prince de Conti, who died lately (in 1709), had good sense, courage, and so many agreeable qualities as to make himself generally beloved. But he had also some bad points in his character, for he was false, and loved no person but himself.

It is said that he caused his own death by taking stimulating medicines, which destroyed a constitution naturally feeble. There had been some talk of making him King of Poland.—[In 1696, after the death of John Sobiesky.]

SECTION XXIX.—THE GREAT PRINCESSE DE CONTI, DAUGHTER OF LA VALLIERE.

This is of all the King's illegitimate daughters the one he most loves. She is by far the most polite and well-bred, but she is now totally absorbed by devotion.

SECTION XXX.—THE PRINCESS PALATINE, MARIE-THERESE DE BOURBON, WIFE OF FRANCOIS-LOUIS,

PRINCE DE CONTI.

This Princess is the only one of the House of Conde who is good for anything. I think she must have some German blood in her veins. She is little, and somewhat on one side, but she is not hunchbacked. She has fine eyes, like her father; with this exception, she has no pretensions to beauty, but she is virtuous and pious. What she has suffered on account of her husband has excited general compassion; he was as jealous as a fiend, though without the slightest cause. She never knew where she was to pass the night. When she had made arrangements to sleep at Versailles, he would take her from Paris to Chantilly, where she supposed she was going to stay; then she was obliged to set out for Versailles. He tormented her incessantly in all possible ways, and he looked, moreover, like a little ape. The late Queen had two paroquets, one of which was the very picture of the Prince, while the other was as much like the Marechal de Luxembourg as one drop of water is like another.

Notwithstanding all that the Princess has suffered, she daily regrets the loss of her husband. I am often quite angry to see her bewailing her widowhood instead of enjoying the repose which it affords her; she wishes that her husband were alive again, even although he should torment her again as much as before.

She was desirous that Mademoiselle de Conde should marry the late Margrave; this lady was incomparably more handsome than her sister; but I think he had a greater inclination for Mademoiselle de Vendome, because she seemed to be more modest and quiet.

The Princess, who has been born and educated here, had not the same dislike that I felt to her son's marrying an illegitimate child, and yet she has repented it no less. She is exceedingly unhappy with respect to her children. The Princesse de Conti, mother of the Prince de Conti, who is rather virtuous than otherwise, is nevertheless a little simpleton, and is something like the Comtesse Pimbeche Orbeche, for she is always wishing to be engaged in lawsuits against her mother; who, on her part, has used all possible means, but without success, to be reconciled to her. On Thursday last (10th March, 1720) she lost her cause, and I am very glad of it, for it was an unjust suit. The younger Princess wished the affair to be referred to arbitration; but the son would have the business carried through, and made his counsel accuse his mother of falsehood. The advocate of the Princess replied as follows:

"The sincerity of the Princesse de Conti and of the Princess her daughter are so well known that all the world can judge of them." This has amused the whole palace.

SECTION XXXI.—LOUISE-ELIZABETH, PRINCESSE DE CONTI, CONSORT OF LOUIE-ARMAND DE CONTI.

She is a person full of charms, and a striking proof that grace is preferable to beauty. When she chooses to make herself agreeable, it is impossible to resist her. Her manners are most fascinating; she is full of gentleness, never displaying the least ill-humour, and always saying something kind and obliging. It is greatly to be regretted that she is not in the society of more virtuous persons, for she is herself naturally very good; but she is spoiled by bad company. She has an ugly fool for her husband, who has been badly brought up; and the examples which are constantly before her eyes are so pernicious that they have corrupted her and made her careless of her reputation. Her amiable, unaffected manners are highly delightful to foreigners. Among others, some Bavarians have fallen in love with her, as well as the Prince Ragotzky; but she disgusted him with her coquetry.

She does not love her husband, and cannot do so, no less on account of his ugly person than for his bad temper. It is not only his face that is hideous, but his whole person is frightful and deformed. She terrified him by placing some muskets and swords near her bed, and assuring him that if he came there again with his pistols charged, she would take the gun and fire upon him, and if she missed, she would fall upon him with the sword. Since this time he has left off carrying his pistols.

Her husband teased her, and made her weep so much that she has lost her child, and her health is again injured.

SECTION XXXII.—LOUIE-ARMAND, PRINCE DE CONTI.

It cannot be denied that his whole appearance is extremely repulsive. He is a horribly ill-made little man, and is always absent-minded, which gives him a distracted air, as if he were really crazy. When it could be the least expected, too, he will fall over his own walking-stick. The folks in the palace were so much accustomed to this in the late King's time, that they used always to say, when they heard anything fall,

"It's nothing; only the Prince de Conti tumbling down."

He has sense, but he has been brought up like a scullion boy; he has strange whimsies, of which he is quite aware himself, but which he cannot control. His wife is a charming woman, and is much to be pitied for being in fear of her life from this madman, who often threatens her with loaded pistols. Fortunately, she has plenty of courage and does not fear him. Notwithstanding this, he is very fond of her; and this is the more surprising, because his love for the sex is not very strong; and although he visits improper places occasionally, it is only for the purpose of tormenting the poor wretches who are to be found there. Before he was married he felt no, affection for any woman but his mother, who also loved him very tenderly. She is now vexed at having no longer the same ascendency over her son, and is jealous of her daughter-in-law because the Prince loves her alone. This occasions frequent disturbances in the house. The mother has had a house: built at some distance from her son. When they are good friends, she dismisses the workmen; but when they quarrel, she doubles the number and hastens the work, so that one may always tell, upon a mere inspection of the building, upon what terms the Princesse de Conti and her son are living. The mother wished to have her grandson to educate; her daughter-in-law opposed it because she preferred taking care of him herself; and then ensued a dog-and-cat quarrel. The wife, who is cunning enough, governs her husband entirely, and has gained over his favourites to be her creatures. She is the idol of the-whole house.

In order to prevent the Prince de Conti from going to Hungary, the government of Poitou has been bought for him, and a place in the Council of the Regency allotted to him; by this means they have retained the wild beast.

Our young Princess says her husband has a rheum in his eyes.

To amuse her, he reads aloud Ovid in the original; and although she does not understand one word of Latin, she is obliged to listen and to remain silent, even though any one should come in; for if anybody interrupts him he is angry, and scolds all who are in the apartment.

At the last masked ball (4th March, 1718) some one who had dressed himself like the Prince de Conti, and wore a hump on his back, went and sat beside him. "Who are you, mask?" asked the Prince.

The other replied, "I am the Prince de Conti."

Without the least ill-temper, the Prince took off his mask, and, laughing, said, "See how a man may be deceived. I have been fancying for the last twenty years that I was the Prince de Conti." To keep one's temper on such an occasion is really an uncommon thing.

The Prince thought himself quite cured, but he has had a relapse in Spain, and, although he is a general of cavalry, he cannot mount his horse. I said on Tuesday last (17th July, 1719) to the young Princesse de Conti that I heard her husband was not entirely recovered. She laughed and whispered to me,—

"Oh, yes, he is quite well; but he pretends not to be so that he may avoid going to the siege, where he may be killed, for he is as cowardly as an ape." I think if I had as little inclination for war as he has, I would not engage in the campaign at all; there is nothing to oblige him to do so-it is to reap glory, not to encounter shame, that men go into the army. His best friends, Lanoue and Cleremont, for example, have remonstrated with him on this subject, and he has quarrelled with them in consequence. It is an unfortunate thing for a man not to know himself.

The Prince is terribly afflicted with a dysentery. They wanted to carry him to Bayonne, but he has so violent a fever that he would not be able to support the journey. He is therefore obliged to stay with the army (25th August, 1719).

He has been back nine or ten days, but I have heard nothing of him yet; he is constantly engaged in the Rue de Quincampoix, trying to gain money among the stock-jobbers (19th September, 1719).

At length he has been to see me. Perhaps there was this morning less stock-jobbing than usual in the Rue de Quincampoix, for there he has been ever since his return. His cousin, the Duke, is engaged in the same pursuit. The Prince de Conti has not brought back much honour from the campaign; he is too much addicted to debauchery of all kinds.

Although he can be polite when he chooses, no one can behave more brutally than he does occasionally, and he becomes more and more mad daily.

At one of the last opera balls he seized a poor little girl just come from the country, took her from her mother's side, and, placing her between his own legs, amused himself by slapping and fillipping her until he made her nose and mouth bleed. The young girl, who had done nothing to offend him, and who did not even know him, wept bitterly; but he only laughed, and said, "Cannot I give nice fillips?" All who were witnesses of this brutal scene pitied her; but no one dared come to the poor child's assistance, for they were afraid of having anything to do with this violent madman. He makes the most frightful grimaces, and I, who am extremely frightened at crazy people, tremble whenever I happen to be alone with him.

His wicked pranks remind me of my own. When I was a child I used to take touchwood, and, placing pieces of it over my eyes and in my mouth, I hid myself upon the staircase for the purpose of terrifying the people; but I was then much afraid of ghosts, so that I was always the first to be frightened. It is in the same way that the Prince de Conti does; he wishes to make himself feared, and he is the most timid person in the world.

The Duke and his mother, as well as Lasse, the friend of the latter, have gained several millions. The Prince has gained less, and yet his winnings, they say, amount to millions.

[He had four wagons loaded with silver carried from Law's bank, in exchange for his paper money; and this it was that accelerated Law's disgrace, and created a kind of popularity for the Prince de Conti.]

The two cousins do not stir from the Rue de Quincampoix, which has given rise to the following epigram:

*Prince dites nous vos exploits Que faites vous pour votre gloire?
Taisez-vous sots!—Lisez l'histoire De la rue de Quincampoix.*

But the person who had gained most by this affair is Dantin, who is horridly avaricious.

The Princesse de Conti told me that she had had her son examined in his infancy by Clement, for the purpose of ascertaining whether he was in every respect well made; and that he, having found the child perfectly well made, went to the Prince de Conti, and said to him: "Monseigneur, I have examined the shape of the young Prince who is just born: he is at all points well formed, let him sleep without a bolster that he may remain so; and only imagine what grief it would occasion to the Princesse de Conti, who has brought him into the world straight, if you should make him crooked."

The Prince de Conti wished to speak of something else, but Clement still returned to the same topic, saying, "Remember, Monseigneur, he is straight as a wand, and do not make him crooked and hunchbacked."

The Prince de Conti, not being able to endure this, ran away.

SECTION XXXIII.—THE ABBE DUBOIS.

My son had a sub-governor, and he it was who appointed the Abbe, a very learned person, to be his tutor. The sub-governor's intention was to have dismissed the Abbe as soon as he should have taught my son sufficiently, and, excepting during the time occupied by the lessons, he never suffered him to remain with his pupil. But this good gentleman could not accomplish his design; for being seized with a violent colic, he died, unhappily for me, in a few hours. The Abbe then proposed himself to supply his place. There was no other preceptor near at hand, so the Abbe remained with my son, and assumed so adroitly the language of an honest man that I took him for one until my son's marriage; then it was that I discovered all his knavery. I had a strong regard for him, because I thought he was tenderly attached to my son, and only desired to promote his advantage; but when I found that he was a treacherous person, who thought only of his own interest, and that, instead of carefully trying to preserve my son's honour, he plunged him into ruin by permitting him to give himself up to debauchery without seeming to perceive it, then my esteem for this artful priest was changed into disgust. I know, from my son himself, that the Abbe, having one day met him in the street, just as he was about to enter a house of ill-fame, did nothing but laugh at him, instead of taking him by the arm and leading him home again. By this culpable indulgence, and by the part he took in my son's marriage, he has proved that there is neither faith nor honesty in him. I know that I do him no wrong in suspecting him to have contributed to my son's marriage; what I say I have from my son himself, and from people who were living with that old Maintenon at the time, when the Abbe used to go nightly for the purpose of arranging that intrigue with her, the object of which was to sell and betray his master. He deceives himself if he fancies that I do not know all this. At first he had declared in my favour, but after the old woman had sent for him two or three times he suddenly changed his conduct. It was not, however, on this that the King afterwards took a dislike to him, but for a nefarious scheme in which he was engaged with the Pere La Chaise. Monsieur was as much vexed as I. The King and the old woman threatened to dismiss all his favourites, which made him consent to everything; he repented afterwards, but it was then too late.

I would to God that the Abbe Dubois had as much religion as he has talent! but he believes in nothing—he is treacherous and wicked—his falsehood may be seen in his very eyes. He has the look of a fox; and his device is an animal of this sort, creeping out of his hole and watching a fowl. He is unquestionably a good scholar, talks well, and has instructed my son well; but I wish he had ceased to visit his pupil after his tuition was terminated. I should not then have to regret this unfortunate marriage, to which I can never reconcile myself. Excepting the Abbe Dubois there is no priest in my son's favour. He has a sort of indistinctness in his speech, which makes it sometimes necessary for him to repeat his words; and this often annoys me.

If there is anything which detracts from the Abbe's good sense it is his extreme pride; it is a weak side upon which he may always be successfully attacked. I wish my son had as little confidence in him as I have; but what astonishes me most is that, knowing him as he does, better than I do, he will still trust him. My son is like the rest of his family; he cannot get rid of persons to whom he is accustomed, and as the Abbe has been his tutor, he has acquired a habit of suffering him to say anything he chooses. By his amusing wit, too, he always contrives to restore himself to my son's good graces, even when the latter has been displeased with him.

If the Abbe had been choked with his first lie he had been dead long ago. Lying is an art in which he excels, and the more eminently where his own interest is concerned; if I were to enumerate all the lies I have known him to utter I should have a long list to write. He it was who suggested to the King all that was necessary to be said to him respecting my son's marriage, and for this purpose he had secret interviews with Madame de Maintenon. He affects to think we are upon good terms, and whatever I say to him, however disagreeable, he takes it all with a smile.

My son has most amply recompensed the Abbe Dubois; he has given him the place of Secretary of the King's Cabinet, which M. Calieres formerly held, and which is worth 22,000 livres; he has also given him a seat in the Council of Regency for the Foreign Affairs.

My son assures me that it is not his intention to make the Abbe Dubois a Cardinal, and that the Abbe himself does not think about it (17th August, 1717).

On the 6th of March, this disagreeable priest came to me and said, "Monseigneur has just nominated me Archbishop of Cambrai." I replied, "I congratulate you upon it; but has this taken place today? I heard of it a week ago; and, since you were seen to take the oaths on your appointment, no one has doubted it." It is said that the Duc de Mazarin said, on the Abbe's first Mass, "The Abbe Dubois is gone to his first communion;" meaning that he had never before taken the communion in all his life. I embarrassed my son by remarking to him that he had changed his opinion since he told me the Abbe should never become Bishop or Archbishop, and that he did not think of being Cardinal. My son blushed and answered, "It is very true; but I had good reason for changing my intention." "Heaven grant it may be so," I said, "for it must be by God's mercy, and not from the exercise of your own reason."

The Archbishop of Cambrai is the declared enemy of our Abbe Saint-Albin. The word arch is applicable to all his qualities; he is an arch-cheat, an arch-hypocrite, an arch-flatterer, and, above all, an arch-knave.

It is reported that a servant of the Archbishop of Rheims said to a servant of the Archbishop of Cambrai, "Although my master is not a Cardinal, he is still a greater lord than yours, for he consecrates the Kings."

"Yes," replied the Abbe Dubois' servant, "but my master consecrates the real God, who is still greater than all Kings."

SECTION XXXIV.—MR. LAW.

Mr. Law is a very honest and a very sensible man; he is extremely polite to everybody, and very well bred. He does not speak French ill—at least, he speaks it much better than Englishmen in general. It is said that when his brother arrived in Paris, Mr. Law made him a present of three millions (of livres); he has good talents, and has put the affairs of the State in such good order that all the King's debts have been paid. He is admirably skilled in all that relates to finance. The late King would have been glad to employ him, but, as Mr. Law was not a Catholic, he said he ought not to confide in him (19th Sept., 1719).

He (Law) says that, of all the persons to whom he has explained his system, there have been only two who have properly comprehended it, and these are the King of Sicily and my son; he was quite astonished at their having so readily understood it. He is so much run after, that he has no repose by day or by night. A Duchess even kissed his hand publicly.

If a Duchess can do this, what will not other ladies do?

Another lady, who pursued him everywhere, heard that he was at Madame de Simiane's, and immediately begged the latter to permit her to dine with her. Madame de Simiane went to her and said she must be excused for that day, as Mr. Law was to dine with her. Madame de Bouchu replied that it was for this reason expressly she wished to be invited. Madame de Simiane only repeated that she did not choose to have Mr. Law troubled, and so quitted her. Having, however, ascertained the dinner-hour, Madame de Bouchu passed before the house in her coach, and made her coachman and footman call out "Fire!" Immediately all the company quitted the table to know where the fire was, and among them Mr. Law appeared. As soon as Madame de Bouchu saw him, she jumped out of her carriage to speak to him; but he, guessing the trick, instantly disappeared.

Another lady ordered her carriage to be driven opposite to Mr. Law's hotel and then to be overturned. Addressing herself to the coachman, she said, "Overturn here, you blockhead—overturn!" Mr. Law ran out to her assistance, when she confessed to him that she had done this for the sole purpose of having an interview with him.

A servant had gained so much in the Rue de Quincampoix, that he was enabled to set up his equipage. When his coach was brought home, he forgot who he was, and mounted behind. His servant cried out, "Ah, sir! what are you doing? this is your own carriage."

"That is true," said the quondam servant; "I had forgotten."

Mr. Law's coachman having also made a very considerable sum, demanded permission to retire from his service. His master gave it him, on condition of his procuring him another good coachman. On the next day, the wealthy coachman made his appearance with two persons, both of whom were, he said, good coachmen; and that Mr. Law had only to choose which of them he liked, while he, the coachman, would take the other.

People of all nations in Europe are daily coming to Paris; and it has been remarked that the number of souls in the capital has been increased by 250,000 more than usual. It has been necessary to make granaries into bedrooms; there is such a profusion of carriages that the streets are choked up with them, and many persons run great danger.

Some ladies of quality seeing a well-dressed woman covered with diamonds, and whom nobody knew, alight from a very handsome carriage, were curious to know who it was, and sent to enquire of the lackey. He replied, with a sneer, "It is a lady who has recently tumbled from a garret into this carriage." This lady was probably of the same sort as Madame Bejon's cook. That lady, being at the opera, some days back, saw a person in a costly dress, and decorated with a great quantity of jewels, but very ugly, enter the theatre. The daughter said, "Mamma, unless I am very much deceived, that lady so dressed out is Mary, our cook-maid."

"Hold your tongue, my dear," said the mother, "and don't talk such nonsense."

Some of the young people, who were in the amphitheatre, began to cry out, "Mary, the cook-maid! Mary, the cook-maid!"

The lady in the fine dress rose and said, "Yes, madam, I am Mary, the cook-maid; I have gained some money in the Rue de Quincampoix; I like to be well-dressed; I have bought some fine gowns, and I have paid for them. Can you say so much for your own?"

Mr. Law is not the only person who has bought magnificent jewels and extensive estates. The Duke, too, has become immensely rich, as well as all those who have held stock. Mr. Law has made his abjuration at Melun; he has embraced the Catholic religion, with his children, and his wife is in utter despair at it.

[The abjuration did not take place at Paris, because the jokes of the Parisians were to be dreaded. The Abbe Tencin was so fortunate as to have the office of converting Mr. Law. "He gained by this pious labour," says Duclos, "a large sum in bank-notes and stock."]

It is amusing enough to see how the people run after him in crowds only to be looked at by him or his son. He has had a terrible quarrel with the Prince de Conti, who wished Mr. Law to do at the bank a thing which my son had forbidden. The Prince de Conti said to Mr. Law, "Do you know who I am?"

"Yes, Prince," replied Law, "or I should not treat you as I have done."

"Then," said the Prince, "you ought to obey me."

"I will obey you," replied Law, "when you shall be Regent;" and he withdrew.

The Princesse de Leon would be taken to the bank, and made her footmen cry out, "Room for the Princesse de Lion." At the same time she, who is very little, slipped into the place where the bankers and their clerks were sitting.

"I want some stock," said she.

The clerk replied, "You must have patience, madame, the certificates are delivered in rotation, and you must wait until those who applied before you are served."

At the same time he opened the drawer where the stock-papers were kept; the Princess snatched at them; the clerk tried to prevent her, and a fight ensued. The clerk was now alarmed at having beaten a lady of quality, and ran out to ask the servants who the Princesse de Leon was. One of the footmen-said, "She is a lady of high rank, young and beautiful."

"Well, then," said the clerk, "it cannot be she."

Another footman said, "The Princesse de Leon is a little woman with a hunch before and another behind, and with arms so long that they nearly reach the ground."

"Then," replied the clerk, "that is she."

Mr. Law is not avaricious; he gives away large soma in charity, and assists many indigent people.

When my son wanted some Duchess to accompany my daughter to Geneva, some one, who heard him speaking about it, said, "if, Monsieur, you would like to select from a number of Duchesses, send to Mr. Law's; you will find them all there."

Lord Stair cannot conceal his hatred of Mr. Law, and yet he has gained at least three millions by him.

Mr. Law's son was to have danced in the King's ballet, but he has been attacked by the small-pox (9th Feb., 1720).

....

My son has been obliged to displace Mr. Law. This person, who was formerly worshipped like a god, is now not sure of his life; it is astonishing how greatly terrified he is. He is no longer Comptroller-General, but continues to hold the place of Director-General of the Bank and of the East India Company; certain members of the Parliamentary Council have, however, been joined with him to watch over the business of the Bank.

[In the Council of the Regency, the Duc d'Orleans was obliged to: admit that Law issued papers to the amount of 1,200 millions above the legal sum; and that he (the Regent) had protected him from all responsibility by decrees of the Council which had been ante-dated. The total, amount of bank-notes in circulation was 2,700,000,000 livres.]

His friend, the Duc d'Antin wanted to get the place of Director.

The Duke at first spoke strongly against Law; but it is said that a sum of four millions, three of which went to him and one to Madame de Prie, has engaged him to undertake Law's defence. My son is not timid, although he is threatened on all sides, and is very much amused with Law's terrors (25th June, 1720).

At length the latter is somewhat recovered, and continues to be great friends with the Duke: this is very pleasant to the Duc de Conti, and makes him behave so strangely that his infirmity is observed by the people. It is fortunate for us that Law is so great a coward, otherwise he would be very troublesome to my son, who, learning that he was joining in a cabal against him, told his wife of it. "Well, Monsieur," said she, "what would you have him do? He likes to be talked of, and he has no other way of accomplishing it. What would people have to say of him if he did not?"

On the 17th of June, while I was at the Carmelites, Madame de Chateau-Thiers came to me in my chamber, and said, "M. de Simiane is just come in from the Palais Royal, and he thinks it fit you should know that upon your return you will find the court of the Palais Royal filled with people, who, though they do not say anything, will not disperse."

At six o'clock this morning they brought in three dead bodies, which M. Le Blanc ordered to be carried away immediately.

Mr. Law has taken refuge in the Palais Royal. The populace have done him no harm, but his coachman has been pelted on his return, and the carriage broken to pieces. It was the coachman's own fault, who said aloud that the people were rabble, and ought to be all hanged. I saw immediately that it would not do to display any fear, and I set off. There was such a stoppage of the carriages that I was obliged to wait half an hour before I could get into the Palais Royal. During this time I heard the people talking; they said nothing against my son, and bestowed benedictions upon me, but they all wished Law to be hanged. When I reached the Palais Royal all was calm again; my son came to me immediately, and, notwithstanding the alarm I had felt, he made me laugh; as for himself, he had not the least fear. He told me that the first president had made a good impromptu upon this affair. Having occasion to go down into the court, he heard what the people had done with Law's carriage, and, upon returning to the Salon, he said with great gravity:

"Messieurs, bonne nouvelle, *Le carrosse de Law est en canelle.*"

Is not this a becoming jest for such serious personages? M. Le Blanc went into the midst of the people with great firmness, and made a speech to them; he afterwards had Law escorted home and all became tranquil.

It is almost impossible that Law should escape, for the same soldiers who protect him from the fury of the people will not permit him to go out of their hands. He is by no means at his ease, and yet I think the people do not now intend to pursue him any farther, for they have begun to make all kinds of songs about him.

Law is said to be in such an agony of fear that he has not been able to venture to my son's at Saint Cloud, although he sent a carriage to fetch him. He is a dead man; he is as pale as a sheet, and it is said can never get over his last panic. The people's hatred of the Duke arises from his being the friend of Law, whose children he carried to Saint Maur, where they remain.

M. Boursel, passing through the Rue Saint Antoine in his way from the Jesuits' College, had his carriage stopped by a hackney coachman, who would neither come on nor go back. M. Boursel's footman, enraged at his obstinacy, struck the coachman, and, M. Boursel getting out of his coach to restrain his servant's rage, the coachman resolved to be avenged of both master and man, and so began to cry out, "Here is Law going to kill me; fall upon him."

The people immediately ran with staves and stones, and attacked Boursel, who took refuge in the church of the Jesuits. He was pursued even to the altar, where he found a little door opened which led into the convent. He rushed through and shut it after him, by which means he saved his life.

M. de Chiverni, the tutor of the Duc de Chartres, was going into the Palais Royal in a chair, when a child about eight years old cried out, "There goes Law!" and the people immediately assembled. M. Chiverni, who is a little, meagre-faced, ugly old man, said pleasantly enough, "I knew very well I had nothing to fear when I should show them my face and figure."

As soon as they saw him they suffered him to get quietly into his chair and to enter the gates of the palace.

On the 10th of December (1720), Law withdrew; he is now at one of his estates about six miles from Paris. The Duke, who wished to visit him, thought proper to take Mdlle. de Prie's post-chaise, and put his footman into a grey livery, otherwise the people would have known and have maltreated him.

Law is gone to Brussels; Madame de Prie lent him her chaise. When he returned it, he wrote thanking her, and at the same time sent her a ring worth 100,000 livres. The Duke provided him with relays, and made four of his own people accompany him. When he took leave of my son, Law said to him, "Monsieur, I have committed several great faults, but they are merely such as are incident to humanity; you will find neither malice nor dishonesty in my conduct." His wife would not go away until she had paid all their debts; he owed to his rotisseur alone 10,000 livres.

[Mr. Law retired to Venice, and there ended his days. Some memoirs state that he was not married to the Englishwoman who passed for his wife.]

BOOK 4.

Victor Amadeus II. The Grand Duchess, Consort of Cosimo II. of Florence The Duchesse de Lorraine, Elizabeth-Charlotte d'Orleans The Duc du Maine The Duchesse du Maine Louvois Louis XV. Anecdotes and Historical Particulars of Various Persons Explanatory Notes

SECTION XXXV.—VICTOR AMADEUS, KING OF SICILY.

It is said that the King of Sicily is always in ill humour, and that he is always quarrelling with his mistresses. He and Madame de Verrue have quarrelled, they say, for whole days together. I wonder how the good Queen can love him with such constancy; but she is a most virtuous person and patience itself. Since the King had no mistresses he lives upon better terms with her. Devotion has softened his heart and his temper.

Madame de Verrue is, I dare say, forty-eight years of age (1718). I shared some of the profits of her theft by buying of her 160 medals of gold, the half of those which she stole from the King of Sicily. She had also boxes filled with silver medals, but they were all sold in England.

[The Comtesse de Verrue was married at the age of thirteen years. Victor Amadeus, then King of Sardinia, fell in love with her. She would have resisted, and wrote to her mother and her husband, who were both absent. They only joked her about it. She then took that step which all the world knows. At the age of eighteen, being at a dinner with a relation of her husband's, she was poisoned. The person she suspected was the same that was dining with her; he did not quit her, and wanted to have her blooded. Just at this time the Spanish Ambassador at Piedmont sent her a counter-poison which had a happy effect: she recovered, but never would mention whom she suspected. She got tired of the King, and persuaded her brother, the Chevalier de Lugner, to come and carry her off, the King being then upon a journey. The rendezvous was in a chapel about four leagues distant from Turin. She had a little parrot with her. Her brother arrived, they set out together, and, after having proceeded four leagues on her journey, she remembered that she had forgotten her parrot in the chapel. Without regarding the danger to which she exposed her brother, she insisted upon returning to look for her parrot, and did so. She died in Paris in the beginning of the reign of Louis XV. She was fond of

literary persons, and collected about her some of the best company of that day, among whom her wit and grace enabled her to cut a brilliant figure. She was the intimate friend of the poet La Faye, whom she advised in his compositions, and whose life she made delightful. Her fondness for the arts and pleasure procured for her the appellation of 'Dame de Volupte', and she wrote this epitaph upon herself: "Ci git, dans un pais profonde, Cette Dame de Volupte, Qui, pour plus grande surete, Fit son Paradis dans ce monde."]

SECTION XXXVI.—THE GRAND DUCHESS, WIFE OF COSMO II. OF FLORENCE.

The Grand Duchess has declared to me, that, from the day on which she set out for Florence, she thought of nothing but her return, and the means of executing this design as soon as she should be able.

No one could approve of her deserting her husband, and the more particularly as she speaks very well of him, and describes the manner of living at Florence as like a terrestrial paradise.

She does not think herself unfortunate for having travelled, and looks upon all the grandeur she enjoyed at Florence as not to be compared with the unrestrained way of living in which she indulges here. She is very amusing when she relates her own history, in the course of which she by no means flatters herself.

"Indeed, cousin," I say to her often, "you do not flatter yourself, but you really tell things which make against you."

"Ah, no matter," she replies, "I care not, provided I never see the Grand Duke again."

She cannot be accused of any amorous intrigue.

Her husband furnishes her with very little money; and at this moment (April, 1718) he owes her fifteen months of her pension. She is now really in want of money to enable her to take the waters of Bourbon. The Grand Duke, who is very avaricious, thinks she will die soon, and therefore holds back the payments that he may take advantage of that event when it shall happen.

SECTION XXXVII.—THE DUCHESSE DE LORRAINE, ELIZABETH-CHARLOTTE PHILIPPINE D'ORLEANS, CONSORT OF LEOPOLD JOSEPH-CHARLES DE LORRAINE.

My daughter is ugly; even more so than she was, for the fine complexion which she once had has become sun-burnt. This makes a great difference in the appearance, and causes a person to look old. She has an ugly round nose, and her eyes are sunken; but her shape is preserved, and, as she dances well, and her manners are easy and polished, any one may see that she is a person of breeding. I know many people who pique themselves upon their good manners, and who still have not so much reason as she has. At all events I am content with my child as she is; and I would rather see her ugly and virtuous than pretty and profligate like the rest.

Whenever the time of her accouchement approaches, she never fails to bid her friends adieu, in the notion that she will die. Fortunately she has hitherto always escaped well.

When jealousy is once suffered to take root, it is impossible to extirpate it—therefore it is better not to let it gain ground. My daughter pretends not to be affected by hers, but she often suffers great affliction from it. This is not astonishing, because she is very fond of her children; and the woman with whom the Duke is infatuated, together with her husband, do not leave him a farthing; they completely ruin his household. Craon is an accursed cuckold and a treacherous man. The Duc de Lorraine knows that my daughter is acquainted with everything, and I believe he likes her the better that she does not remonstrate with him, but endures all patiently. He is occasionally kind to her, and, provided that he only says tender things to her, she is content and cheerful.

I should almost believe that the Duke's mistress has given him a philtre, as Neidschin did to the Elector of Saxony. When he does not see her, it is said he perspires copiously at the head, and, in order that the cuckold of a husband may say nothing about the affair, the Duke suffers him to do whatever he pleases. He and his wife, who is gouvernante, rule everything, although neither the one nor the other has any feeling of honour. She is to come hither, it seems, with the Duke and Duchess.

The Duc de Lorraine is here incog.

[He came to Paris for the purpose of soliciting an arrondissement in Champagne and the title of Royal Highness. Through the influence of his mother-in-law he obtained both the one and the other. By virtue of a treaty very disadvantageous for France, but which was nevertheless registered by the Parliament, he increased his states by adding to them a great number of villages.]

under the title of the Comte de Blamont. Formerly the chase was his greatest passion; but now, it seems, the swain is wholly amorous. It is in vain for him to attempt to conceal it; for the more he tries, the more apparent it becomes. When you would suppose he is about to address you, his head will turn round, and his eyes wander in search of Madame Craon; it is quite diverting to see him. I cannot conceive how my daughter can love her husband so well, and not display more jealousy. It is impossible for a man to be more amorous than the Duke is of Craon (19th of April, 1718).

It cannot be denied that she (Madame de Craon) is full of agreeable qualities. Although she is not a beauty, she has a good shape, a fine skin, and a very white complexion; but her greatest charms are her mouth and teeth. When she laughs it is in a very pleasing and modest manner; she behaves properly and respectfully in my daughter's presence; if she did the same when she is not with her, one would have nothing to complain of. It is not surprising that such a woman should be beloved; she really deserves it. But she treats her lover with the utmost haughtiness, as if she were the Duchesse de Lorraine and he M. de Luneville. I never saw a man more passionately attached than he appears to be; when she is not present, he fixes his eyes upon the door with an expression of anxiety; when she appears, he smiles and is calm; it is really very droll to observe him. She, on the contrary, wishes to prevent persons from perceiving it, and seems to care nothing about him. As the Duke was crossing a hall here with her upon his arm, some of the people said aloud, "That is the Duc de Lorraine with his mistress." Madame Craon wept bitterly, and insisted upon the Duke complaining of it to his brother. The Duke did in fact complain; but my son laughed at him, and replied, "that the King himself could not prevent that; that he should despise such things, and seem not to hear them."

Madame Craon was my daughter's fille d'honneur; she was then called Mademoiselle de Ligneville, and there it was that the Duke fell in love with her. M. Craon was in disgrace with the Duke, who was about to dismiss him as a rascal, for having practised a sharping trick at play; but, as he is a cunning fellow, he perceived the Duke's love for Mademoiselle de Ligneville, although he pretended to make a great mystery of it. About this time Madame de Lenoncourt, my daughter's dame d'atour, happened to die. The Duke managed to have Mademoiselle de Ligneville appointed in her room; and Craon, who is rich, offered to marry this poor lady. The Duke was delighted with the plan of marrying her to one who would lend himself to the intrigue; and thus she became Madame de Craon, and dame d'atour. The old gouvernante dying soon afterwards, my daughter thought to gratify her husband, as well as Madame de Craon, by appointing her dame d'honneur; and this it is that has brought such disgrace upon her.

My daughter is in despair. Craon and his wife want to take a journey of ten days, for the purpose of buying a marquisate worth 800,000 livres. The Duke will not remain during this time with his wife, but chooses it for an opportunity to visit all the strong places of Alsatia. He will stay away until the return of his mistress and her husband; and this it is which makes my poor daughter so unhappy. The Duke now neither sees nor hears anything but through Craon, his wife, and their creatures.

I do not think that my daughter's attachment to her husband is so strong as it used to be, and yet I think she loves him very much; for every proof of fondness which he gives her rejoices her so much that she sends me word of it immediately. He can make her believe whatever he chooses; and, although she cannot doubt the Duke's passion for Madame de

Craon, yet, when he says that he feels only friendship for her, that he is quite willing to give up seeing her, only that he fears by doing so he would dishonour her in the eyes of the public, and that there is nothing he is not ready to do for his wife's repose, she receives all he says literally, beseeches him to continue to see Madame de Craon as usual, and fancies that her husband is tenderly attached to her, while he is really laughing at her. If I were in my daughter's place, the Duke's falsehood would disgust me more than his infidelity.

What appears to me the most singular in this intrigue is that the Duke is as fond of the husband as of the wife, and that he cannot live without him. This is very difficult to comprehend; but M. de Craon understands it well, and makes the most of it; he has already bought an estate for 1,100,000 livres.

[The Marquis de Craon was Grand Chamberlain and Prime Minister of the Duc de Lorraine; who, moreover, procured for him from the Emperor of Germany the title of Prince. This favourite married one of his daughters to the Prince de Ligin, of the House of Lorraine.]

The burning of Lundville was not the effect of an accident; it is well known that some of the people stopped a woman's mouth, who was crying out "Fire!" A person was also heard to say, "It was not I who set it on fire." My daughter thinks that Old Maintenon would have them all burnt; for the person who cried out has been employed, it seems, in the house of the Duc de Noailles. For my part, I am rather disposed to believe it was the young mistress, Madame de Craon, who had a share in this matter; for Luneville is my daughter's residence and dowry.

SECTION XXXVIII.—THE DUC DU MAINE, LOUIS-AUGUSTUS.

The Duc du Maine flattered himself that he would marry my daughter. Madame de Maintenon and Madame de Montespan were arranging this project in presence of several merchants, to whom they paid no attention, but the latter, engaging in the conversation, said, "Ladies, do not think of any such thing, for it will cost you your lives if you bring about that marriage."

Madame de Maintenon was dreadfully frightened at this, and immediately went to the King to persuade him to relinquish the affair.

The Duc du Maine possesses talent, which he displays particularly in his manner of relating anything. He knows very well who is his mother, but he has never had the least affection for any one but his gouvernante, against whom he never bore ill-will, although she displaced his mother and put herself in her room. My son will not believe that the Duc du Maine is the King's son. He has always been treacherous, and is feared and hated at Court as an arch tale-bearer. He has done many persons very ill offices with the King; and those in particular to whom he promised most were those who have had the greatest reason to complain of him. His little wife is worse even than he, for the husband is sometimes restrained by fear; but she mingles the pathetic occasionally in her comedies. It is certain that there does not exist a more false and wicked couple in the whole world than they are.

I can readily believe that the Comte de Toulouse is the King's son; but I have always thought that the Duc du Maine is the son of Terme, who was a false knave, and the greatest tale-bearer in the Court.

That old Maintenon had persuaded the King that the Duc du Maine was full of piety and virtue. When he reported evil tales of any persons, she pretended that it was for their good, and to induce the King to correct them. The King was, therefore, induced to fancy everything he did admirable, and to take him for a saint. The confessor, Le Pere Letellier, contributed to keep up this good opinion in order to pay court to the old woman; and the late Chancellor, M. Voisin, by her orders continued to aid the King's delusion.

The Duc du Maine fancied that, since he had succeeded in getting himself declared a Prince of the blood, he should not find it difficult on that account to attain the royal dignity, and that he could easily arrange everything with respect to my son and the other Princes of the blood. For this reason he and the old woman industriously circulated the report that my son had poisoned the Dauphine and the Duc de Berri. The Duc du Maine was instigated by Madame de Montespan and Madame de Maintenon to report things secretly to the King; at first for the purpose of making him bark like a cur at all whom they disliked, and afterwards for the King's diversion, and to make themselves beloved by him.

These bastards are of so bad a disposition that God knows who was their father.

Yesterday the Parliament presented its remonstrance to my son. It is not difficult to guess whence this affair proceeds. They were closeted for four hours together with the Duc and Duchesse du Maine, who had the Councillors brought thither in their coach, and attended by their own livery servants (20th June, 1718).

I believe that my son is only, restrained from acting rigorously against the Duc du Maine because he fears the tears and anger of his wife; and, in the second place, he, has an affection for his other brother-in-law, the Comte de Toulouse.

That old woman must surely think herself immortal, for she still hopes to reign, though at the age of eighty-three years. The Duc du Maine's affair is a severe blow for her. She is, nevertheless, not without hope, and it is said not excessively grieved. This fills me with anxiety, for I know too well how expert the wicked old hussy is in the use of poison.

The first President of Mesmes ought to be friendly towards the Duc du Maine, to whom he is indebted for the office he holds. The Duke keeps all his places; as to that of Grand Master of Artillery, they could not take it away unless they had proceeded to extremities with him.

The Duke became so devout in his prison, and during Passion week he fasted so rigorously, that he fell sick in consequence. He says that he is innocent and that he has gained heaven by the purity of his conduct; this renders him gay and contented. He is not, besides, of a sorrowful temper, but, on the contrary, is fond of jests and merry tales. He does not speak ill of persons publicly; it was only to the King he used to denounce them.

Yesterday my son was requested to permit the Duc du Maine to be reconciled with his wife. His answer was, "They might have been reconciled without speaking to me about it, for whether they become friends again or not, I know what to think of them."

SECTION XXXIX.—THE DUCHESSE DU MAINE, LOUISE-BENOITE, DAUGHTER OF HENRI-JULES DE CONDE.

Madame du Maine is not taller than a child ten years old, and is not well made. To appear tolerably well, it is necessary for her to keep her mouth shut; for when she opens it, she opens it very wide, and shows her irregular teeth. She is not very stout, uses a great quantity of paint, has fine eyes, a white skin, and fair hair. If she were well disposed, she might pass, but her wickedness is insupportable.

She has good sense, is accomplished, and can talk agreeably on most subjects. This brings about her a host of learned men and wits. She flatters the discontented very adroitly, and says all ill things of my son. This is the secret by which she has made her party. Her husband is fond of her, and she in turn piques herself upon her love for him; but I should be sorry to swear to her sincerity. This at least is certain, that she rules the Duc du Maine absolutely. As he holds several offices, he can provide for a great number of persons, either in the regiment of Guards, of which he is General; or in the Artillery, of which he is Grand Master; or in the Carabineers, where he appoints all the officers; without reckoning his regiments, by which he attracts a great number of persons.

Madame du Maine's present lover is the Cardinal de Polignac; but she has, besides, the first Minister and some young men. The Cardinal is accused of having assisted in the refutation of Fitz-Morris's letters, although he has had this very year (1718) a long interview with my son, and has sworn never to engage in anything against his interests, notwithstanding his attachment to the Duchesse du Maine.

The Comte d'Albert, who was here last winter, took some pains to make himself agreeable to Madame du Maine, and succeeded so well as to make the Cardinal de Polignac very jealous. He followed them masked to a ball; but upon seeing the Duchess and the Count tete-a-tete, he could not contain his anger this betrayed him; and when the people learned that a Cardinal had been seen at a masked ball it caused them great diversion.

Her being arrested threw Madame du Maine into such a transport of rage that she was near choking, and only recovered herself by slow degrees.

[The Marquis d'Ancenis, Captain of the Guards, who came early in the morning to arrest the Princess, had supped with her on the preceding evening, when he entered, the Duchess cried out to him, "Mon Dieu! what have I done to you, that you should wake me so early?" The chief domestics of the household were taken to the Bastille or to Vincennes; the Prince of Dombes and the Comte d'Eu were carried to Eu.]

She is now said to be quite calm, and, it is added, she plays at cards all day long. When the play is over, she grows angry again, and falls upon her husband, his children, or her servants, who do not know how to appease her. She is dreadfully violent, and, it is said, has often beaten her husband.

All the time of her residence at Dijon she was playing the Orlando Furioso: sometimes she was not treated with the respect due to her rank; sometimes she complains of other things; she will not understand that she is a prisoner, and that she has deserved even a worse fate. She had flattered herself that when she should reach Chalons-sur-Saone she would enjoy more liberty, and have the whole city for her prison; but when she learnt that she was to be locked up in the citadel, as at Dijon, she would not set out. Far from repenting her treason, she fancies she has done something very praiseworthy.

Melancholy as I am, my son has made me laugh by telling me what has been found in Madame du Maine's letters, seized at the Cardinal de Polignac's. In one of her letters, this very discreet and virtuous personage writes, "We are going into the country tomorrow; and I shall so arrange the apartments that your chamber shall be next to mine. Try to manage matters as well as you did the last time, and we shall be very happy."

The Princess knows very well that her daughter has had an intrigue with the Cardinal, and has endeavoured to break it off. For this purpose she has convinced her by the Cardinal's own letters that he is unfaithful to her, and prefers a certain Montauban to her. This, however, has had no effect. The Duc du Maine has been informed of everything, and he writes to her sister, "I ought not to be put into prison, but into petticoats, for having suffered myself to be so led by the nose."

He has resolved never to see his wife again, although he does not yet know of the Duchess's letter to the Cardinal, nor of the other measures she has taken for the purpose of decorating her husband's brows.

Madame du Maine will eventually become really crazy, for she is dreadfully troubled with the vapours. Her mother has entreated my son to let her daughter be brought to her house at Anet, where she will be answerable for her conduct and suffer her to speak with no one.

My son replied, "that if Madame du Maine had only conspired against his life, he would have pardoned her with all his heart; but that, as her offence had been committed against the State, he was obliged, in spite of himself, to keep her in prison."

It is not true that the Duc du Maine has permission to hunt; he is only allowed to ride upon a hired horse round the citadel, to take the air, in the company of four persons.

The Abbe de Maulevrier and Mademoiselle de Langeron persuaded the Princess that Madame du Maine was at the point of death, and was only desirous of seeing her dear mother before she expired, to receive her last benediction, as she should die innocent. The Princess immediately set out in great anxiety and with deep grief; but was strangely surprised, on arriving at her daughter's house, to see her come to meet her in very good health. Mademoiselle de Langeron said that the Duchess concealed her illness that she might not make her mother unhappy.

After the confession which Madame du Maine thought proper to make, which she has confirmed by writing, my son has set her at liberty, and has permitted her to come to Sceaux. She is terribly mortified at her letter being read in the open Council. As she has declared in her confession that she had done everything without her husband's knowledge, although in his name, he, too, has been permitted to return to his estate of Chavigny, near Versailles.

Madame du Maine had written to my son that, in the event of her having omitted anything in her declaration, he would only have to ask Mademoiselle de Launay about it. He sent in consequence for that lady, to ask her some questions. Mademoiselle de Launay replied: "I do not know whether her imprisonment may have turned my mistress's brain, but it has not had the same effect upon me; I neither know, nor will I say anything."

Madame du Maine had gained over certain gentlemen in all the Provinces, and had tampered with them to induce them to revolt; but none of them would swallow the bait excepting in Brittany.

She has not been at the theatre yet; meaning, by this, to intimate that she is still afflicted at lying under her husband's displeasure. It is said that she has written to him, but that he has returned her letter unopened.

She came some days ago to see my son, and to request him not to oppose a reconciliation between herself and her husband. My son laughed and said, "I will not interfere in it; for have I not learned from Sganarelle that it is not wise to put one's finger between the bark and the tree?" The town says they will be reconciled. If this really should take place, I shall say as my father used: "Agree together, bad ones!"

My son tells me that the little Duchess has again besought him to reconcile her with her husband. My son replied, "that it depended much more upon herself than upon him." I do not know whether she took this for a compliment, or what crotchet she got in her head, but she suddenly jumped up from the sofa, and clung about my son's neck, kissing him on both cheeks in spite of himself (18th June, 1720).

The Duc du Maine is entirely reconciled to his dear moiety. I am not surprised, for I have been long expecting it.

SECTION XL.—LOUVOIS

M. de Louvois was a person of a very wicked disposition; he hated his father and brother, and, as they were my very good friends, this minister made me feel his dislike of them. His hatred was also increased, because he knew that I was acquainted with his ill-treatment of my father, and that I had no reason in the world to like him. He feared that I should seek to take vengeance upon him, and for this reason he was always exciting the King against me. Upon this point alone did he agree with that old, Maintenon.

I believe that Louvois had a share in the conspiracy by which Langhans and Winkler compassed my poor brother's death. When the King had taken the Palatinate, I required him to arrest the culprits; the King gave orders for it, and they were in fact seized, but afterwards liberated by a counter-order of Louvois. Heaven, however, took care of their punishment for the crime which they had committed upon my poor brother; for Langhans died in the most abject wretchedness, and Winkler went mad and beat his own brains out.

There is no doubt that the King spoke very harshly to Louvois, but certainly he did not treat him as has been pretended, for the King was incapable of such an action. Louvois was a brute and an insolent person; but he served the King faithfully, and much better than any other person. He did not, however, forget his own interest, and played his cards very well. He was horribly depraved, and by his impoliteness and the grossness of his replies made himself universally hated. He might, perhaps, believe in the Devil; but he did not believe in God. He had faith in all manner of predictions, but he did not scruple to burn, poison, lie and cheat.

If he did not love me very well, I was at least even with him; and, for the latter part of his time, he conducted himself somewhat better. I was one of the last persons to whom he spoke, and I was even shocked when it was announced that the man with whom I had been conversing a quarter of an hour before, and who did not look ill, was no more.

They have not yet learnt, although I have resided so long in France, to respect my seal. M. de Louvois used to have all my letters opened and read; and M. Corey, following his noble example, has not been more courteous to me. Formerly they used to open them for the purpose of finding something to my prejudice, and now (1718) they open them through mere habit.

SECTION XLI.—LOUIS XV.

It is impossible for any child to be more agreeable than our young King; he has large, dark eyes and long, crisp eyelashes; a good complexion, a charming little mouth, long and thick dark-brown hair, little red cheeks, a stout and well-formed body, and very pretty hands and feet; his gait is noble and lofty, and he puts on his hat exactly like the late King. The shape of his face is neither too long nor too short; but the worst thing, and which he inherits from his mother, is, that he changes colour very frequently. Sometimes he looks ill, but in half an hour his colour will have returned. His manners are easy, and it may be said, without flattery, that he dances very well. He is quick and clever in all that he attempts; he has already (1720) begun to shoot at pheasants and partridges, and has a great passion for shooting.

He is as like his mother as one drop of water is to another; he has sense enough, and all that he seems to want is a little more affability. He is terribly haughty, and already knows what respect is. His look is what may be called agreeable, but his air is milder than his character, for his little head is rather an obstinate and wilful one.

The young King was full of grief when Madame de Ventadour quitted him. She said to him, "Sire, I shall come back this evening; mind that you behave very well during my absence."

"My dear mamma," replied he, "if you leave me I cannot behave well."

He does not care at all for any of the other women.

The Marechal de Villeroi teases the young King sometimes about not speaking to me enough, and sometimes about not walking with me. This afflicts the poor child and makes him cry. His figure is neat, but he will speak only to persons he is accustomed to.

On the 12th August (1717), the young King fell out of his bed in the morning; a valet de chambre, who saw him falling, threw himself adroitly on the ground, so that the child might tumble upon him and not hurt himself; the little rogue thrust himself under the bed and would not speak, that he might frighten his attendants.

The King's brother died of the small-pox in consequence of being injudiciously blooded; this one, who is younger than his brother, was also attacked, but the femme de chambre concealed it, kept him warm, and continued to give him Alicant wine, by which means they preserved his life.

The King has invented an order which he bestows upon the boys with whom he plays. It is a blue and white ribbon, to which is suspended an enamelled oval plate, representing a star and the tent or pavilion in which he plays on the terrace (1717).

SECTION XLII.—ANECDOTES AND HISTORICAL PARTICULARS RELATING TO VARIOUS PERSONS.

Some horrible books had been written against Cardinal Mazarin, with which he pretended to be very much enraged, and had all the copies bought up to be burnt. When he had collected them all, he caused them to be sold in secret, and as if it were unknown to him, by which contrivance he gained 10,000 crowns. He used to laugh and say, "The French are delightful people; I let them sing and laugh, and they let me do what I will."

In Flanders it is the custom for the monks to assist at all fires. It appeared to me a very whimsical spectacle to see monks of all colours, white, black and brown, running hither and thither with their frocks tucked up and carrying pails.

The Chevalier de Saint George is one of the best men in the world, and complaisance itself. He one day said to Lord Douglas, "What should I do to gain the good-will of my countrymen?" Douglas replied, "Only embark hence with twelve Jesuits, and as soon as you land in England hang every one of them publicly; you can do nothing so likely to recommend you to the English people."

It is said that at one of the masked balls at the opera, a mask entered the box in which were the Marechals de Villars and d'Estrees. He said to the former, "Why do you not go below and dance?" The Marshal replied, "If I were younger I could, but not crippled as you see I am."—"Oh, go down," rejoined the mask, "and the Marechal d'Estrees too; you will cut so brilliant a figure, having both of you such large horns." At the same time he put up his fingers in the shape of horns. The Marechal d'Estrees only laughed, but the other was in a great rage and said, "You are a most insolent mask, and I do not know what will restrain me from giving you a good beating."—"As to a good beating;" replied the mask, "I can do a trifle in that way myself when necessary; and as for the insolence of which you accuse me, it is sufficient for me to say that I am masked." He went away as he said this, and was not seen again.

The King of Denmark has the look of a simpleton; he made love to my daughter while he was here. When they were dancing he used to squeeze her hand, and turn up his eyes languishingly. He would begin his minuet in one corner of the hall and finish it in another. He stopped once in the middle of the hall and did not know what to do next. I was quite uneasy at seeing him, so I got up and, taking his hand, led him away, or the good gentleman might have strayed there until this time. He has no notion of what is becoming or otherwise.

The Cardinal de Noailles is unquestionably a virtuous man; it would be a very good thing if all the others were like him. We have here four of them, and each is of a different character. Three of them resemble each other in a certain particular—they are as false as counterfeit coin; in every other respect they are directly opposite. The Cardinal de Polignac is well made, sensible, and insinuating, and his voice is very agreeable; but he meddles too much with politics, and is too much occupied with seeking favour. The Cardinal de Rohan has a handsome face, as his mother had, but his figure is despicable. He is as vain as a peacock, and fancies that there is not his equal in the whole world. He is a tricking intriguer, the slave of the Jesuits, and fancies he rules everything, while in fact he rules nothing. The Cardinal de Bissi is as ugly and clumsy as a peasant, proud, false and wicked, and yet a most fulsome flatterer; his falsehood may be seen in his very eyes; his talent he turns to mischievous purposes. In short, he has all the exterior of a Tartuffe. These Cardinals could, if they chose, sell the Cardinal de Noailles in a sack, for they are all much more cunning than he is.

With respect to the pregnancy of the Queen of England, the consort of James II., whom we saw at Saint-Germain, it is well known that her daughter-in-law maintains that she was not with child; but it seems to me that the Queen might easily have taken measures to prove the contrary. I spoke about it to Her Majesty myself. She replied "that she had begged the Princess Anne to satisfy herself by the evidence of her own senses, and to feel the motion of the child;" but the latter refused, and the Queen added "that she never could have supposed that the persons who had been in the habit of seeing her daily during her pregnancy could doubt the fact of her having been delivered."

[On the dethronement of James II., the party of William, Prince of Orange, asserted that the Prince of Orange was a supposititious child, and accused James of having spirited away the persona who could have proved the birth of the Queen's child, and of having made the midwife leave the kingdom precipitately, she being the only person who had actually seen the child born.]

A song has been made upon Lord Bolingbroke on the subject of his passion for a young girl who escaped from her convent. Some persons say that the girl was a professed nun. She ran after the Duke Regent a long time, but could not accomplish her intention.

Lady Gordon, the grandaunt of Lord Huntley, was my dame d'atour for a considerable period. She was a singular person, and always plunged into reveries. Once when she was in bed and going to seal a letter, she dropped the wax upon her own thigh and burnt herself dreadfully. At another time, when she was also in bed and engaged in play, she threw the dice upon the ground and spat in the bed. Once, too, she spat in the mouth of my first femme de chambre, who happened to be passing at the moment. I think if I had not interposed they would have come to blows, so angry was the femme de chambre. One evening when I wanted my head-dress to go to Court, she took off her gloves and threw them in my face, putting on my head-dress at the same time with great gravity. When she was speaking to a man she had a habit of playing with the buttons of his waistcoat. Saving one day some occasion to talk to the Chevalier Buveon, a Captain in the late Monsieur's

Guard, and he being a very tall man, she could only reach his waistband, which she began to unbutton. The poor gentleman was quite horror-stricken, and started back, crying, "For Heaven's sake, madame, what are you going to do?" This accident caused a great laugh in the Salon of Saint Cloud.

They say that Lord Peterborough, speaking of the two Kings of Spain, said, "What fools we are to cut each other's throats for two such apes."

Monteleon has good reason to be fond of the Princesse des Ursins, for she made his fortune: he was an insignificant officer in the troop, but he had talents and attached himself to this lady, who made of him what he now is (1716).

The Abbess of Maubuisson, Louise Hollandine, daughter of Frederic V., Elector-Palatine of the days of Henri IV., had had so many illegitimate children, that she commonly swore by her body, which had borne fourteen children.

Cardinal Mazarin could not bear to have unfortunate persons about him. When he was requested to take any one into his service, his first question was, "Is he lucky?"

My son has never assisted the Pretender (Prince Edward Stuart), either publicly or privately; and if my Lord Stair had chosen to contract a more close alliance, as my son wished, he would have prevented the Pretender's staying in France and collecting adherents; but as that alliance was declined, he merely confined himself to the stipulations contained in the treaty of peace. He neither furnished the Pretender with arms nor money. The Pope and some others gave him money, but my son could not, for he was too much engaged in paying off the late King's debts, and he would not on account of that treaty. There can be no doubt that an attempt has been made to embroil my son with the King of England; for, at the same time that they were making the King believe my son was sustaining the Pretender's cause, they told my son that Lord Stair had interviews with M. Pentenriedez, the Emperor's Envoy, as well as with the Sicilian Ambassador, the object of which was to make a league with those powers to drive out the King of Spain and to set up the King of France in his place, at the same time that Sicily should be given up to the Emperor—in short, to excite all Europe against France. My son said himself, that, since he was to confine himself to the articles of the treaty of peace, he did not think he had any right to prevent the Pretender's passage through his kingdom; and as the army had been reduced, he could not hinder the disbanded soldiers from taking service wherever they chose. My son had no intention whatever to break with England, although he has been told that there was a majority of two voices only in that nation against declaring it at war with France. He thinks Lord Stair is not his friend, and that he has not faithfully reported to his monarch the state of things here, but would rather be pleased to kindle the flames of a war. If that Minister had honestly explained to the King my son's intentions, the King would not have refused to agree with them.

It is said here that the present Queen of Spain (1716), although she is more beloved by her husband than was the last, has less influence over him. The Abbe Alberoni has them both in his power, and governs them like two children.

The English gentlemen and ladies who are here tell horrible stories of Queen Anne. They say she gets quite drunk, and that besides but that she is inconstant in her affections, and changes often. Lady Sandwich has not told this to me, but she has to my son. I have seen her but seldom, on account of the repugnance I felt at learning she had confessed she had been present at such orgies.

I do not know whether it is true that Louvois was poisoned by that old Maintenon, but it is quite certain that he was poisoned, as well as his physician who committed the crime, and who said when he was dying, "I die by poison, but I deserve it, for having poisoned my master, M. de Louvois; and I did this in the hope of becoming the King's physician, as Madame de Maintenon had promised me." I ought to add that some persons pretend to think this story of Doctor Seron is a mere invention. Old Piety (Maintenon) did not commit this crime without an object; but if she really did poison Louvois, it was because he had opposed her designs and endeavoured to undeceive the King. Louvois, the better to gain his object, had advised the King not to take her with him to the army. The King was weak enough to repeat this to her, and this it was that excited her against Louvois. That the latter was a very bad man, who feared neither heaven nor hell, no man can deny; but it must be confessed that he served his King faithfully.

The Duke de Noailles' grandfather was one of the ugliest men in the world. He had one glass eye, and his nose was like an owl's, his mouth large, his teeth ugly and decayed, his face and head very small, his body long and bent, and he was bitter and ill-tempered. His name was Gluinel. Madame de Cornuel one day was reading his grandson's genealogy, and, when she came to his name, exclaimed, "I always suspected, when I saw the Duc de Noailles, that he came out of the Book of the Lamentations of Jeremiah!"

When James II. took refuge in France from England, Madame de Cornuel went to Saint-Germain to see him. Some time afterwards, she was told of the pains our King was taking to procure his restoration to the throne. Madame de Cornuel shook her head, and said, "I have seen this King James; our monarch's efforts are all in vain; he is good for nothing but to make poor man's sauce. (La sauce au pauvre homme.)"

She went to Versailles to see the Court when M. de Torcy and M. de Seignelay, both very young, had just been appointed Ministers. She saw them, as well as Madame de Maintenon, who had then grown old. When she returned to Paris, some one asked her what remarkable things she had seen. "I have seen," she said, "what I never expected to see there; I have seen love in its tomb and the Ministry in its cradle."

The elder Margrave of Anspach was smitten with Mademoiselle d'Armagnac, but he would not marry her, and said afterwards that he had never intended to do so, because the familiarities which had passed between her and the Marquis de Villequier (1716) had disgusted him. The lady's mother would have liked nothing better than to surprise the Margrave with her daughter in some critical situation: for this purpose he had sufficient opportunities given him, but he was prudent, and conducted himself with so much modesty, that he avoided the snare. To tell the truth, I had given him a hint on the subject, for I was too well acquainted with the mother, who is a very bad woman.

The Cardinal de Richelieu, notwithstanding his wit, had often fits of distraction. Sometimes he would fancy himself a horse, and run jumping about a billiard-table, neighing and snorting; this would last an hour, at the end of which his people would put him to bed and cover him up closely to induce perspiration; when he awoke the fit had passed and did not appear again.

The Archbishop of Paris reprimanded the Bishop of Gap on the bad reputation which he had acquired in consequence of his intercourse with women. "Ah, Monseigneur," replied the Bishop of Gap, "if you knew what you talk of, you would not be astonished. I lived the first forty years of my life without experiencing it; I don't know what induced me to venture on it, but, having done so, it is impossible to refrain. Only try it for once, Monseigneur, and you will perceive the truth of what I tell you."

[This Bishop, whose name was Herve, had lived in prudence and regularity up to the age of fifty, when he began, on a sudden, to lead a very debauched life. They compelled him to give up his Bishopric, which he did on condition of being allowed to stay at Paris as much as he chose. He continued to live in perpetual pleasure, but towards the close of his career he repented of his sins and engaged with the Capuchin missionaries.]

This Bishop is now living in the village of Boulogne, near Paris: he is a little priest, very ugly, with a large head and fiery red face.

Our late King said, "I am, I confess, somewhat piqued to see that, with all the authority belonging to my station in this country, I have exclaimed so long against high head-dresses, while no one had the complaisance to lower them for me in the slightest degree. But now, when a mere strange English wench arrives with a little low head-dress, all the Princesses think fit to go at once from one extremity to another."

A Frenchman who had taken refuge in Holland informed me by letter of what was passing with respect to the Prince of Orange. Thinking that I should do the King a service by communicating to him these news, I hastened to him, and he thanked me for them. In the evening, however, he said to me, smiling, "My Ministers will have it that you have been misinformed, and that your correspondent has not written you one word of truth." I replied, "Time will show which is better informed, your Majesty's Ministers or my correspondent. For my own part, Sire, my intention at least was good."

Some time afterwards, when the report of the approaching accession of William to the throne of England became public, M. de Torcy came to me to beg I would acquaint him with my news. I replied, "I receive none now; you told the King that what I formerly had was false, and upon this I desired my correspondents to send me no more, for I do not love to spread false reports." He laughed, as he always did, and said, "Your news have turned out to be quite correct." I replied, "A great and able Minister ought surely to have news more correct than I can obtain; and I have been angry with myself for having formerly acquainted the King with the reports which had reached me. I ought to have recollected that his clever Ministers are acquainted with everything." The King therefore said to me, "You are making game of my Ministers."—"Sire," I replied, "I am only giving them back their own."

M. de Louvois was the only person who was well served by his spies; indeed, he never spared his money. All the Frenchmen who went into Germany or Holland as dancing or fencing-masters, esquires, etc., were paid by him to give him information of whatever passed in the several Courts. After his death this system was discontinued, and thus it is that the present Ministers are so ignorant of the affairs of other nations.

Lauzun says the drollest things, and takes the most amusing, roundabout way of intimating whatever he does not care to say openly. For example, when he wished the King to understand that the Count de Marsan, brother of M. Legrand, had attached himself to M. Chamillard, the then Minister, he took the following means: "Sire," said he, with an air of the utmost simplicity, as if he had not the least notion of malice, "I wished to change my wigmaker, and employ the one who is now the most in fashion; but I could not find him, for M. de Marsan has kept him shut up in his room for several days past, making wigs for his household, and for M. de Chamillard's friends."

The adventures of Prince Emmanuel of Portugal are a perfect romance. His brother, the King, was desirous, it is said, at first, to have made a priest and a Bishop of him; to this, however, he had an insuperable objection, for he was in love. The King sent for him, and asked him if it was true that he had really resolved not to enter the Church. On the Prince's replying in the affirmative, the King, his brother, struck him. The Prince said, "You are my King and my brother, and therefore I cannot revenge myself as I ought upon you; but you have put an insult upon me which I cannot endure, and you shall never again see me in the whole course of your life." He is said to have set out on that very night. His brother wrote to him, commanding his return from Paris to Holland; as he made no reply to this command, his Governor and the Ambassador had no doubt that it was his intention to obey it. In the course of last week he expressed a desire to see Versailles and Marly. The Ambassador made preparations for this excursion, and together with his wife accompanied the Prince, whose Governor and one of his gentlemen were of the party. Upon their return from Versailles, when they reached the courtyard, the Prince called out to stop, and asked if there were any chaises ready:

"Yes, Monseigneur," replied a voice, "there are four."—"That will be sufficient," replied the Prince. Then addressing the Ambassador, he expressed his warmest thanks for the friendly attention he had shown him, and assured him that he desired nothing so much as an opportunity to testify his gratitude. "I am now going to set out," he added, "for Vienna; the Emperor is my cousin; I have no doubt he will receive me, and I shall learn in his army to become a soldier in the campaign against the Turks." He then thanked the Governor for the pains he had bestowed upon his education; and promised that, if any good fortune should befall him, his Governor should share it with him. He also said something complimentary to his gentleman. He then alighted, called for the post-chaises, and took his seat in one of them; his favourite, a young man of little experience, but, as it is said, of considerable talent, placed himself in another, and his two valets de chambre into the third and fourth. That nothing may be wanting to the romantic turn of his adventures, it is said, besides, that Madame de Riveira was the object of his affection in Portugal before she was married; that he even wished to make her his wife, but that his brother would not permit it. A short time before his departure, the husband, who is a very jealous man, found him at his wife's feet; and this hastened the Prince's departure.

Henri IV. had been one day told of the infidelity of one of his mistresses. Believing that the King had no intention of visiting her, she made an assignation with the Duc de Bellegarde in her own apartment. The King, having caused the time of his rival's coming to be watched, when he was informed of his being there, went to his mistress's room. He found her in bed, and she complained of a violent headache. The King said he was very hungry, and wanted some supper; she replied that she had not thought about supper, and believed she had only a couple of partridges. Henri IV. desired they should be served up, and said he would eat them with her. The supper which she had prepared for Bellegarde, and which consisted of much more than two partridges, was then served up; the King, taking up a small loaf, split it open, and, sticking a whole partridge into it, threw it under the bed. "Sire," cried the lady, terrified to death, "what are you doing?"—"Madame," replied the merry monarch, "everybody must live." He then took his departure, content with having frightened the lovers.

I have again seen M. La Mothe le Vayer; who, with all his sense, dresses himself like a madman. He wears furred boots, and a cap which he never takes off, lined with the same material, a large band, and a black velvet coat.

We have had few Queens in France who have been really happy. Marie de Medicis died in exile. The mother of the King and of the late Monsieur was unhappy as long as her husband was alive. Our Queen Marie-Therese said upon her death-bed, "that from the time of her becoming Queen she had not had a day of real happiness."

Lauzun sometimes affects the simpleton that he may say disagreeable things with impunity, for he is very malicious. In order to hint to Marechal de Tesse that he did wrong in being so familiar with the common people, he called out to him one night in the Salon at Marly, "Marshal, pray give me a pinch of snuff; but let it be good—that, for example, which I saw you taking this morning with Daigremont the chairman."

In the time of Henri IV. an Elector-Palatine came to France; the King's household was sent to meet him. All his expenses were paid, as well as those of his suite; and when he arrived at the Court he entered between the Dauphin and Monsieur and dined with the King. I learned these particulars from the late Monsieur. The King, under the pretence of going to the chase, went about a league from Paris, and, meeting the Elector, conducted him in his carriage. At Paris he was always attended by the King's servants. This treatment is somewhat different from that which, in my time, was bestowed upon Maximilian Maria, the Elector of Bavaria. This Elector often enraged me with the foolish things that he did. For example, he went to play and to dine with M. d'Antin, and never evinced the least desire to dine with his own nephews. A sovereign, whether he be Elector or not, might with propriety dine either at the Dauphin's table or mine; and, if the Elector had chosen, he might have come to us; but he was contented to dine with M. d'Antin or M. de Torcy, and some ladies of the King's suite. I am angry to this day when I think of it. The King used often to laugh at my anger on this subject; and, whenever the Elector committed some new absurdity, he used to call to me in the cabinet and ask me, "Well, Madame, what have you to say to that?" I would reply, "All that the Elector does is alike ridiculous." This made the King laugh heartily. The Elector had a Marshal, the Count d'Arco, the brother of that person who had married in so singular a manner the Prince's mistress, Popel, which marriage had been contracted solely upon his promise never to be alone with his wife. The Marshal, who was as honest as his brother was accommodating, was terribly annoyed at his master's conduct; he came at first to me to impart to me his chagrin whenever the Elector committed some folly; and when he behaved better he used also to tell me of it. I rather think he must have been forbidden to visit me, for latterly I never saw him. None of the Elector's suite have visited me, and I presume they have been prevented. This Prince's amorous intrigues have been by no means agreeable to the King. The Elector was so fond of grisettes that, when the King was giving names to each of the roads through the wood, he was exceedingly anxious that one of them should be called L'Allee des Grisettes; but the King would not consent to it. The Elector has perpetuated his race in the villages; and two country girls have been pointed out to me who were pregnant by him at his departure.

His marriage with a Polish Princess is a striking proof that a man cannot avoid his fate. This was not a suitable match for him, and was managed almost without his knowledge, as I have been told. His Councillors, having been bought over, patched up the affair; and when the Elector only caused it to be submitted for their deliberation, it was already decided on.

This Elector's brother must have been made a Bishop of Cologne and Munster without the production of proof of his nobility being demanded; for it is well known that the King Sobieski was a Polish nobleman, who married the daughter of Darquin, Captain of our late Monsieur's Swiss Guards. Great suspicions are entertained respecting the children of the Bavaria family, that is, the Elector and his brothers, who are thought to have been the progeny of an Italian doctor named Simoni. It was said at Court that the doctor had only given the Elector and his wife a strong cordial, the effect of which had been to increase their family; but they are all most suspiciously like the doctor.

I have heard it said that in England the people used to take my late uncle, Rupert, for a sorcerer, and his large black dog for the Devil; for this reason, when he joined the army and attacked the enemy, whole regiments fled before him.

A knight of the Palatinate, who had served many years in India, told me at Court in that country the first Minister and the keeper of the seals hated each other mortally. The latter having one day occasion for the seals, found they had been taken from the casket in which they were usually kept. He was of course greatly terrified, for his head depended upon their production. He went to one of his friends, and consulted with him what he should do. His friend asked him if he had any enemies at Court. "Yes," replied the keeper of the seals, "the chief Minister is my mortal foe."—"So much the better," replied his friend; "go and set fire to your house directly; take out of it nothing but the casket in which the seals were kept, and take it directly to the chief Minister, telling him you know no one with whom you can more safely deposit it; then go home again and save whatever you can. When the fire shall be extinguished, you must go to the King, and request him to order the chief Minister to restore you the seals; and you must be sure to open the casket before the Prince. If the seals are there, all will be explained; if the Minister has not restored them, you must accuse him at once of having stolen them; and thus you will be sure to ruin your enemy and recover your seals." The keeper of the seals followed his friend's advice exactly, and the seals were found again in the casket.

As soon as a royal child, which they call here un Enfant de France, is born, and has been swaddled, they put on him a grand cordon; but they do not create him a knight of the order until he has communicated; the ceremony is then performed in the ordinary manner.

The ladies of chancellors here have the privilege of the tabouret when they come to the toilette; but in the afternoon they are obliged to stand. This practice began in the days of Marie de Medicis, when a chancellor's wife happened to be in great favour. As she had a lame foot and could not stand up, the Queen, who would have her come to visit her every morning, allowed her to sit down. From this time the custom of these ladies sitting in the morning has been continued.

In the reign of Henri IV. the King's illegitimate children took precedence of the Princes of the House of Lorraine. On the day after the King's death, the Duc de Verneuil was about to go before the Duc de Guise, when the latter, taking him by the arm, said, "That might have been yesterday, but to-day matters are altered."

Two young Duchesses, not being able to see their lovers, invented the following stratagem to accomplish their wishes. These two sisters had been educated in a convent some leagues distant from Paris. A nun of their acquaintance happening to die there, they pretended to be much afflicted at it, and requested permission to perform the last duties to her, and to be present at her funeral. They were believed to be sincere, and the permission they asked was readily granted them. In the funeral procession it was perceived that, besides the two ladies, there were two other persons whom no one knew. Upon being asked who they were, they replied they were poor priests in need of protection; and that, having learnt two Duchesses were to be present at the funeral, they had come to the convent for the purpose of imploring their good offices. When they were presented to them, the young ladies said they would interrogate them after the service in their chambers. The young priests waited upon them at the time appointed, and stayed there until the evening. The Abbess, who began to think their audience was too long, sent to beg the priests would retire. One of them seemed very melancholy, but the other laughed as if he would burst his sides. This was the Duc de Richelieu; the other was the Chevalier de Guemene, the younger son of the Duke of that name. The gentlemen themselves divulged the adventure.

The King's illegitimate children, fearing that they should be treated in the same way as the Princes of the blood, have for some months past been engaged in drawing a strong party of the nobility to their side, and have presented a very unjust petition against the Dukes and Peers. My son has refused to receive this petition, and has interdicted them from holding assemblies, the object of which he knows would tend to revolt. They have, nevertheless, continued them at the instigations of the Duc du Maine and his wife, and have even carried their insolence so far as to address a memorial to my son and another to the Parliament, in which they assert that it is within the province of the nobility alone to decide between the Princes of the blood and the legitimated Princes. Thirty of them have signed this memorial, of whom my son has had six arrested; three of them have been sent to the Bastille, and the other three to Vincennes; they are MM. de Chatillon, de Rieux, de Beaufremont, de Polignac, de Clermont, and d'O. The last was the Governor of the Comte de Toulouse, and remains with him. Clermont's wife is one of the Duchesse de Berri's ladies. She is not the most discreet person in the world, and has been long in the habit of saying to any one who would listen to her, "Whatever may come of it, my husband and I are willing to risk our lives for the Comte de Toulouse." It is therefore evident that all this proceeds from the bastards. But I must expose still further the ingratitude of these people. Chatillon is a poor gentleman, whose father held a small employment under M. Gaston, one of those offices which confer the privilege of the entree to the antechambers, and the holders of which do not sit in the carriage with their masters. The two descendants, as they call themselves, of the house of Chatillon, insist that this Chatillon, who married an attorney's daughter, is descended from the illegitimate branches of that family. His son was a subaltern in the Body Guard. In the summer time, when the young officers went to bathe, they used to take young Chatillon with them to guard their clothes, and for this office they gave him a crown for his supper. Monsieur having taken this poor person into his service, gave him a cordon bleu, and furnished him with money to commence a suit which he subsequently gained against the House of Chatillon, and they were compelled to recognize him. He then made him a Captain in the Guards; gave him a considerable pension, which my son continued, and permitted him also to have apartments in the Palais Royal. In these very apartments did this ungrateful man hold those secret meetings, the end of which was proposed to be my son's ruin. Rieux's grandfather had neglected to uphold the honour to which he was entitled, of being called the King's cousin. My son restored him to this honour, gave his brother a place in the gendarmerie, and rendered him many other services. Chatillon tried particularly to excite the nobility against my son; and this is the recompense for all his kindness. My son's wife is gay and content, in the hope that all will go well with her brothers.

That old Maintenon has continued pretty tranquil until the termination of the process relating to the legitimation of the bastards. No one has heard her utter a single expression on the subject. This makes me believe that she has some project in her head, but I cannot tell what it is.

A monk, who was journeying a few days ago to Luzarche, met upon the road a stranger, who fell into conversation with him. He was an agreeable companion, and related various adventures very pleasantly. Having learned from the monk that he was charged with the rents of the convent, to which some estates in the neighbourhood of Luzarche belonged, the stranger told him that he belonged to that place, whither he was returning after a long journey; and then observing to the monk that the road they were pursuing was roundabout, he pointed out to him a nearer one through the forest. When they had reached the thickest part of the wood, the stranger alighted, and, seizing the bridle of the monk's horse, demanded his money. The monk replied that he thought he was travelling with an honest man, and that he was astonished at so singular a demand. The stranger replied that he had no time for trifling, and that the monk must either give up his money or his life. The monk replied, "I never carry money about me; but if you will let me alight and go to my servant, who carries my money, I will bring you 1,000 francs."

The robber suffered the monk to alight, who went to his servant, and, taking from him the 1,000 francs which were in a purse, he at the same time furnished himself with a loaded pistol which he concealed in his sleeve. When he returned to the thief, he threw down the purse, and, as the robber stooped to pick it up, the monk fired and shot him dead;

then, remounting his horse, he hastened to apply to the police, and related his adventure. A patrole was sent back with him to the wood, and, upon searching the robber, there were found in his pockets six whistles of different sizes; they blew the largest of the number, upon which ten other armed robbers soon afterwards appeared; they defended themselves, but eventually two of them were killed and the others taken.

The Chevalier Schaub, who was employed in State affairs by Stanhope, the English Minister, brought with him a secretary, to whom the Prince of Wales had entrusted sixty guineas, to be paid to a M. d'Isten, who had made a purchase of some lace to that amount for the Princess of Wales; the brother of M. d'Isten, then living in London, had also given the same secretary 200 guineas, to be delivered to his brother at Paris. When the secretary arrived he enquired at the Ambassador's where M. d'Isten lived, and, having procured his address, he went to the house and asked for the German gentleman. A person appeared, who said, "I am he." The secretary suspecting nothing, gave him the Prince of Wales' letter and the sixty guineas. The fictitious d'Isten, perceiving that the secretary had a gold watch, and a purse containing fifty other guineas, detained him to supper; but no sooner had the secretary drank some wine than he was seized with an invincible desire to go to sleep. "My good friend," said his host, "your journey has fatigued you; you had better undress and lie down on my bed for a short time." The secretary, who could not keep his eyes open, consented; and no sooner had he lain down than he was asleep. Some time after, his servant came to look for him, and awoke him; the bottles were still standing before the bed, but the poor secretary's pockets were emptied, and the sharper who had personated M. d'Isten had disappeared with their valuable contents.

The Princesse Maubuisson was astonishingly pleasant and amiable. I was always delighted to visit her, and never felt myself tired in her society. I soon found myself in much greater favour than any other of her nieces, because I could converse with her about almost everybody she had known in the whole course of her life, which the others could not. She used frequently to talk German with me, which she knew very well; and she told me all her adventures. I asked her how she could accustom herself to the monastic life. She laughed and said, "I never speak to the nuns but to give orders." She had a deaf nun with her in her own chamber, that she might not feel any desire to speak. She told me that she had always been fond of a country life, and that she still could fancy herself a country girl. "But," I asked her, "how do you like getting up and going to church in the middle of the night?" She replied that she did as the painters do, who increase the splendour of their light by the introduction of deep shadows. She had in general the faculty of giving to all things a turn which deprived them of their absurdity.

I have often heard M. Bernstorff spoken of by a person who was formerly very agreeable to him; I mean the Duchess of Mecklenbourg, the Duc de Luxembourg's sister. She praised his talents very highly, and assured me that it was she who gave him to the Duke George William.

The wife of the Marechal de Villars is running after the Comte de Toulouse. My son is also in her good graces, and is not a whit more discreet. Marechal de Villars came one day to see me; and, as he pretends to understand medals, he asked to see mine. Baudelot, who is a very honest and clever man, and in whose keeping they are, was desired to show them; he is not the most cautious man in the world, and is very little acquainted with what is going on at Court. He had written a dissertation upon one of my medals, in which he proved, against the opinion of other learned men, that the horned head which it displayed was that of Pan and not of Jupiter Ammon. Honest Baudelot, to display his erudition, said to the Marshal, "Ah, Monseigneur, this is one of the finest medals that Madame possesses: it is the triumph of Cornificius; he has, you see, all sorts of horns. He was like you, sir, a great general; he wears the horns of Juno and Faunus. Cornificius was, as you probably well know, sir, a very able general." Here I interrupted him. "Let us pass on," I said, "to the other medal; if you stop in this manner at each, you will not have time to show the whole."

But he, full of his subject, returned to it. "Ah, Madame," he went on, "this is worthy of more attention than perhaps any other; Cornificius is, indeed, one of the most rare medals in the world. Look at it, Madame; I beg you to observe it narrowly; here, you see, is Juno crowned, and she is also crowning this great general." All that I could say to him was not sufficient to prevent Baudelot talking to the Marshal of horns. "Monseigneur," he said, "is well versed in all these matters, and I want him to see that I am right in insisting that these horns are those of Faunus, not those of Jupiter Ammon."

All the people who were in the chamber, with difficulty refrained from bursting into a loud laugh. If the plan had been laid for the purpose, it could not have succeeded better. When the Marshal had gone, I, too, indulged myself by joining in the laugh. It was with great difficulty that I could make Baudelot understand he had done wrong.

The same Baudelot, one day at a masked ball, had been saying a great many civil things to the Dowager Madame, who was there masked, and whom, therefore, he did not know. When he came and saw that it was Madame, he was terrified with affright: the Princess laughed beyond measure at it.

Our Princes here have no particular costume. When they go to the Parliament they wear only a cloak, which, in my opinion, has a very vulgar appearance; and the more so, as they wear the 'collet' without a cravat. Those of the Royal Family have no privileges above the other Dukes, excepting in their seats and the right of crossing over the carpet, which is allowed to none but them. The President, when he addresses them, is uncovered, but keeps his hat on when he speaks to everybody else. This is the cause of those great disputes which the Princes of the blood have had with the bastards, as may be seen by their memorial. The Presidents of the Parliament wear flame-coloured robes trimmed with ermine at the neck and sleeves.

The Comtesse de Soissons, Angelique Cunegonde, the daughter of Francois-Henri de Luxembourg, has, it must be confessed, a considerable share of virtue and of wit; but she has also her faults, like the rest of the world. It may be said of her that she is truly a poor Princess. Her husband, Louis-Henri, Chevalier de Soissons, was very ugly, having a very long hooked nose, and eyes extremely close to it. He was as yellow as saffron; his mouth was extremely small for a man, and full of bad teeth of a most villanous odour; his legs were ugly and clumsy; his knees and feet turned inwards, which made him look when he was walking like a parrot; and his manner of making a bow was bad. He was rather short than otherwise; but he had fine hair and a large quantity of it. He was rather good-looking when a child. I have seen portraits of him painted at that period. If the Comtesse de Soissons' son had resembled his mother, he would have been very well, for her features are good, and nothing could be better than her, eyes, her mouth, and the turn of her face; only her nose was too large and thick, and her skin was not fine enough.

Whoever is like the Prince Eugene in person cannot be called a handsome man; he is shorter than his elder brother, but, with the exception of Prince Eugene, all the rest of them are good for nothing. The youngest, Prince Philippe, was a great madman, and died of the small-pox at Paris. He was of a very fair complexion, had an ungraceful manner, and always looked distracted. He had a nose like a hawk, a large mouth, thick lips, and hollow cheeks; in all respects I thought he was like his elder brother. The third brother, who was called the Chevalier de Savoie, died in consequence of a fall from his horse. The Prince Eugene was a younger brother: he had two sisters, who were equally ugly; one of them is dead, and the other is still living (1717) in a convent in Savoy. The elder was of a monstrous shape, but a mere dwarf. She led a very irregular life. She afterwards ran away with a rogue, the Abbe de la Bourlie, whom she obliged to marry her at Geneva; they used to beat each other. She is now dead.

Prince Eugene was not in his younger days so ugly as he has become since; but he never was good-looking, nor had he any nobility in his manner. His eyes were pretty good, but his nose, and two large teeth which he displayed whenever he opened his mouth, completely spoilt his face. He was besides always very filthy, and his coarse hair was never dressed.

This Prince is little addicted to women, and, during the whole time that he has been here, I never heard one mentioned who has pleased him, or whom he has distinguished or visited more than another.

His mother took no care of him; she brought him up like a scullion, and liked better to stake her money at play than to expend it upon her youngest son. This is the ordinary practice of women in this country.

They will not yet believe that the Persian Ambassador was an impostor;

[This embassy was always equivocal, and even something more. From all that can be understood of it, it would seem that a Minister of one of the Persian provinces, a sort of Intendant de Languedoc, as we might say, had commissioned this pretended Ambassador to manage for him some commercial affairs with certain merchants, and that for his own amusement the agent chose to represent the Persian Ambassador. It is said, too, that Pontchartrain, under whose department this affair fell, would not expose the trick, that the King might be amused, and that he might recommend himself to His Majesty's favour by making him believe that the Sophy had sent him an Ambassador.—Notes to Dangeau's Journal.]

it is quite certain that he was a clumsy fellow, although he had some sense. There was an air of magnificence about the way in which he gave audience. He prevailed upon a married woman, who was pregnant by him, to abjure Christianity. It is true she was not a very respectable person, being the illegitimate daughter of my son's chief almoner, the Abbe de Grancey, who always kept a little seraglio. In order to carry her away with him, the Ambassador had her fastened up in a box filled with holes, and then begged that no person might be allowed to touch it, being, as he said, filled with the sacred books written by Mahomet himself, which would be polluted by the contact of Christians. Upon this pretence the permission was given, and by these means the woman was carried off. I cannot believe the story which is told of this Ambassador having had 10,000 louis d'or given him.

I had the misfortune to displease the Margrave John Frederic of Anspach. He brought me a letter from my brother and his wife, both of whom begged I would assist him with my advice. I therefore thought that by counselling him as I should have counselled my own brother I should be rendering him the best service. When he arrived he was in deep mourning for his first wife, who had then not been dead three months. I asked him what he proposed to do in France? He replied "that he was on his way to England, but that before his departure he should wish to pay his respects to the King." I asked him if he had anything to solicit from the King or to arrange with him. He replied "he had not."—"Then," I said, "I would advise you, if you will permit me, to send the principal person of your suite to the King to make your compliments, to inform him that you are going to England, and that you would not have failed to wait upon him, but that, being in mourning for your wife, your respect for him prevented your appearing before him in so melancholy a garb."—"But," he rejoined, "I am very fond of dancing, and I wish to go to the ball; now I cannot go thither until I have first visited the King."—"For God's sake," I said, "do not go to the ball; it is not the custom here. You will be laughed at, and the more particularly so because the Marechal de Grammont, who presented you to the King some years ago, said that you could find nothing to praise in the whole of France, with the exception of a little goldfinch in the King's cabinet which whistled airs. I recommend you not to go to see the King, nor to be present at the ball." He was angry, and said "he saw very well that I discountenanced German Princes, and did not wish them to be presented to the King." I replied "that the advice I had given him sprang from the best intentions, and was such as I would have given to my own brother." He went away quite angry to Marechal Schomberg's, where he complained of my behaviour to him. The Marshal asked him what I had said, which he repeated word for word. The Marshal told him that I had advised him well, and that he was himself of my opinion. Nevertheless, the Margrave persisted on being presented to the King, whither he prevailed upon the Marshal to accompany him, and went the next day to the ball. He was extremely well dressed in half-mourning, with white lace over the black, fine blue ribands, black and white laces, and rheingraves, which look well upon persons of a good figure; in short, he was magnificently dressed, but improperly, for a widower in the first stage of his mourning. He would have seated himself within the King's circle, where none but the members of the Royal Family and the King's grandchildren are allowed to sit; the Princes of the blood even are not allowed to do so, and therefore foreign Princes can of course have no right. The Margrave then began to repent not having believed me, and early the next morning he set off.

Prince Ragotzky is under great obligations to his wife, who saved his life and delivered him from prison. Some person was repeating things to her disadvantage, but he interrupted them by saying, "She saved my head from the axe, and this prevents my having any right to reprove too strictly whatever she may choose to do; for this reason I shall not thank any person who speaks to me upon the subject."

[Louis XIV. gave to the Prince Ragotsky, who in France took the title of Comte de Saaross, 200,000 crowns upon the Maison de Ville, and a pension of 2,000 crowns per month besides.]

Beatrice Eleanora, the Queen of James II., was always upon such good terms with Maintenon that it is impossible to believe our late King was ever fond of her. I have seen a book, entitled "L'ancien Ward protecteur du nouveau," in 12mo, in which is related a gallantry between the Queen and the Pere la Chaise. The confessor was then eighty years of age, and not unlike an ass; his ears were very long, his mouth very wide, his head very large, and his body very long. It was an ill-chosen joke. This libel was even less credible than what was stated about the King himself.

The Monks of Saint Mihiel possess the original manuscripts of the Memoirs of Cardinal Retz. They have had them printed and are selling them at Nancy; but in this copy there are many omissions. A lady at Paris, Madame Caumartin, has a copy in which there is not a word deficient; but she obstinately refused to lend it that the others may be made complete.

When an Ambassador would make his entry at Paris he has himself announced some days before by the officers whose duty it is to introduce Ambassadors, in order that the usual compliments may be paid him. To royal Ambassadors a chevalier d'honneur is sent, to those from Venice or Holland the first equerry, and when he is absent or unwell the chief Maitre d'Hotel, who is also sent to the Ambassador from Malta.

The English ladies are said to be much given to running away with their lovers. I knew a Count von Konigsmark, whom a young English lady followed in the dress of a page. He had her with him at Chambord, and, as there was no room for her in the castle, he lodged her under a tent which he had put up in the forest. When we were at the chase one day he told me this adventure. As I had a great curiosity to see her, I rode towards the tent, and never in my life did I see anything prettier than this girl in the habit of a page. She had large and beautiful eyes, a charming little nose, and an elegant mouth and teeth. She smiled when she saw me, for she suspected that the Count had told me the whole story. Her hair was a beautiful chestnut colour, and hung about her neck in large curls. After their departure from Chambord, while they were at an inn upon their way to Italy, the innkeeper's wife ran to the Count, crying, "Sir, make haste upstairs, for your page is lying-in." She was delivered of a girl, and the mother and child were soon afterwards placed in a convent near Paris. While the Count lived he took great care of her, but he died in the Morea, and his pretended page did not long survive him; she displayed great piety in the hour of death. A friend of the Count's, and a nephew of Madame de Montespan, took care of the child, and after his death the King gave the little creature a pension. I believe she is still (1717) in the convent.

The Abbe Perrault founded an annual funeral oration for the Prince de Conde in the Jesuits' Church, where his heart is deposited. I shall not upon this occasion call to mind his victories, his courage in war, or his timidity at Court; these are things well known throughout France.

A gentleman of my acquaintance at Paris heard a learned Abbe, who was in the confidence of Descartes, say that the philosopher used often to laugh at his own system, and said, "I have cut them out some work: we shall see who will be fools enough to undertake it."

That old Beauvais, the Queen-mother's first femme de chambre, was acquainted with the secret of her marriage, and this obliged the Queen to put up with whatever the confidante chose to do. From this circumstance has arisen that custom which gives femmes de chambre so much authority in our apartments. The Queen-mother, the widow of Louis XIII., not contented with loving Cardinal Mazarin, went the absurd length of marrying him. He was not a priest, and therefore was not prevented by his orders from contracting matrimony. He soon, however, got very tired of the poor Queen, and treated her dreadfully ill, which is the ordinary result in such marriages. But it is the vice of the times to contract clandestine marriages. The Queen-mother of England, the widow of Charles II., made such an one in marrying her chevalier d'honneur, who behaved very ill to her; while the poor Queen was in want of food and fuel, he had a good fire in his apartment, and was giving great dinners. He called himself Lord Germain, Earl of St. Albans; he never addressed a kind expression to the Queen. As to the Queen-mother's marriage, all the circumstances relating to it are now well enough known. The secret passage by which he went nightly to the Palais Royal may still be seen; when she used to visit him, he was in the habit of saying, "what does this woman want with me?" He was in love with a lady of the Queen's suite, whom I knew very well: she had apartments in the Palais Royal, and was called Madame de Bregie. As she was very pretty, she excited a good deal of passion; but she was a very honest lady, who served the Queen with great fidelity, and was the cause of the Cardinal's living upon better terms with the Queen than before. She had very good sense. Monsieur loved her for her fidelity to the Queen his mother. She has been dead now four-and-twenty years (1717).

The Princesse de Deux Ponts has recently furnished another instance of the misfortune which usually attends the secret marriages of ladies of high birth. She married her equerry, was very ill-treated by him, and led a very miserable life; but she deserved all she met with and I foresaw it. She was with me at the Opera once, and insisted at all events that her equerry should sit behind her. "For God's sake," I said to her, "be quiet, and give yourself no trouble about this Gerstorf; you do not know the manners of this country; when folks perceive you are so anxious about that man, they will think you are in love with him." I did not know then how near this was to the truth. She replied, "Do people, then, in this country take no care of their servants?"—"Oh, yes," I said, "they request some of their friends to carry them to the Opera, but they do not go with them."

M. Pentenrieder is a perfect gentleman, extremely well-bred, totally divested of the vile Austrian manners, and speaks good German instead of the jargon of Austria. While he was staying here, the Fair of Saint-Germain commenced; a giant, who came to Paris for the purpose of exhibiting himself, having accidentally met M. Pentenrieder, said as soon as he saw him, "It's all over with me: I shall not go into the fair; for who will give money to see me while this man shows himself for nothing?" and he really went away. M. Pentenrieder pleased everybody. Count Zinzendorf, who succeeded him, did not resemble him at all, but was a perfect Austrian in his manners and his language.

I have heard that it was from the excitement of insulted honour that Ravaillac was induced to murder Henri IV.; for that the King had seduced his sister, and had abandoned her during her pregnancy: the brother then swore he would be avenged on the King. Some persons even accuse the Duc d'Epernon, who was seated in the coach in such a manner that he might have warded off the blow, but he is said to have drawn back and given the assassin an opportunity to strike.

When I first came to France I found in it such an assemblage of talent as occurs but in few ages. There was Lulli in music; Beauchamp in ballets; Corneille and Racine in tragedy; Moliere in comedy; La Chamelle and La Beauval, actresses; and Baron, Lafleur, Toriliere, and Guerin, actors. Each of these persons was excellent in his way. La Ducloa and La Raisin were also very good; the charms of the latter had even penetrated the thick heart of our Dauphin, who loved her very tenderly: her husband was excellent in comic parts. There was also a very good harlequin, and as good a scaramouch. Among the best performers at the Opera were Clediere, Pomereuil, Godenarche, Dumenil, La Rochechouard, Maury, La Saint Christophe, La Brigogne, La Beaucreux. All that we see and hear now do not equal them.

That which pleased me most in Beauvernois' life is the answer he made to the Prince of Vaudemont. When he was fleeing, and had arrived at Brussels, he gave himself out for a Prince of Lorraine. M. de Vaudemont sent for him, and, upon seeing him, said,—"I know all the Princes of Lorraine, but I do not know you."—"I assure you, sir," replied Beauvernois, "that I am as much a Prince of Lorraine as you are."

I like that Mercy who tricked his master, the Duc de Lorraine. When he reached Nancy he requested the Duke to recruit three regiments, which he said should be his own. The Duke did recruit them, fully persuaded they were to be his; but when the companies were filled, Mercy begged the Emperor to give them to him, and he actually obtained them; so that the Duke had not the appointment of a single officer.

The poor Duchess of Mecklenbourg, the wife of Christian Louis, was a very good woman when one was thoroughly acquainted with her. She told me the whole history of her intrigue with Bernstorff. She regulated her household very well, and had always two carriages. She did not affect the splendour of a sovereign; but she kept up her rank better than the other Duchesses, and I liked her the better for this. The husband, Christian Louis of Mecklenbourg, was a notable fool. He one day demanded an audience of the King, under the pretence of having something of importance to say to him. Louis XIV. was then more than forty years old. When the Duke found himself in the King's presence, he said to him, "Sire, you seem to me to have grown." The King laughed, and said, "Monsieur, I am past the age of growing."—"Sire," rejoined the Duke, "do you know everybody says I am very much like you, and quite as good-looking as you are?"—"That is very probable," said the King, still laughing. The audience was then finished, and the Duke went away. This fool could never engage his brother-in-law's favour, for M. de Luxembourg had no regard for him.

When the Queen had the government of the country, all the females of the Court, even to the very servants, became intriguers. They say it was the most ridiculous thing in the world to see the eagerness with which women meddled with the Queen-mother's regency. At the commencement she knew nothing at all. She made a present to her first femme de chambre of five large farms, upon which the whole Court subsisted. When she went to the Council to propose the affair, everybody laughed, and she was asked how she proposed to live. She was quite astonished when the thing was explained to her, for she thought she had only given away five ordinary farms. This anecdote is very true and was related to me by the old Chancellor Le Tellier, who was present at the Council. She is said often to have laughed as she confessed her ignorance. Many other things of a similar nature happened during the regency.

There is a Bishop of a noble family, tolerably young but very ugly, who was at first so devout that he thought of entering La Trappe; he wore his hair combed down straight, and dared not look a woman in the face. Having learned that in the city where he held his see there was a frail fair one, whose gallantries had become notorious, he felt a great desire to convert her and to make her come to the confessional. She was, it is said, a very pretty woman, and had, moreover, a great deal of wit.

No sooner had the Bishop began to visit than he began to pay attention to his hair: first he powdered it, and then he had it dressed. At length he swallowed the bait so completely, that he neither quitted the fair siren by night nor by day. His clergy ventured to exhort him to put an end to this scandal, but he replied that, if they did not cease their remonstrances, he would find means of making them. At length he even rode through the city in his carriage with his fair penitent.

The people became so enraged at this that they pelted him with stones. His relations repaired to his diocese for the purpose of exhorting him in their turn, but he would only receive his mother, and would not even follow her advice. His relations then applied to the Regent to summon the lady to Paris. She came, but her lover followed and recovered her; at length she was torn from him by a lettre-de-cachet, and taken from his arms to a house of correction. The Bishop is in a great rage, and declares that he will never forgive his family for the affront which has been put upon him (1718).

The Queen-mother is said to have eaten four times a day in a frightful manner, and this practice is supposed to have brought on that cancer in the breast, which she sought to conceal by strong Spanish perfumes, and of which she died.

Those female branches of the French Royal Family, who are called Enfants de France, all bear the title of Madame. For this reason it is that in the brevets they are called Madame la Duchesse de Berri; Madame la Duchesse d'Orleans; but in conversation they are called the Duchesse de Berri, the Duchesse d'Orleans; or, rather, one should say, Madame de Berri will have it so with respect to herself. The title of Duchesse d'Orleans belongs to Madame la Duchesse d'Orleans, as granddaughter. Such is the custom prevalent here. The brother and the sister-in-law of the King are called simply Monsieur and Madame, and these titles are also contained in my brevets; but I suffer myself to be called commonly Madame la Duchesse d'Orleans. Madame de Berri will be called Madame la Duchess de Berri, because, being only an Enfant de France of the third descent, she has need of that title to set off her relationship. There is nothing to be said for this: if there were any unmarried daughters of the late King, each would be called Madame, with the addition of their baptismal name.

It seems that Queen Mary of England was something of a coquette in Holland. Comte d'Avaux, the French Ambassador, told me himself that he had had a secret interview with her at the apartments of one of the Queen's Maids of Honour, Madame Treslane. The Prince of Orange, becoming acquainted with the affair, dismissed the young lady, but invented some other pretext that the real cause might not be known.

Three footmen had a quarrel together; two of them refused to admit the third to their table, saying, "as he and his master only serve a president's wife, he cannot presume to compare himself with us, who serve Princesses and Duchesses." The rejected footman called another fellow to his aid, and a violent squabble ensued. The commissaire was called: he found that they served three brothers, the sons of a rich merchant at Rouen; two of them had bought companies in the French Guards; one of the two had an intrigue with the wife of Duc d'Abret, and the other with the Duchesse de Luxembourg, while the third was only engaged with the wife of a president. The two former were called Colande and Maigremont; and, as at the same time the Duc d'Abret, the son of the Duc de Bouillon, was in love with the lady of the President Savari.

The Envoy from Holstein, M. Dumont, was very much attached to Madame de La Rochefoucauld, one of Madame de Berri's 'dames du palais'. She was very pretty, but gifted with no other than personal charms. Some one was joking her on this subject, and insinuated that she had treated her lover very favourably. "Oh! no," she replied, "that is impossible, I assure you, entirely impossible." When she was urged to say what constituted the impossibility, she replied, "If I tell, you will immediately agree with me that it is quite impossible." Being pressed still further, she said, with a very serious air, "Because he is a Protestant!"

When the marriage of Monsieur was declared, he said to Saint-Remi, "Did you know that I was married to the Princesse de Lorraine?"—

"No, Monsieur," replied the latter; "I knew very well that you lived with her, but I did not think you would have married her."

Queen Marie de Medicis, the wife of Henri IV., was one day walking at the Tuileries with her son, the Dauphin, when the King's mistress came into the garden, having also her son with her. The mistress said very, insolently, to the Queen, "There are our two Dauphins walking together, but mine is a fairer one than yours." The Queen gave her a smart box on the ear, and said at the same time, "Let this impertinent woman be taken away." The mistress ran instantly to Henri IV. to complain, but the King, having heard her story, said, "This is your own fault; why did you not speak to the Queen with the respect which you owe to her?"

Madame de Fiennes, who in her youth had been about the Queen-mother, used always to say to the late Monsieur, "The Queen, your mother, was a very silly woman; rest her soul!" My aunt, the Abbess of Maubuisson, told me that she saw at the Queen's a man who was called "the repairer of the Queen's face;" that Princess, as well as all the ladies of the Court, wore great quantities of paint.

On account of the great services which the House of Arpajon in France had rendered to the Order of Malta, a privilege was formerly granted that the second son of that family, should at his birth become a Knight of the Order without the necessity of any proof or any inquiry as to his mother.

The Czar Peter I. is not mad; he has sense enough, and if he had not unfortunately been so brutally educated he would have made a good prince. The way in which he behaved to his Czarowitz (Alexis) is horrible. He gave his word that he would do him no injury, and afterwards poisoned him by means of the Sacrament. This is so impious and abominable that I can never forgive him for it (1719).

The last Duc d'Ossuna had, it is said, a very beautiful, but at the same time a passionate and jealous wife. Having learnt that her husband had chosen a very fine stuff for the dress of his mistress, an actress, she went to the merchant and procured it of him. He, thinking it was intended for her, made no scruple of delivering it to her. After it was made up she put it on, and, showing it to her husband, said, "Do not you think it is very beautiful?" The husband, angry at the trick, replied, "Yes, the stuff is very beautiful, but it is put to an unworthy use." "That is what everybody says of me," retorted the Duchess.

At Fontainebleau in the Queen's cabinet may be seen the portrait of La Belle Terronniere, who was so much beloved by Francois I., and who was the unwitting cause of his death.

I have often walked at night in the gallery at Fontainebleau where the King's ghost is said to appear, but the good Francois I. never did me the honour to show himself. Perhaps it was because he thought my prayers were not efficacious enough to draw him from purgatory, and in this I think he was quite right.

King James II. died with great firmness and resolution, and without any bigotry; that is to say, very differently from the manner in which he had lived. I saw and spoke to him four-and-twenty hours before his death. "I hope," I said, "soon to hear of your Majesty's getting better." He smiled and said, "If I should die, shall I not have lived long enough?"

I hardly know how to rejoice at the accession of our Prince George to the Throne of England, for I have no confidence in the English people. I remember still too well the fine speeches which were made here not long ago by Lord Peterborough. I would rather that our Elector was Emperor of Germany, and I wish that the King who is here (James II.) was again in possession of England, because the kingdom belongs to him. I fear that the inconstancy of the English will in the end produce some scheme which may be injurious to us. Perhaps there was never in any nation a King who had been crowned with more eclat, or tumultuous joy than James II.; and yet the same nation since persecuted him in the most pitiless manner, and has so tormented his innocent son that he can scarcely find an asylum after all his heavy misfortunes.

[The Duchesse D'Orleans was, by the mother's side, granddaughter of James I, which explains the interest she took in the fate of the Stuart family.]

If the English were to be trusted I should say that it is fortunate the Parliaments are in favour of George; but the more one reads the history of English Revolutions, the more one is compelled to remark the eternal hatred which the people of that nation have had towards their Kings, as well as their fickleness (1714).

Have I not reason to fear on George's account since he has been made King of England, and knowing as I do the desire he had to be King of another country? I know the accursed English too well to trust them. May God protect their Majesties the Princes, and all the family, but I confess I fear for them greatly (1715).

The poor Princess of Wales

[Wilhelmina-Dorothea-Charlotte, daughter of John Frederick, Margrave of Anspach, born in 1682, married to the Prince of Wales in 1706. The particulars of the quarrel between George I. and his son, the Prince of Wales, will be found in Cose's "Memoirs of Sir Robert Walpole."]

has caused me great uneasiness since her letter of the 3rd (15th) of February (1718). She has implored the King's pardon as one implores the pardon of God, but without success. I know nothing about it, but dread lest the Prince should partake his mother's disgrace. I think, however, since the King has declared the Prince to be his son, he should treat him as such, and not act so haughtily against the Princess, who has never offended him, but has always treated him with the respect due to a father. Nothing good can result from the present state of affairs; and the King had better put an end to a quarrel which gives occasion to a thousand impertinences, and revives awkward stories which were better forgotten.

The King of England has returned to London in good health (1719). The Prince of Wales causes me great anxiety. He thought he should do well to send one of his gentlemen to his father, to assure him in most submissive terms of the joy he felt at his happy return. The King not only would not receive the letter, but he sent back the gentleman with a very harsh rebuke, revoking at the same time the permission, which before his journey he had given to the Prince of Wales, to see his daughter, whom the Prince loves very tenderly; this really seems too severe. It may be said that the King is rather descended from the race of the Czar than from that of Brunswick and the Palatinate. Such conduct can do him no good.

M. d'Entremont, the last Ambassador from Sicily, was upon the point of departing, and had already had his farewell audience, when some circumstance happened which compelled him to stay some time longer. He found himself without a lodging, for his hotel had been already let. A lady seeing the embarrassment in which Madame d'Entremont was thus placed, said to her, "Madame, I have pleasure in offering you my house, my own room, and my own bed." The Ambassador's lady not knowing what to do, accepted the offer with great readiness. She went to the lady's house, and as she is old and in ill health, she went to bed immediately. Towards midnight she heard a noise like that of some person opening a secret door. In fact, a door in the wall by the bedside was opened. Some one entered, and began to undress. The lady called out, "Who is there?" A voice replied, "It is I; be quiet." "Who are you?" asked the lady. "What is the matter with you?" was the reply. "You were not wont to be so particular. I am undressing, and shall come to bed directly." At these words the lady cried out, "Thieves!" with all her might, and the unknown person dressed himself quickly, and withdrew.

When the Electoral Prince of Saxony came hither, he addressed a pretty compliment to the King, which we all thought was his own, and we therefore conceived a very favourable notion of his parts. He did not, however, keep up that good opinion, and probably the compliment was made for him by the Elector-Palatine. The King desired the Duchesse de Berri to show him about Marly. He walked with her for an hour without ever offering her his arm or saying one word to her. While they were ascending a small hill, the Palatine, his Governor, nodded to him; and as the Prince did not understand what he meant, he was at length obliged to say to him, "Offer your arm to the Duchesse de Berri." The Prince obeyed, but without saying a word. When they reached the summit, "Here," said the Duchesse de Berri, "is a nice place for blindman's buff." Then, for the first time, he opened his mouth, and said, "Oh, yes; I am very willing to play." Madame de Berri was too much fatigued to play; but the Prince continued amusing himself the whole day without offering the least civility to the Duchess, who had taken such pains for him. This will serve to show how puerile the Prince is.

....

We have had here several good repartees of Duke Bernard von Weimar. One day a young Frenchman asked him, "How happened it that you lost the battle?"—"I will tell you, sir," replied the Duke, coolly; "I thought I should win it, and so I lost it. But," he said, turning himself slowly round, "who is the fool that asked me this question?"

Father Joseph was in great favour with Cardinal Richelieu, and was consulted by him on all occasions. One day, when the Cardinal had summoned Duke Bernard to the Council, Father Joseph, running his finger over a map, said, "Monsieur, you must first take this city; then that, and then that." The Duke Bernard listened to him for some time, and at length said, "But, Monsieur Joseph, you cannot take cities with your finger." This story always made the King laugh heartily.

....

M. de Brancas was very deeply in love with the lady whom he married. On his wedding-day he went to take a bath, and was afterwards going to bed at the bath-house. "Why are you going to bed here, sir?" said his valet de chambre; "do you not mean to go to your wife?"—"I had quite forgotten," he replied. He was the Queen-mother's chevalier d'honneur. One day, while she was at church, Brancas forgot that the Queen was kneeling before him, for as her back was very round, her head could hardly be seen when she hung it down. He took her for a prie-dieu, and knelt down upon her, putting his elbows upon her shoulders. The Queen was of course not a little surprised to find her chevalier d'honneur upon her back, and all the bystanders were ready to die with laughing.

Dr. Chirac was once called to see a lady, and, while he was in her bedchamber, he heard that the price of stock had considerably decreased. As he happened to be a large holder of the Mississippi Bonds, he was alarmed at the news; and being seated near the patient, whose pulse he was feeling, he said with a deep sigh, "Ah, good God! they keep sinking, sinking, sinking!" The poor sick lady hearing this, uttered a loud shriek; the people ran to her immediately. "Ah," said she, "I shall die; M. de Chirac has just said three times, as he felt my pulse, 'They keep sinking!'" The Doctor recovered himself soon, and said, "You dream; your pulse is very healthy, and you are very well. I was thinking of the Mississippi stocks, upon which I lose my money, because their price sinks." This explanation satisfied the sick lady.

The Duc de Sully was subject to frequent fits of abstraction. One day, having dressed himself to go to church, he forgot nothing but his breeches. This was in the winter; when he entered the church, he said, "Mon Dieu, it is very cold to-day." The persons present said, "Not colder than usual!"—"Then I am in a fever," he said. Some one suggested that he had perhaps not dressed himself so warmly as usual, and, opening his coat, the cause of his being cold was very apparent.

Our late King told me the following anecdote of Queen Christina of Sweden: That Princess, instead of putting on a nightcap, wrapped her head up in a napkin. One night she could not sleep, and ordered the musicians to be brought into her bedroom; where, drawing the bed-curtains, she could not be seen by the musicians, but could hear them at her ease. At length, enchanted at a piece which they had just played, she abruptly thrust her head beyond the curtains, and cried out, "Mort diable! but they sing delightfully!" At this grotesque sight, the Italians, and particularly the castrati, who are not the bravest men in the world, were so frightened that they were obliged to stop short.

In the great gallery at Fontainebleau may still be seen the blood of the man whom she caused to be assassinated; it was to prevent his disclosing some secrets of which he was in possession that she deprived him of life. He had, in fact, begun to chatter through jealousy of another person who had gained the Queen's favour. Christina was very vindictive, and given up to all kinds of debauchery.

Duke Frederick Augustus of Brunswick was delighted with Christina; he said that he had never in his life met a woman who had so much wit, and whose conversation was so truly diverting; he added that it was impossible to be dull with her for a moment. I observed to him that the Queen in her conversation frequently indulged in very filthy discussions. "That is true," replied he, "but she conceals such things in so artful a manner as to take from them all their disgusting features." She never could be agreeable to women, for she despised them altogether.

Saint Francois de Sales, who founded the order of the Sisters of Saint Mary, had in his youth been extremely intimate with the Marechal de Villeroi, the father of the present Marshal. The old gentleman could therefore never bring himself to call his old friend a saint. When any one spoke in his presence of Saint Francois de Sales, he used to say, "I was delighted when I saw M. de Sales become a saint; he used to delight in talking indecently, and always cheated at play; but in every other respect he was one of the best gentlemen in the world, and perhaps one of the most foolish."

M. de Cosnac, Archbishop of Aix, was at a very advanced age when he learnt that Saint Francois de Sales had been canonized. "What!" cried he, "M. de Geneve, my old friend? I am delighted at his good fortune; he was a gallant man, an amiable man, and an honest man, too, although he would sometimes cheat at piquet, at which we have often played together."—"But, sir," said some one present, "is it possible that a saint could be a sharper at play?"—"No," replied the Archbishop, "he said, as a reason for it, that he gave all his winnings to the poor." [Loisirs d'un homme d'etat, et Dictionnaire Historique, tom. vii. Paris, 1810.]

While Frederick Charles de Wurtemberg, the administrateur of that duchy, was staying at Paris, the Princesse Marianne de Wurtemberg, Duke Ulric's daughter, was there also with her mother. Expecting then to marry her cousin,

[The learned Journal of Gottengin for the year 1789, No. 30, observes there must be some mistake here, because in 1689, when this circumstance is supposed to have occurred, the administrateur had been married seven years, and had children at Stuttgard.]

she had herself painted as Andromeda and her cousin as Perseus as the latter wore no helmet, everybody could of course recognize him. But when he went away without having married her, she had a casque painted, which concealed the face, and said she would not have another face inserted until she should be married. She was then about nineteen years old. Her mother said once at Court, "My daughter has not come with me to-day because she is gone to confess; but, poor child, what can she have to say to her confessor, except that she has dropped some stitches in her work." Madame de Fiennes, who was present, whispered, "The placid old fool! as if a stout, healthy girl of nineteen had no other sins to confess than having dropped some stitches."

106

A village pastor was examining his parishioners in their catechism. The first question in the Heidelberg catechism is this: "What is thy only consolation in life and in death?" A young girl, to whom the pastor put this question, laughed, and would not answer. The priest insisted. "Well, then," said she at length, "if I must tell you, it is the young shoemaker who lives in the Rue Agneaux."

The late Madame de Nemours had charitably brought up a poor child. When the child was about nine years old, she said to her benefactress, "Madame, no one can be more grateful for your charity than I am, and I cannot acknowledge it better than by telling everybody I am your daughter; but do not be alarmed, I will not say that I am your lawful child, only your illegitimate daughter."

The Memoirs of Queen Margaret of Navarre are merely a romance compared with those of Mdlle. de La Force. The authoress's own life was a romance. Being extremely poor, although of an ancient and honourable family, she accepted the office of demoiselle d'honneur to the Duchesse de Guise. Here the Marquis de Nesle, father of the present Marquis (1720), became enamoured of her, after having received from her a small bag to wear about his neck, as a remedy against the vapours. He would have married her, but his relations opposed this intention on the score of Mdlle. de La Force's poverty, and because she had improperly quitted the Duchesse de Guise. The Great Conde, the Marquis de Nesle's nearest relation, took him to Chattillon that he might forget his love for Mdlle. de La Force; all the Marquis's relations were there assembled for the purpose of declaring to him that they would never consent to his marriage with Mdlle. de La Force; and he on his part told them that he would never while he lived marry any other person. In a moment of despair, he rushed out to the garden and would have thrown himself into the canal, but that the strings, with which Mdlle. de La Force had tied the bag about his neck, broke, and the bag fell at his feet. His thoughts appeared to undergo a sudden change, and Mdlle. de La Force seemed to him to be as ugly as she really is. He went instantly to the Prince and his other relations who were there, and told them what had just happened. They searched about in the garden for the bag and the strings, and, opening it, they found it to contain two toads' feet holding a heart wrapped up in a bat's wing, and round the whole a paper inscribed with unintelligible cyphers. The Marquis was seized with horror at the sight. He told me this story with his own mouth. Mdlle. de La Force after this fell in love with Baron, but as he was not bewitched, the intrigue did not last long: he used to give a very amusing account of the declaration she made to him. Then a M. Briou, the son of a Councillor of that name, became attached to her; his relations, who would by no means have consented to such a marriage, shut the young man up. La Force, who has a very fertile wit, engaged an itinerant musician who led about dancing bears in the street, and intimated to her lover that, if he would express a wish to see the bears dance in the courtyard of his own house, she would come to him disguised in a bear's skin. She procured a bear's skin to be made so as to fit her, and went to M. Briou's house with the bears; the young man, under the pretence of playing with this bear, had an opportunity of conversing with her and of laying their future plans. He then promised his father that he would submit to his will, and thus having regained his liberty he immediately married Mdlle. de La Force, and went with her to Versailles, where the King gave them apartments, and where Madame de Briou was every day with the Dauphine of Bavaria, who admired her wit and was delighted with her society. M. de Briou was not then five-and-twenty years of age, a very good-looking and well-bred young man. His father, however, procured a dissolution of the marriage by the Parliament, and made him marry another person. Madame de Briou thus became once more Mdlle. de La Force, and found herself without husband and money. I cannot tell how it was that the King and her parents, both of whom had consented to the marriage, did not oppose its dissolution. To gain a subsistence she set about composing romances, and as she was often staying with the Princesse de Conti, she dedicated to her that of Queen Margaret.

We have had four Dukes who have bought coffee, stuffs, and even candles for the purpose of selling them again at a profit. It was the Duke de La Force who bought the candles. One evening, very recently, as he was going out of the Opera, the staircase was filled with young men, one of whom cried out, as he passed, "His purse!"—"No," said another, "there can be no money in it; he would not risk it; it must be candles that he has bought to sell again." They then sang the air of the fourth act of 'Phaeton'.

[The Duke, together with certain other persons, made considerable purchases of spice, porcelain, and other merchandizes, for the purpose of realizing the hope of Law's Banks. As he was not held in estimation either by the public or by the Parliament, the Duke was accused of monopoly; and by a decree of the Parliament, in concert with the Peers, he was enjoined "to use more circumspection for the future, and to conduct himself irreproachably, in a manner as should be consistent with his birth and his dignity as a Peer of France."]

The Queen Catherine (de Medicis) was a very wicked woman. Her uncle, the Pope, had good reason for saying that he had made a bad present to France. It is said that she poisoned her youngest son because he had discovered her in a common brothel whither she had gone privately. Who can wonder that such a woman should drink out of a cup covered with designs from Aretino. The Pope had an object in sending her to France. Her son was the Duc d'Alencon; and as they both remained incog. the world did not know that they were mother and son, which occasioned frequent mistakes.

The young Count Horn, who has just been executed here (1720), was descended from a well-known Flemish family; he was distinguished at first for the amiable qualities of his head and for his wit. At college he was a model for good conduct, application, and purity of morals; but the intimacy which he formed with some libertine young men during his stay at the Academy of Paris entirely changed him. He contracted an insatiable desire for play, and even his own father said to him, "You will die by the hands of the executioner." Being destitute of money, the young Count took up the trade of a pickpocket, which he carried on in the pit of the theatres, and by which he made considerable gains in silver-hilted swords and watches. At length, having lost a sum of five-and-twenty thousand crowns at the fair of Saint-Germain, he was led to commit that crime which he has just expiated on the scaffold. For the purpose of discharging the debt he had contracted, he sent for a banker's clerk to bring him certain bank bills, which he proposed to purchase. Having connected himself with two other villains, he attacked the clerk as soon as he arrived, and stabbed him with poniards which he had bought three days before on the Pont Neuf. Hoping to conceal the share which he had taken in this crime, he went immediately after its perpetration to the Commissaire du Quartier, and told him, with a cool and determined air, that he had been obliged, in his own defence, to kill the clerk, who had attacked him and put him in danger of his life. The Commissaire looking at him steadfastly, said, "You are covered with blood, but you are not even wounded; I must retain you in custody until I can examine this affair more minutely." At this moment the accomplice entered the room. "Here, sir," said the Count to the Commissaire, "is one who can bear testimony that the account I have given you of this business is perfectly true." The accomplice was quite terrified at hearing this; he thought that Count Horn had confessed his crime, and that there could be no advantage in continuing to deny it; he therefore confessed all that had taken place, and thus the murder was revealed. The Count was not more than two-and-twenty years of age, and one of the handsomest men in Paris. Some of the first persons in France solicited in his favour, but the Duke Regent thought it necessary to make an example of him on account of the prevalent excess of crime. Horn was publicly broken on the wheel with his second accomplice; the other died just before: they were both gentlemen and of noble families. When they arrived at the place of punishment, they begged the people to implore the pardon of Heaven upon their sins. The spectators were affected to tears, but they nevertheless agreed in the just severity of their punishment. The people said aloud after the execution, "Our Regent has done justice."

One lady was blaming another, her intimate friend, for loving a very ugly man. The latter said, "Did he ever speak to you tenderly or passionately?"—"No," replied the former. "Then you cannot judge," said her friend, "whether I ought to love him or not."

Madame de Nemours used to say, "I have observed one thing in this country, 'Honour grows again as well as hair.'"

An officer, a gentleman of talent, whose name was Hautmont, wrote the following verses upon Cardinal Mazarin, for which he was locked up in the Bastille for eighteen months:

> *A ce Jules nouveauu beau,*
> *Creusons tous le tombeau*
> *Cherchons un nouveau Brute.*
> *Si nous voyions sa chute!*
> *A qui nous persecute;*
> *Que le jour serait*

The Queen-mother could not endure Boisrobert on account of his impiety; she did not like him to visit her sons, the King and Monsieur, in their youth, but they were very fond of him because he used to amuse them. When he was at the point of death, the Queen-mother sent some priests to convert him and to prepare him for confession. Boisrobert appeared inclined to confess. "Yes, mon Dieu," said he, devoutly joining his hands, "I sincerely implore Thy pardon, and confess that I am a great sinner, but thou knowest that the Abbe de Villargeau is a much greater sinner than I am."

Cardinal Mazarin sent him once to compliment the English Ambassador on his arrival. When he reached the hotel, an Englishman said to him, "Milord, il est pret; my ladi, il n'est pas pret, friselire ses chevaux, prendre patience." The late King used to relate stories of this same Boisrobert in a very whimsical manner.

The life which folks lead at Paris becomes daily more scandalous; I really tremble for the city every time it thunders. Three ladies of quality have just committed a monstrous imprudence. They have been running after the Turkish Ambassador; they made his son drunk and kept him with them three days; if they go on in this way even the Capuchins will not be safe from them. The Turks must needs have a very becoming notion of the conduct of ladies of quality in a Christian country. The young Turk is said to have told Madame de Polignac, who was one of the three ladies, "Madame, your reputation has reached Constantinople, and I see that report has only done you justice." The Ambassador, it is said, is very much enraged with his son, and has enjoined him to keep his adventure profoundly a secret, because he would risk the top of his head on his return to Constantinople if it were known that he had associated with Christian women. It is to be feared that the young man will get safely out of France. Madame de Polignac has fleeced all the young men of quality here. I do not know how her relations and those of her husband choose to suffer her to lead so libertine a life. But all shame is extinct in France, and everything is turned topsy-turvy.

It is very unfortunate that noblemen like the Elector-Palatine John William should suffer themselves to be governed by the priesthood; nothing but evil can result from it. He would do much better if he would follow the advice of able statesmen, and throw his priest into the Necker. I would advise him to do so, and I think I should advise him well.

I cannot conceive why the Duke Maximilian (brother of George I. of England)

[*Prince Maximilian of Hanover, the second brother of George I., had, after the death of his brother, Frederick Augustus, certain rights over the Bishopric of Osnaburgh; love and his monks caused him to embrace the catholic faith.*]

changed his religion, for he had very little faith in general; none of his relations solicited him to do so, and he was induced by no personal interest.

I have heard a story of this Prince, which does him little honour. I have been told that he complained to the Emperor of his mother, who bred him tenderly, but who had not sent him eight thousand crowns which he had asked her for. This is abominable, and he can hope for happiness neither in this nor in the next world; I can never forgive him for it. The first idea of this must have originated with Father Wolff, who has also excited him against Prince Edward Augustus.—[Maximilian contested the Bishopric of Osnaburgh with his younger brother.]—What angers me most with this cursed monk is, that he will not suffer Duke Maximilian to have a single nobleman about him; he will only allow him to be approached by beggars like himself.

Printed in Great Britain
by Amazon